Praise for *Fix Injustice, Not Ki[...]* for Transformative Eq[...]

MW00603857

"So what can I do?" is a question that so many p[...] in equity work at school. This is not the inquiry [...] book asks and answers a more powerful question: "If I care about children, their communities, and their futures, *who do I need to become?*"

—**Cornelius Minor,** author of
We Got This: Equity, Access, and the Quest to Be Who Our Students Need Us to Be

Fix Injustice, Not Kids and Other Principles for Transformative Equity Leadership is exactly the book we need today when conversations about equity, diversity, and justice often are hijacked and distorted. This is a must-read for education leaders and professionals everywhere.

—**Gloria Ladson-Billings,** professor emerita,
University of Wisconsin–Madison

Drawing on their extensive experience and research confronting injustice in education, Gorski and Swalwell's *Fix Injustice, Not Kids and Other Principles for Transformative Equity Leadership* is a gift to all who are committed to moving schools and school leaders from good intentions to powerful practices. Rooted by a most radical sense of equity, and grounded in real-life, supremely applicable approaches to making school structures more just and equitable, *Fix Injustice, Not Kids* needs to be read by current and future education leaders everywhere.

—**Wayne Au,** professor, University of Washington Bothell
and editor, *Rethinking Schools*

Paul Gorski and Katy Swalwell offer fresh insights on the cumulative and multifaceted dimensions of inequity through their prescient and timely "equity literacy framework" that is chock-full of conceptual tools and strategies for the outright transformation of institutional cultures that reach beyond diversity and inclusion to foster genuine equity.

—**Angela Valenzuela, PhD,** author of
Subtractive Schooling and *Growing Critically Conscious Teachers: A Social Justice Curriculum for Educators of Latino/a Youth*

Gorski and Swalwell have crafted for educational leaders a clear and courageous pathway beyond easy assumptions and good intentions—and toward decisive equity-literate skills and actions. Guided by scholarship, grown from their many years of practical experience in schools, and grounded in the reality of structural inequities—this is a foundational and transformational resource for achieving equitable and just schooling.

—**Gary Howard,** author of
We Can't Lead Where We Won't Go: An Educator's Guide to Equity

As leaders, we should all strive to disrupt inequity. But just how do we do that? Look no further than Gorski and Swalwell's *Fix Injustice, Not Kids and Other Principles for Transformative Equity Leadership.* They provide a framework for moving beyond high-optics equity initiatives that only yield low-impact institutional results. Instead, they help leaders recognize inequity with a sharper lens and know how to disrupt it at its core.

—**Zaretta Hammond,** author of
Culturally Responsive Teaching and the Brain: Promoting Authentic Engagement and Rigor Among Culturally and Linguistically Diverse Students

This insightful book asks us to look beyond the current zeitgeist of antiracist work and helps us develop principles about the work we're seeking to do. As a justice-oriented educator, I appreciate how Gorski and Swalwell delineate how to do this work with integrity, curiosity, and willingness to push boundaries on the status quo.

—**José Luis Vilson,** veteran educator, executive director of EduColor, and author of *This Is Not a Test: A New Narrative on Race, Class, and Education*

With their basic principles of equity literacy, Gorski and Swalwell share a vision for the transformative power of collective action toward living and breathing equity not only at work, but also in our personal lives, so that we become threats to inequity everywhere we go.

—**Dena Simmons,** founder of LiberatED

Fix Injustice, Not Kids and Other Principles for Transformative Equity Leadership is a compelling and sometimes uncomfortable book for educators who are willing to confront the conditions that perpetuate inequity and who have the courage to take actions that actually cultivate equity. It sheds a bright light on how the difference between doing "something" in the name of equity and taking meaningful action can change the educational trajectory for young people who are marginalized by much of what we continue to do in schools and classrooms.

—**Carol Ann Tomlinson,** author of *How to Differentiate Instruction in Academically Diverse Classrooms*, 3rd Edition

I appreciated the authors' emphasis on transformative over mitigative equity, and the rich principles and examples to illuminate the difference. This will help educators consider the impact of their efforts. Equity-focused educators serious about deepening their practice will benefit immensely from the explanation of action steps through the compelling equity literacy approach, powerful narratives, and relevant exercises. Get this book.

—**Mark Anthony Gooden,** author of *Five Practices for Equity-Focused School Leadership*

Transformational change through the lens of antiracism is a monumental undertaking—one that Paul Gorski and Katy Swalwell do not shy away from. Rather, in *Fix Injustice, Not Kids and Other Principles for Transformative Equity Leadership,* Gorski and Swalwell help educators and school communities confront that lift directly, moving past surface-level good intentions and towards changed, antiracist outcomes—long overdue for Black and Brown youth.

—**Kass Minor,** author of *Teaching Fiercely: Spreading Joy and Justice in Our Schools* and cofounder, The Minor Collective

FIX INJUSTICE, NOT KIDS

and Other Principles for Transformative Equity Leadership

PAUL GORSKI   KATY SWALWELL

FIX INJUSTICE, NOT KIDS

and Other Principles for Transformative Equity Leadership

Arlington, Virginia USA

2800 Shirlington Road, Suite 1001 • Arlington, VA 22206 USA
Phone: 800-933-2723 or 703-578-9600 • Fax: 703-575-5400
Website: www.ascd.org • Email: member@ascd.org
Author guidelines: www.ascd.org/write

Penny Reinart, *Deputy Executive Director*; Genny Ostertag, *Managing Director,
Book Acquisitions & Editing*; Susan Hills, *Senior Acquisitions Editor*; Mary Beth Nielsen,
Director, Book Editing; Liz Wegner, *Editor*; Thomas Lytle, *Creative Director*; Donald Ely,
Art Director; Daniela Aguero/The Hatcher Group, *Graphic Designer*; Cynthia Stock,
Typesetter; Kelly Marshall, *Production Manager*; Shajuan Martin, *E-Publishing Specialist*

PAPERBACK ISBN: 978-1-4166-3196-5   ASCD product #120012   n6/23
PDF EBOOK ISBN: 978-1-4166-3197-2; see Books in Print for other formats.
Quantity discounts are available: email programteam@ascd.org or call 800-933-2723,
ext. 5773, or 703-575-5773. For desk copies, go to www.ascd.org/deskcopy.

Library of Congress Cataloging-in-Publication Data
Names: Gorski, Paul, author. | Swalwell, Katy M., author.
Title: Fix injustice, not kids and other principles for transformative
    equity leadership / Paul Gorski and Katy Swalwell.
Description: Arlington, VA : ASCD, 2023. | Includes bibliographical
    references and index.
Identifiers: LCCN 2023002275 (print) | LCCN 2023002276 (ebook) | ISBN
    9781416631965 (paperback) | ISBN 9781416631972 (pdf)
Subjects: LCSH: Educational leadership—Social aspects—United States. |
    Educational equalization—United States. | Social justice and
    education—United States.
Classification: LCC LB2805 .G648 2023 (print) | LCC LB2805 (ebook) | DDC
    371.2/011—dc23/eng/20230203
LC record available at https://lccn.loc.gov/2023002275
LC ebook record available at https://lccn.loc.gov/2023002276

32 31 30 29 28 27 26 25 24 23   1 2 3 4 5 6 7 8 9 10 11 12

For Marceline, Haseena, Taharee, Seema, and Katy.
I am honored to be part of a team of people I so
deeply love and respect.

—*Paul*

————————————————

For the students and teachers over the years who
have summoned, strengthened, and sustained me.
I owe you so much.

—*Katy*

FIX INJUSTICE, NOT KIDS

and Other Principles for Transformative Equity Leadership

Letter to Readers

We've been friends and colleagues for years. We have written together before, but this project felt different. Frankly, it was *much* more difficult than we anticipated. A pandemic hit at the same time each of us welcomed new babies into our families, alongside difficult diagnoses of loved ones. It was not the easiest time to write a book, to say the least.

What we found most challenging, however, was not the chaos in our lives but the fact that this book represents the culmination of decades we've spent collaborating with students and educators to make schools more equitable and just. It is not hyperbole to say that inequity in schools is a life-and-death issue. We know that students, families, and staff desperately need classrooms and schools to be better *now*. We believed we had an opportunity to help move the needle, and we didn't want to blow it.

In this book, we share a set of principles for leading unequivocally in ways that disrupt inequity at its roots—for becoming, and helping others become, transformative equity leaders. We draw on scholarship about educational equity as well as our decades of experience as teachers, administrators, professors, researchers, and facilitators of systems-level change. Over the years we've heard from readers and participants in our workshops how helpful this combination of scholarship and stories has been. Together, the research and personal accounts can help us jump-start long overdue conversations and actions, provide support for work that is under attack, and affirm what so many families have been advocating for generations.

Of course, we harbor no illusion that one set of principles or one book about them will be a cure-all for the many interlocking oppressions that have thrived in schools, especially when so many aspects of schooling were designed to protect and reproduce those inequities (Au, 2010; Ewing, 2018; González, 2007). Nor do we think so highly of ourselves that we believe that what we have written is the final or only word on educational equity. In particular, we understand that our identities afford us certain publishing opportunities and presumptions of credibility: namely, we are straight, cisgender, white, non-disabled, economically stable, non-Native, fluent English speakers and documented U.S. citizens with PhDs who have held tenured positions at research-intensive universities. We know that such opportunities and presumptions are not always equally extended to brilliant educators who are LGBQ+, transgender, Black and Brown, Indigenous, disabled, undocumented, economically marginalized, masters of languages other than English, non-Christian, or not similarly credentialed (Gutiérrez y Muhs et al., 2012).

We believe the positions and privileges afforded us by our identities obligate us to name injustice directly and unequivocally, to never soften or fluff up the conversation out of concern for the comfort of similarly privileged readers. This obligation is one way we try to leverage the oppressive reality that some leaders may feel more comfortable learning from us because of who we are. As one way to amplify voices of people whose lives are directly and negatively affected by inequity in schools, we were deliberate about citing work and shouting out organizations led by people who are fighting for liberation while also contending with the inequities we examine in this book. We urge readers to engage with these incredible educators and organizations and to direct resources their way.

We also want to be clear that we are not above the problems we identify in this book. Throughout the following pages, we strive to stay humble and point out moments from our own practice when we've missed the mark. Nevertheless, we are sure there are important points or nuances we have missed. On top of that, inequities within school and the language to address them keep evolving. Because we are dedicated to eviscerating inequity and cultivating equity, we are constantly pushing ourselves to learn more, to take greater risks, and to seek critical feedback to sharpen our own equity literacy skills. In that spirit, this book is as much an inward-facing challenge, an expression of self-accountability, as it is an outward-facing challenge to you, the reader.

Acknowledgments

None of this would be possible without friends, colleagues, and family members who have pushed, pulled, and promoted us throughout our lives and work. Although there are too many people to name, a few explicit appreciations are in order. First and foremost, we are grateful for the educational leaders who have invited us into their spaces and for the students and staff within those schools who have been willing to share their experiences with us in the hope that it will help inspire change. We have learned and continue to learn so much from them and feel deeply obligated to do right by them in this book and everything we do. We are forever indebted to our friends and colleagues, and even to scholars and activists we've never met, who have shaped our ideas and inspired us for years. We cite many of them in this book.

We particularly want to thank Vidya Iyer and Gabriel Rodriguez for their feedback on various versions of this book. And we want to thank Marceline DuBose and Daniel Spikes, our closest collaborators, whose ideas and passion helped inform this book and much of the other work we do. We are better people, scholars, and educators because of their critical friendship, research, teaching, and organizing.

We express deep gratitude for our editor, Susan Hills, for infinite patience with us through the writing process.

Last but not least, we want to thank you, reader, for giving this book a chance. We hope you feel both supported and challenged by it.

Introduction

We stood in the main doorway of Green Fields High School's cafeteria during the busiest lunch period of the day. Michael, a dean at Green Fields, pointed toward a table on the left side of the cafeteria where a group of Black students talked, laughed, and ate. Then he nodded toward the table directly in front of us, where a group consisting primarily of second- and third-generation Korean American students did the same.

We were visiting the school at Michael's request. He had called us earlier that week. "We have a race problem at Green Fields," he explained. "We need help understanding and fixing it."

He pointed again to the tables where Black and Korean American students were eating. "See what I mean about the race problem?" he asked.

By all accounts, Michael, a middle-aged, white, cisgender man, was well-liked by students, including students of color. Colleagues at Green Fields, a predominately white but increasingly racially diverse school, recognized him as a champion for diversity. He sponsored the student Multicultural Club. He decorated his office like a shrine to inclusion, with a "Safe Space" sticker on his door and a "Unity Through Diversity" poster pinned to the wall behind his desk.

Despite his enthusiasm for inclusion, despite his engagement with the Multicultural Club and diversity decor, Michael couldn't quite manage to recognize how inequity operated right in front of him. He didn't lack goodwill. He wasn't a rabid racist or a zealous xenophobe. Truth is, although the relatively small number of rabid racists and zealous xenophobes we've come across in schools do a great deal of damage, even greater and more dangerous damage can be done by diversity-minded educators like Michael: leaders who don't intend to do damage (Lewis & Diamond, 2015). More on that in a moment.

As Michael pointed to those two tables as though the problem was too obvious to miss, we responded that, no, we did not see what he meant. Were we missing something?

"Look," he said, "the problem is that the students of color segregate themselves. It's like they don't want to integrate and be part of the school." It was a scene straight out of Beverly Daniel Tatum's (2017) book, *Why Are All the Black Kids Sitting Together in the Cafeteria? And Other Conversations About Race.*

We scanned the room. Sure, the cafeteria was fairly segregated in the same way we observe in many racially and ethnically diverse middle and high schools. Yes, Black and Korean American students filled those two tables. At the most surface level, we could see what Michael saw. The trouble was, Michael seemed to see only those two tables: the ones full of two groups of color in a veritable sea of whiteness. Those two tables sat at the outer edges, the literal margins, of a cafeteria where 20 tables were filled almost entirely with white students.

It hadn't occurred to Michael that perhaps the *white* students were segregating themselves, or that the Black and Korean American students were simply finding a few moments of ease and safety in a school where they often were the only students of their racial or ethnic identities in their classes, where there were no Korean American teachers, only two Black teachers, and no administrators or counselors of color. We shared this observation with Michael, attempting to help him interpret what he saw in a more nuanced, more equity-literate way.

Looking around the cafeteria, he responded, humbly, "I've never seen it that way before."

The Trouble, the Struggle, and the Commitment

The trouble at Green Fields, like the trouble at many schools we visit, was not a shortage of people who cared about their students or who valued diversity. Michael and his colleagues cared deeply about their students. They had plenty of diversity- or inclusion-related programs and initiatives. Instead, the trouble was that Michael and many of his colleagues struggled to recognize with sufficient depth how bias and inequity operated at their school. They struggled ideologically to understand the lived realities of students of color and how the Multicultural Club and diversity decorations did not remedy those realities. Their shaky awareness undermined their abilities to devise suitable and sustainable solutions for their equity problems.

The leaders at Green Fields struggled to interpret concerns such as disparate rates of extracurricular participation, disparate patterns of discipline referrals, or even disparate test score data through an equity lens. They struggled to recognize the inequity embedded in their policies and practices. So, despite their efforts, as we learned when we facilitated a series of student focus groups, Black students experienced significant racial bias at Green Fields, and Korean American students largely felt invisible. That reality meant that no matter what leaders thought they were doing in the name of racial *equity*, the impact tended to cement racial *inequity*. These students' barriers and frustrations were more related to educators' ideologies and misinterpretation than to practical strategy, programming, complete inattention, or explicit bigotry.

In fact, the trouble in many schools is the desire, and sometimes even the desperation, to prescribe equity *solutions* without understanding the equity *problems*. Bad equity solutions almost always increase inequity. That's where Michael was stuck.

We asked Michael how he intended to address what he interpreted as Green Fields's "race problem": students of color segregating themselves. He shared that the school's administrative team had considered force-integrating the cafeteria. They explored the possibility of assigning students to specific tables but worried that a mutiny might ensue if they tried to enforce table assignments. It hadn't occurred to them that for some students at Green Fields, lunchtime was a respite.

Because that hadn't occurred to them, it also hadn't occurred to them that the real problem might be that Black students, Korean American students, and other students of color at Green Fields *needed* a respite. They needed a respite from racial microaggressions they experienced from peers and adults at the school. They needed a respite from the social and cultural pressures they felt to conform to an institutional culture that largely rendered them invisible. They needed a respite from the curricular erasure, from being "the only" in their classes, from teachers responding inadequately to racist comments and jokes. They needed a respite from the racism. And they needed Michael and his administrative peers to be more concerned with the racism students faced at Green Fields and less with where they sat during lunch.

From Good Intentions to Good Actions

In our experience, the situation at Green Fields illustrates a bit of an epidemic among school and district leaders. Sure, part of schools' equity problem stems from the beliefs and actions of rabid racists and zealous xenophobes, as we said earlier, along with calculating cisgenderists and enthusiastic sexists. But perhaps a bigger portion comes down to the beliefs and actions of people like Michael: people with real concern, people with ostensibly good intentions, people who appreciate diversity but may struggle to understand how injustice operates with enough depth to eliminate it.

We want to be clear about this: there's no shame in that struggle. The reality is, most of us do well recognizing and understanding the kinds of inequity we experience but labor to recognize and understand the kinds of injustice from which our identities and positionalities protect us. As people who have committed our lives to fighting for equity and justice in education, we find ourselves perpetually in this struggle.

The shame is in choosing *not* to be in that struggle when students, families, and colleagues who are being harmed desperately need us to be in it. To opt out is an expression of privilege and entitlement, because the people being harmed can't opt out.

Part of what we ask you to do while reading this book is to stay with us in that struggle. When we find ourselves feeling defensive or clinging onto old ideas like security blankets, we know it's time to engage more deeply rather than less deeply.

Consider an example. As we discuss in greater detail later, researchers who have studied why Black students are suspended or expelled from school at higher rates than their classmates have concluded that the disparity is trackable largely to racial bias, not to Black students misbehaving more often or their families not valuing school enough. What do we know? We know that Black students are suspended and expelled at higher rates than white students, for example. Based on big national studies, including one examining more than a million office referrals (Girvan et al., 2017), we know that the biggest cause of this disparity comes down to differences in how educators interpret and respond to subjective behaviors—*the student is behaving in a "disrespectful manner"* or *the student is being "insubordinate"*— leading to higher rates of subjective office referrals for Black students who are behaving in ways for which their white classmates aren't as likely to be referred.

We should wonder, then, why most of the popular solutions for addressing racial disparities in discipline seem to focus on everything other than the only possible solution: eliminating this racism. Perhaps we adopt Positive Behavioral Interventions and Supports (PBIS) so that we can be clearer about behavior expectations. Perhaps we embrace trauma-sensitive approaches so that we can respond to the underlying causes of behaviors. Perhaps we offer students training in mindfulness and emotion regulation.

At best, these are bad solutions based on significant misunderstandings of the problem. At worst, they appear to be purposeful dodging: a way to sustain racist experiences and outcomes while creating the illusion of antiracist concern. The research is clear: the problem isn't a lack of clarity about behavior expectations, a mindfulness deficiency, or some innate cultural value that keeps students from "behaving"; the problem is racial bias and inequitable applications of discipline policies. Perhaps the biggest barrier to equity progress is the struggle among people who value diversity or belonging to understand that offering mindfulness and emotion regulation to students as solutions to racial discipline disparities or interrupting Black or Korean American students' respite from racism while failing to attend to the racism is a way we actually perpetuate racism.

Again, the typical trouble is not that leaders aren't doing *something* about racial discipline disparities or other inequities. Schools generally appear to be doing a whole lot of *something*. The trouble instead is that most of what that something comprises poses no real threat to the disparities or inequities. Because the something is usually ineffectual, it's also usually inefficient—a misuse of the energy, time, and emotional labor that educators invest in their jobs. Why would we spend precious resources on "equity" approaches, strategies, and initiatives that are bound to fail?

As far as we can see, we might answer this question in a couple of ways. Neither lands us at particularly good news.

The first possible answer is that it's purposeful. We know, at the very least, that many leaders feel pressure to demonstrate the optics of movement on equity and justice. Unfortunately, that's what often seems to be rewarded or prioritized in school systems: *optics.* In fact, when we ask school and district leaders to share the most important thing they're doing when it comes to equity, they most commonly describe cool-sounding student programs: a diversity assembly, perhaps, or an antibullying workshop. These sorts of initiatives are high on optics but generally low on impact. They don't identify or eliminate institutional racism, heterosexism, or ableism. They don't change institutional conditions any more than Michael force-integrating the Green Fields cafeteria would change institutional conditions. It's hard not to read the evasion as purposeful after watching school leaders respond to inequitable conditions, not with plans to transform institutional cultures around an antiracist or anti-ableist commitment, but instead with decontextualized community dialogues or statements about how *diversity is our strength.*

Again, these are high-equity-optics, low-institutional-impact responses. We can do better.

One way to do better is to begin questioning the presumption of good intentions. After all, how many generations of educational leaders with good equity intentions does it take to substantially transform schools, to wipe out all or even most of the predictable bias and inequity? The courageous move is to put an expiration date on good intentions—our own and one another's. When is *actual* movement going to be rewarded more than the *illusion* of movement or the ostensible *intention* of movement? This is the sort of individual and collective reckoning we should embrace if we are serious about educational equity.

This answer to our question, that the problem is purposeful evasion, sounds discouraging, we know. That's why we constructed this book around the second answer, for leaders who don't want their efforts to be about optics, who genuinely want to do right by students and staff, who are horrified to learn that what they've been doing in the name of diversity might perpetuate harm. We're not naive enough to believe that this description covers *everybody*, including everybody working in education. We have our determined inequitable system-sustainers just like every other field and system. But we do presume that, with deeper understanding and more transformative equity commitments and skills, Michael and other educational leaders can become strong, effective equity leaders. As we discuss in more detail later, we constructed this book on the assumption that you'll read it because you desire equity and have the will to do something about inequity. You want to embrace the most transformative approach possible, because that is what is required to fulfill this equity desire.

To be sure, these transformations do not come without resistance and backlash. We return to this point several times throughout this book: inequitable systems do not pass quietly into the night. But if we have the knowledge, skills, and will to push through the backlash, we *can* effect deep change (Theoharis, 2007). We can, and we must. (We discuss backlash in more detail in Chapter 8.)

But this change can happen only when we are willing to embrace transformative ideas, when we shake free of the kinds of ideological blockages with which Michael and his colleagues struggled, when we embrace new ways of looking at things based on a deep and layered commitment to equity. We can't *celebrate diversity* our way to equity. We can't rely on good intentions that aren't buttressed by good actions. We must reimagine and reconstruct almost everything in our spheres of influence. We need the knowledge to understand the difference between celebrating diversity and eliminating inequity; we need the skills to enact an active, transformative equity vision. Through this commitment we can strengthen what we call our *equity literacy*: our *literacy* when it comes to understanding, cultivating, and sustaining *equity*.

A Brief Introduction to the Rest of This Book

This commitment captures the essence of where we're going in the following chapters. In our view, this book's most important feature is detailed descriptions of what we call the basic principles of equity literacy. We conceived these principles to help educational leaders avoid the misunderstandings and missteps so commonly employed in the name of equity and instead embrace and enact deep, transformative approaches to equity leadership.

In Chapter 1, we define *equity* and *inequity* and distinguish between *mitigative* and *transformative* approaches to equity. In Chapter 2, we introduce key concepts, components, and tenets of the equity literacy framework. This includes the four key building blocks of *equity desire, equity knowledge, equity abilities,* and *equity will*—the will to lead transformatively for equity. The framework also includes what we call the five abilities of equity literacy: *recognizing* inequity, *responding to* inequity, *redressing* inequity, *sustaining* equity, and *actively cultivating* equity.

After introducing the framework, we dive into the principles of equity literacy with a chapter dedicated to each. We use case scenarios, student voices, and other tools to illustrate why the principles are important and to demonstrate them in action. Throughout, we provide reflection prompts that challenge readers to apply the concepts and principles to their own leadership practice.

The *direct confrontation principle,* which we discuss in Chapter 3, reminds us that the path to equity requires direct, decisive action. We begin by recognizing the ways inequity related to race, ability, sex, socioeconomic status, gender identity and expression, sexual identity, size, ethnicity, language, citizenship status, religion, and other identities operate in our spheres of influence. Then we ask of our equity efforts: *To what extent is what we're doing a real threat to inequity and injustice? To what extent does it activate and accelerate equity and justice?* Celebrating diversity by itself doesn't do that. Cultural competence by itself doesn't do that. We can hold the cultures of people who are culturally different from us in high esteem while still enacting policies that harm them racially, economically, or otherwise. The direct confrontation principle is not simply about confronting people but about honestly naming and directly addressing the conditions that perpetuate inequity.

In Chapter 4, we explore the *fix injustice, not kids principle.* This principle challenges us to reconsider programs and initiatives that attempt to achieve equity by adjusting the cultures, mindsets, values, behaviors, grittiness, or attitudes of the people who are experiencing inequity. Equity is never about fixing or adjusting students and families who are racially, economically, or otherwise marginalized, an approach often called *deficit ideology* (Fergus, 2021; Gorski, 2016). Instead, it's about eliminating the conditions that marginalize students and families. In this chapter, we outline ways we can root out deficit approaches and bridge ourselves and one another to what we call a *structural* equity approach. When we do so, we equip ourselves to more clearly recognize and more effectively attend to the root causes of disparities and inequities.

The *prioritization principle,* the focus of Chapter 5, challenges leaders to learn how to intentionally prioritize the best interests, joys, needs, and access of students and families who historically have been, and presently continue to be, denied equitable access and opportunity. The only way to do this with the level of transformation required is to reimagine policies and practices and rebuild institutional cultures in ways that account for historical and present inequity and its ramifications. We must commit to pacing equity efforts in ways that prioritize the people most desperate for equity and justice rather than stepping gingerly, protecting the people most resistant to equity and justice. This is not just ideological posturing; it's consistent with organizational change theory and research about how to lead significant institutional change.

In Chapter 6, we introduce the *just access principle*, which insists that we move beyond concerns about access and outcomes to nurture truly transformative equity. Too often school policies, practices, and initiatives, including those posing as something new, uphold historical efforts to assimilate, marginalize, police, and punish students. For example, so much of our curriculum has been focused on the values, beliefs, and assumptions that perpetuate discrimination and oppression, even when these intentions are hidden behind promising-sounding initiatives such as *advanced coursework* or *character education* or *social-emotional learning*. We reconsider what we are working so hard to provide equitable access to, and whether it is itself equitable.

Chapter 7 examines the *evidence-based equity principle* and the ways conventional approaches to collecting and analyzing data can cloud our understandings of inequity and hinder our ability to eliminate it. We point to the need to gather more meaningful data to help us assess a school's equity health.

Finally, in Chapter 8, we share the *care, joy, and sustainability principle*. As we finished writing this book, the pushback against educational equity efforts was increasingly organized and well-funded. It can be hard not to despair at the resistance to even the most menial inclusion efforts. However, the push for equity also has never been stronger or the need for it more apparent. This principle emphasizes the importance of joy and community-building in cultivating and sustaining transformative equity. We also discuss self- and community care for equity leaders who face blowback and reprisals for taking strong equity stands.

Starting Assumptions

Before we jump into Chapter 1, we want to be as clear as possible about our givens. These are the assumptions we carry into this book.

Assumption One: Equity Leadership Does Not Require Positional Authority

In many schools and districts, the most important, most transformative equity leadership comes not from principals or other people with positional authority but from teachers, counselors, parents, students, and others who, despite not having positional authority, do everything they can to push equity efforts forward. In fact, sometimes the most substantive equity leadership we witness is provided by people who are doing everything in their power to lead transformative change *despite* inaction and insufficient support from positional leaders. We have been blown away, for example, by the equity leadership assumed by student and alumni groups who are organizing on social media to demand that school and district leaders pay more serious attention to racism, heterosexism, cisgenderism, and other forms of oppression.

Of course, principals, superintendents, and other positional leaders can be—*ought to* be—equity leaders too. Many of the examples of equity leadership we offer throughout this book draw on our experiences with people who have positional authority. The best-case scenario is that positional leaders work alongside all those other leaders, the people our brilliant colleague Marceline DuBose calls *passion leaders*, to enact and sustain equity efforts. After all, positional leaders have the authority to quicken the pace of change, and often passion leaders have the experience and expertise to understand most clearly what change needs to happen.

We share all of this to say that we wrote this book not just for principals, equity directors, and central office administrators, but also for anybody bent on leading transformative equity efforts. Whatever your sphere of influence or official role, if you are advocating for equity, we believe the principles in this book will help you do so in the most transformative way possible.

Assumption Two: There Is No Magic Equity Blueprint

If you're looking for a book that describes "10 strategies you can implement tomorrow, making all things equitable," this is not that.

And if you find a book claiming to be that, our recommendation is, don't trust it.

This is the first cognitive challenge we pose to many educational leaders. Let go of the expectation that equity leadership is about this or that strategy, program, or initiative. We understand that in an education culture where the supposed building blocks of good schooling often are marketed as what we call the "shiny new things," this cognitive shift can be difficult. But ask yourself this: How have those programs and initiatives been working so far? Have they helped us eliminate any disparities?

The reality is that, for generations, we in education have churned through program after program, initiative after initiative—all the shiny new things—and for the most part they have made little or no difference when it comes to equity and justice, especially when implemented in a sort of mindless plug-and-play fashion. It's time for a different approach.

We remember when "learning styles" was the shiny new thing, embraced in many schools as a salve for achievement disparities. It wasn't. It couldn't be, because attending to learning styles has nothing to do with identifying and eliminating the racism, cisgenderism, sexism, ableism, or other oppressive conditions that cause and sustain inequity. It also couldn't be the salve because, as it turns out, the notion that adjusting teaching to students' learning styles improves learning is among the most thoroughly debunked presumptions in education (Pashler et al., 2008). But it sure was marketed as a salve for a good decade before research demonstrated its ineffectiveness, in the same way some more recent studies have suggested growth mindset interventions have little impact on learning (Sisk et al., 2018).

Neither is resilience or antibullying or diversity programming or SEL or PBIS the salve. If we start with a school where, say, socioeconomic inequity operates in a variety of ways and we sprinkle all of this in—the diversity programming, the cultural competence, the kindness—we're still left with socioeconomic inequity, because none of these ingredients poses any substantial threat to inequity. Which of these ingredients identifies and eliminates inequitable policies and practices? Which substantially addresses the root causes of discipline disparities? Which transforms institutional cultures not just to celebrate diversity but also to normalize conversations about and actions toward justice? The problem here is not that we as educational leaders don't *recognize* the problem of inequity but rather that we *misunderstand* it. As a result, our solutions pose no serious threat to it. Again, it's a lot of optics with no serious potential for change (Stevenson, 2014).

This reality doesn't mean some of these shiny new things aren't beneficial to children and families. For example, we're proponents of SEL when it is informed with an equity lens. It just means that no combination of them can, in itself, make schools more equitable or just, especially schools where leaders refuse to embrace more transformative equity commitments. So we must let go of the expectation that there's an outline or equation that tells us which practices and initiatives to stir together to concoct the equity potion. Nothing replaces the hard work of identifying inequity, eliminating inequity, and actively cultivating equity. There's no blueprint for that. But there are some key understandings and abilities to help us do it. Those are the principles we detail in this book.

Assumption Three: Ideological Shifts Drive Practical Shifts

In the spirt of Assumption One, we offer in this book something that we have learned is more valuable and, in a way, even more practical than practices: the critical understandings we need to make those transformative commitments and lead for equity in meaningful ways. These are the principles, the values, that can guide the programs, practices, and literally everything else we do. They help achieve clarity about our ends so that we can embrace the best possible means. We offer a framework to inform *all* of the doing rather than a step-by-step guide to the doing.

In other words, the shifts we're proposing are, as much as anything, ideological and institutional adjustments. The fix injustice, not kids principle, for example, requires that we ditch deficit perspectives and quit grit as solutions for educational disparities, and focus instead on addressing the conditions that marginalize students and create the disparities. Doing so requires an ideological shift for many educators. Without that shift, equitable practices aren't sustainable anyway.

This step, the ideological shift, is one we too often skip in education. Bad ideology explains why there are more initiatives focusing on resilience, social-emotional learning, and behavior adjustment than on antiracism in schools that desperately need antiracism. Bad ideology doesn't mean bad people. It means we need to prepare ourselves to understand more precisely why conditions exist so that we can address them deeply rather than dancing around them.

So our third assumption grows out of our belief that there is no shortage of equity-related programs and initiatives, but there is a shortage of equity because those efforts are almost always (1) built on misunderstandings or evasions, such as professional development on debunked concepts such as the "mindset of poverty"; or (2) not specifically constructed with equity in mind, such as PBIS. When we address the misunderstandings and evasions and embrace deep equity principles that facilitate profound understandings and more direct and effective eradications of inequity, we will prepare ourselves to lead more transformatively for equity. If we choose instead to hold onto our ideological blockages, we render ourselves incapable of serious change.

Assumption Four: Desiring Equity Is Not Enough

In the same spirit, we start with the assumption that you, like Michael and his Green Fields colleagues, want to lead for equity. We also assume, as Michael illustrated, that the *desire* to lead for equity is an unsuitable, and maybe even dangerous, stand-in for the knowledge and skills necessary to lead for equity. As Martin Luther King Jr. wrote in his "Letter from Birmingham Jail," "Shallow understanding from people of good will is more frustrating than absolute misunderstanding from people of ill will." Without deep understanding and just *actions*, good intentions—talking the equity talk—add up to precisely no meaningful equity movement. This book is about how we can leverage deep understanding and goodwill to promote transformative action in equity leadership.

We also start with the assumption that we do not need to convince you that equity and justice matter, or that sexism, racism, ableism, classism, colonialism, and other forms of oppression exist and wreak havoc in and out of schools. Nor do we try to convince readers that we all are responsible for attending to inequity and injustice in serious, transformative ways. They do, and we are. That's our point of departure.

Instead, our guiding questions are *What does serious, transformative equity leadership look like? On what values and understandings is it conceived?* Based on the work we've done with hundreds of schools and districts, and considering the values embraced in schools we've observed making substantial strides versus those that expend substantial resources but make little progress, we ask these questions: *What are the basic principles and values that can guide transformative equity leadership? What ideals and understandings do effective equity leaders embrace that other, perhaps well-intentioned, leaders fail to, or choose not to, embrace?*

Assumption Five: We Must Listen to Students

As you read this book, you'll notice we often refer to lessons we've learned from students, especially those who experience substantial inequity in their schools. Sometimes these lessons come from the hundreds of focus groups we've conducted, and sometimes they are from individual, even informal, conversations we've had with students. Sure, we cite other sorts of evidence where appropriate, including big national quantitative studies, but we have learned that nothing can replace what we call the *listen and believe* commitment. Listen to students' stories about how they experience school and believe what they say. If we're going to be evidence-informed, we should ask ourselves what kinds of evidence we're ignoring. Stories and counter-stories are evidence—valuable, powerful evidence. We come back to this point throughout the book, but especially in Chapter 7.

Students' stories also illustrate the impacts of inequitable conditions in classrooms and schools, so we draw on them a lot. We do so both because they are vital evidence, important illustrations, but also because we worry that so much equity work in schools is guided by presumptions about what students need rather than what they are explicitly demanding.

Conclusion

In the rest of this book, we describe an approach to equity leadership that eases our reliance on prepackaged, nonlocalized, plug-and-play strategies—all the stuff that tends to be high on optics and low on impact. We build our approach on well-evidenced principles for transformative and sustainable equity leadership, relevant both to individual leaders and to schools, districts, and other educational institutions. It starts with strengthening our equity literacy.

1

More Than Mitigations: Embracing Transformative Equity

The tricky thing about defining *equity* is that the people who commit their careers to enacting it don't always agree on what it means. It's a buzzword in schools today; we know that much. It's fashionable the way *multicultural education* was when we began our careers. We also know that when concepts associated with transformative ideas become trendy, that usually means the teeth have been filed out of them. Eventually schools tend to adopt them in ways that are barely distinguishable from the conditions they were meant to transform.

For example, the educators most responsible for conceptualizing multicultural education decades ago generally described it as an antiracist, anti-oppressive approach for reimagining all aspects of education (e.g., Nieto & Bode, 2017). Unfortunately, schools that embraced multicultural education often—perhaps *usually*—did so in softer and far less transformative ways, through gentle cultural exchanges, student multicultural clubs, and diversity assemblies. Gloria Ladson-Billings (2014) expressed similar concerns about how schools commonly enact culturally relevant pedagogy, omitting its transformative roots while embracing minor and sometimes stereotypical "cultural diversity" strategies. Using a call-and-response pedagogy, for example, does not make a school riddled with racism less racist.

Diversity, *Equity*, and Inclusion

Something similar is happening with equity. In what commonly is called "DEI" work, *equity* is tucked between two softer, less transformative concepts: *diversity* and *inclusion*. Most school equity statements we've seen are not equity statements at all, but rather diversity and inclusion statements: "Diversity is our strength" and "All students are welcome" and that sort of thing. We don't disagree that diversity can and should be a strength, but without equity it's a strength borne of local demographics, not of institutional transformation. Nearly all schools are diverse to some extent, if not racially or linguistically or religiously, then economically, and almost always along lines of ethnicity, gender identity and expression, sexual orientation, and disability. Most schools also are full of inequities, big and small, implicit and explicit, purposeful and unintentional.

Having diversity without equity is most definitely possible; but without equity, diversity itself is not any institution's strength—at least not for the people who are denied equity. So we should be careful not to conflate diversity, equity, and inclusion. When we do, we risk obscuring the demands that equity makes of us that diversity and inclusion without equity don't make. We can lead a school that is racially or economically diverse, but if our "diverse" school is full of racism and class inequity, we can't say it's equitable. That's why we put equity and justice at the center of the conversation: robust, healthy diversity and inclusion cannot exist without equity.

In Chapter 2, we introduce the equity literacy framework, the building blocks of the principles described in this book. In preparation for that task, we offer a conception of equity grounded in a transformative view that demands something more than celebrating diversity or surface-level inclusion. We won't insist that our way of understanding equity is the only useful or transformative one. It *is*, however, an approach that has enabled us to help educational leaders embrace a deep, profound, layered understanding of equity. It's meant to ensure we aren't fooled into embracing an approach to equity that has no real chance at cultivating equity.

Something More Than "Giving Individuals What They Need"

When we ask fellow educators how they define *equity*, they most commonly respond with something like "providing all students with what they need to achieve to their fullest capabilities." We appreciate the distinction between *equity* and *equality* implied by this definition. We will explore that distinction shortly. From an equity literacy point of view, this is a decent start. We absolutely want to attend to the unique academic, social, emotional, and other needs of each student; we want to provide all students with tools and support tailored to their individual needs, passions, and desires.

The limitation of this Multi-Tiered Systems of Support–style definition of equity is that if all we're doing is building individual relationships, determining individual needs, and responding to those needs without any real contextual or institutional understanding of how inequity may be operating, we're actually missing *most* of the inequity. We need to be careful not to individualize equity so much that we fail to attend to the biases and inequities that are embedded in school and classroom cultures, policies, practices, and systems: the curricular erasure of Indigenous communities, the practices and procedures that punish families experiencing poverty for their poverty, the ways that racism and ableism have shaped who has access to certain schools and academic tracks. We need to understand what Sonia Nieto and Patty Bode (2017) call the "sociopolitical context of schooling," including how societal forms of injustice operate through, and inform what we do in, schools.

For example, our strong personal connections to individual LGBQ+ students or students who do not conform to rigid categories of gender identity or expression do not substantially protect them from the oppressive impact of an institutionalized health or history curriculum that renders them invisible and ignores their needs and concerns. Those connections don't protect them from schools' tendencies to address heterosexism and cisgenderism only as a one-on-one bullying problem and not as an institutional concern wrapped into school cultures, policies, and presumptions. Finding ways to help students survive that bullying or the heterosexist, cisgenderist curriculum while we ignore the conditions in classrooms and schools that oppress them is just another layer of inequity.

At some point we must transform the curriculum. Then we must understand that the heterosexist, cisgenderist curriculum is just a symptom or manifestation of something bigger. We need to transform the aspects of institutional culture and ideology that resulted in that curriculum, that had a building full of caring adults implementing it, many perhaps not realizing what was wrong with it. Beyond cultivating good interpersonal relationships and supports with them, LGBQ+ students need us to address the conditions that may cause them to experience curricular erasure and other forms of heterosexism at school. Transgender students need to be able to come to school without worrying how they will experience transphobia. And those LGBQ+ and transgender students who are also students of color, disabled, undocumented, or otherwise marginalized face additional structural barriers. Responding to and refusing to recreate these barriers are *institutional* endeavors, not just *interpersonal* ones.

Our starting point, then, is embracing an understanding of equity that has a more transformative, more institutional bent layered atop the popular notion of addressing individual needs. In fact, we generally use the word *equity* to refer to anti-oppression and justice efforts, commitments, and conditions within specific institutions like schools. We use *equity* in schools or districts the way we might use *social justice* to refer to bigger societal movements for, and commitments to, antiracism, antisexism, economic justice, disability justice, and other forms of justice. We don't advocate losing that more individual notion of providing all students what they need. Instead, we want to think about needs and equity more robustly by understanding them in the context of institutions and systems, not just interpersonal relationships.

So this is one important role of equity leaders: helping to transition the people around us to a more layered, more transformative understanding of equity built on something more robust than addressing individual needs within inequitable systems. As we work through the principles in upcoming chapters, we will provide the framing and strategies needed to do that. Of course, it starts with adopting a layered, transformative understanding ourselves.

Understanding Inequity

The second most common response when we ask educators to define equity is something like "equal outcomes." We appreciate the spirit of this response as well. We agree that, all things being equitable, we should not be able to predict patterns of test scores, graduation rates, suspensions and expulsions, assignments to advanced classes or special education, or grade point averages across, say, socioeconomic status. (Of course, all things being equitable, we also would not have such enormous disparities in socioeconomic status more generally, so there's that.) Similarly, all things being equitable, we might expect to observe consistent ranges of traditional measures of achievement across ethnicity, home language, and other identities. Perhaps more important, all things being equitable, we wouldn't expect that we could predict consistent distinctions in how students *experience* school based on socioeconomic status, ethnicity, or gender identity.

More Than Test Score Disparities

But all things aren't equitable. Not even close. They aren't equitable within schools, where, for example, students experiencing poverty are routinely denied learning opportunities that their wealthier peers might take for granted, perhaps because their families can't afford to pay extra fees or because schools with significant numbers of students experiencing poverty tend to be less well-funded and resourced than even the underfunded, underresourced schools with more middle class students (Gorski, 2018). Things aren't equitable or just outside schools either, where many families experiencing poverty are denied basic services and resources such as preventive healthcare, access to healthy food, and safe and affordable housing (Berliner, 2013).

Imagine how different those test scores and graduation rates would be if every student had access to these basic human rights. Imagine how different their experiences would be if we, as a society, attended in serious ways to the injustice they face.

This is another key understanding for equity leaders: inequity both in and out of school causes disparities in educational outcome. These disparities are not the result of a shortage of grit or the undervaluing of education among families experiencing poverty, families who are masters of languages other than English, or families of color. If we fail to address the inequity, then we have no shot at eliminating the outcome disparities.

We want to make this point as clearly as possible. We worry that, during this educational era, when many leaders feel pressured to obsess over comparisons of quantitative achievement, too big a portion of the equity conversation has shifted from attending to how injustice operates in classrooms and schools to focus almost exclusively on decontextualized quantitative data. As a result, inequity in too many contexts has been redefined as test score disparities, and equity has been reimagined simply as *raising test scores*. This reframing of the equity conversation also takes those test scores for granted as objective measures when, in reality, they are flawed when it comes to measuring ability or potential (Au, 2010). We discuss this in more detail in Chapter 7.

Although it might exist, we've never seen a school whose primary strategy for raising test scores is *eliminate the racism* or *stamp out the economic injustice*. But we've seen many schools whose strategies include *help students become more resilient while ignoring the racism* or *disproportionately deny students experiencing poverty access to the arts so they can have more time in math*. Does this sound like equity?

This is why we define inequity as *an unfair or unjust distribution of material and nonmaterial access and opportunity resulting in outcome disparities and experience disparities that are predictable* by race, socioeconomic status, gender identity and expression, sexual orientation, religion, ethnicity, immigrant status, home language, and (dis)ability, among other identifiers. This unjust distribution of access and opportunity is what we're out to eliminate. Let's pause here and consider what it means.

When Access and Opportunity Are Divvied Up Unjustly

First, the *unjust distribution of access and opportunity* refers to situations in which some students or families are denied the kinds or levels of educational access and opportunity enjoyed by other students or families. Often this happens because of policies, practices, or aspects of institutional culture that protect the interests of students or families with more privileged identities at the expense of other students or families. Perhaps we deny students experiencing poverty opportunities to participate in events scheduled before or after school because we refuse to run an early or late bus. Or we presume that students who are learning English as a second or third or fourth language have learning disabilities and assign them to special education classes. Or we subject girls and young women to dress code policies that police what they wear for fear it might distract heterosexual boys and young men. Or we are careful not to hold school events on Christian holidays or church nights but don't think twice about doing so during other religions' observances. These are *inequitable conditions.*

We also want to consider how inequity operates *accumulatively,* because the unjust distribution of access and opportunity rarely works through single, isolated conditions. It's the extracurricular fees *and* the outrageously expensive yearbook *and* the scheduling of family engagement in ways that are inaccessible to parents working multiple jobs, *and, and, and.* As we discuss when we define equity, we must learn how to recognize inequity in individual manifestations of the unjust distribution of access and opportunity, and we must learn how to recognize and understand the accumulative impact, the patterns or *systems* of advantage and disadvantage built into many schools and districts.

Distinguishing Material and Nonmaterial Access and Opportunity

Second, we distinguish in our definition between *material* and *nonmaterial* access and opportunity. We might reflect on material access using this question: *What are the sorts of material items or services—items or services that cost money—to which some students have access and other students do not?* Think specifically about resources or services that could provide an educational advantage to students who have access to them.

You might be thinking about school supplies, technology, and private tutoring. But there's also preventive healthcare, consistent housing, and transportation. There's the financial means to weather the consequences of a family crisis such as the unexpected death of a parent or a social crisis such as a global pandemic. We might even argue that time itself is a sort of material resource: time to study, time to participate in extracurricular activities, time to prepare healthy meals, time to rest. Not needing to provide childcare to younger siblings or work after school to support the family: this too is a sort of material advantage.

Wrapping our minds around *nonmaterial* access can be a little trickier. It refers to matters of institutional culture, practice, and policy. When we're assessing how schools distribute nonmaterial access, we might ask, *Who has access in school to policies that are constructed around their lived realities rather than somebody else's lived realities? Who has access to teachers and counselors who are attuned to their lives, who they can be reasonably sure don't have sweeping biases about them or their communities? Who has access to a curriculum in which people who share their identities are reflected consistently, honestly, and deeply rather than dishonestly or tokenistically? Who has access to institutional cultures that are built around their cultural norms; who feels, instead, like they cross a cultural border each time they enter a classroom or school? Who is free to be entirely themselves and who might need to spend energy hiding parts of who they are?* We could ask similar questions about the kinds of nonmaterial access students and even educators have outside school because, of course, this could affect their school lives as well.

Notice again that we cannot solve the conditions surrounding these questions at the individual, interpersonal level. We can't solve them by adjusting something about, say, students who aren't Christian or students who are learning English. We can solve them only through institutional commitments and action, through a redistribution of access and opportunity, through the transformation of institutional culture, policy, and practice. We'll return to this idea when we define equity.

Predictable Disparities

Finally, in our definition we refer to disparities that are *predictable* by race, class, and other identifiers. We could stop at the mere existence of disparities, but the predictability is important. Virtually all of the disparities we observe in classrooms, schools, and districts is predictable because they largely follow regional or national patterns. This is true whether we are referring to racial disparities in discipline, gender disparities in enrollment in advanced computer science courses, socioeconomic disparities in assignment to advanced courses (or, if "schools" rather than "students" is our unit of analysis, disparities in the availability of advanced courses) and special education, or sexual orientation disparities in the extent to which students feel represented adequately in school culture. These disparities exist nearly everywhere diversities exist. When we acknowledge this reality in our own institutions, we impose important institutional accountability because it forces us, or *should* force us, to ask ourselves: *If we could have predicted these inequities simply by a brief review of literature on educational equity, then how did we let them happen? Or, if we inherited these conditions from previous leaders, why have we allowed them to persist?*

Either we didn't know something very basic that we should have known and that we need to learn in our effort to be equitable educational leaders, or we knew what we needed to know and didn't respond in a way that was sufficiently transformative. That's a difficult acknowledgment, but it's a critical one if we want to grow as equity leaders.

In conclusion, inequity is the accumulative impact of the largely predictable and persistent outcome and experience disparities that result from past and present unjust distributions of nonmaterial and material access and opportunity. But it's also the set of institutional conditions that allow disparities to exist and persist. It's the inaction, the pretend action, and the insufficient action we take while members of our school community continue to suffer the impacts of sexism, racism, ableism, and other forms of injustice.

We'll explore several examples of these inequities, and what to do about them, in later chapters. For now, take a moment to generate a list of inequities related to material and nonmaterial access and opportunities that are currently operating in your classroom, school, or district. Are these inequities *predictable*, in that they reflect regional or national trends of inequity?

Defining Equity

We use the word *equity* in a couple of interrelated ways. In the most basic sense, equity is a commitment to action. It refers to the process of reimagining and reconstructing classrooms and schools to be anti-oppressive and just across the board. We transcend equity as a philosophical commitment (such as being "equity-minded") to enacting our commitment with clear, decisive, just actions. In this sense, we fully embrace equity only when we adopt specific actions that redistribute access and opportunity and that do so in ways that account for, and counteract the impact of, the historical and present realities of inequity.

So we define equity as *the active process for identifying and eliminating inequity and its underlying oppressions* (such as racism, ableism, and economic injustice). It's also *the active process for intentionally cultivating justice* (including racial justice, disability justice, and economic justice).

Try this: Make a list of everything you're doing in your school or district in the name of diversity, equity, and inclusion. Then cross off your list everything that falls short of eliminating—not helping students navigate or having conversations about, but *eliminating*—inequity or actively cultivating equity. How have you transformed institutional culture, reimagined (rather than just made small changes to) curricula, reconsidered hiring procedures, or recrafted policy in ways that clearly and specifically protect the best interests of the families who until now had been the most marginalized families in your school or district? For every item you cross out, ask yourself what you could do instead that would be a threat to the existence of inequity. Doing those things constitutes equity. We discuss this in more detail when we introduce the direct confrontation principle in Chapter 3.

We also use the term *equity* to describe an institutional way of being. This is what schools and districts ought to aspire to. In this sense, an equitable school is one where biases, inequities, and predictable disparities do not exist. Equitable schools and districts are free of racism, heterosexism, ableism, and other forms of oppression. We call this the *aspirational* side of equity because we've never seen a school or district achieve it. Not completely. In fact, it's probably impossible for a school to be fully equitable when it sits in a society brimming over with inequities or when it is full of people socialized in that society. Whether or not it's fully realizable, though, every school and district, every school and district leader, should actively, intensely pursue it.

There's no equity purity, no equity perfection. The challenge is to claw our way as close to that as possible. We designed the principles we discuss in this book to guide equity leaders in that direction.

Transforming Rather Than Mitigating

As you've probably noticed, in the context of the equity literacy framework, which we describe in detail in Chapter 2, we often use the term *transformative equity*. True equity efforts are, by nature, transformative. Still, we use the word *transformative* because, in our experience, most of what people embrace in the name of equity is *mitigative*, not *transformative*. In other words, the tendency is to nibble around the edges of inequity or offer support to people who have been harmed rather than wholly transforming the conditions that perpetuate harm.

Equality, Equity, and Those Softball Stadium Cartoons

You're probably familiar with the popular cartoons, originating from one created by Angus Maguire, distinguishing between *equality* and *equity*. The most widely distributed of these cartoons depicts three people of different heights attempting to peer over an outfield fence to watch a softball game. In the first frame, each stands on a box, which provides a boost to see over the fence. This helps one of the three, who is just tall enough to see over the fence when standing on the box. Of the other two, one doesn't need a box to see over the fence and one is unable to see over the fence despite standing on a box. The boxes are distributed *equally*. Only two of the fans can watch the game.

In the next frame, meant to illustrate *equity*, the boxes are distributed differently. The fan who is tall enough not to require a boost doesn't have any boxes. The fan who can just see over the fence standing on one box has the necessary box. The one who couldn't see over the fence despite standing on one box now has two boxes and can finally see the game. The boxes, this frame claims, are now distributed *equitably*. All three fans presumably have what they need to watch the game.

As we mentioned earlier, we believe meaningful equity leadership requires a more sophisticated understanding of equity. Yes, we must ensure individual students are provided the tailored combination of learning, emotional, social, and other supports that will help them succeed. But we can't stop at that individualistic view. Beyond those individual supports, what students need is to not experience racism at school. What students need is to know they won't be cheated out of learning opportunities because their families can't afford to pay extra fees to access certain programs. They need us to identify sexism, eliminate sexism, and actively cultivate antisexism in policies, practices, and institutional culture before they are plowed under by sexism. This is institutional, transformative work, not just individual work.

The primary trouble in these cartoons is the presence of the fence and the fact that some people are outside it; the fence represents the access and opportunity gap. In this view, that second frame supposedly illustrating equity does not illustrate equity at all. Instead, it represents the way we might *mitigate* structural disadvantage by providing students with supports that help them adjust to it. It's akin to providing resilience and coping strategies in the face of institutional racism when we need racial justice instead.

After all, equity is not about mitigating disadvantage or helping students adjust to a barrier. It's not about tinkering around the edges of injustice, making small adjustments to inequitable conditions, creating the illusion of access and opportunity. It's about transforming conditions by identifying and eliminating inequity and actively cultivating equity. Remove the wall. From a systems point of view, rearranging the boxes is like ignoring the well-documented racial bias in discipline practices we described earlier while offering Black students emotion-regulation strategies, mindfulness practices, or clearer understandings of behavior expectations. We're doing *something*, perhaps, but at best that something is no real threat to inequity. At worst, it is racist or sexist or ableist in its presumptions and evasions.

We call this tinkering a *mitigative* approach to equity. What we're looking for is a *transformative* approach. We want to reimagine the ballpark (or the school) with equity and justice in mind. We want to drive out the ableism, the cisgenderism, the economic injustice, and rebuild institutional policies, practices, and cultures around a commitment to equity and justice.

Sure, in the immediate term we should rearrange the boxes. But we can't let that distract us from addressing the deeper systemic conditions that require the boxes.

Of course, it's important for students who are facing injustice at schools to have strategies for how to navigate and fight it. Many students develop those strategies as a survival mechanism or learn them from members of their community who have faced similar barriers. The problem is when an educator looks at a student who is denied equitable access and opportunity and, instead of addressing that denial, only offers a mitigative salve.

Transformative equity's key task is not to help people overcome a barrier while we ignore the barrier itself. It's not about making a racially inequitable curriculum a little less racist or a transphobic practice slightly less transphobic and then checking off the inclusivity box. What even the equity version of the cartoon fails to depict is the accumulated advantage for the people who always have been able to see over the fence. It does not help us make sense of the order of operations, whether we're redistributing boxes, tearing down the fence, or incorporating fans into the game.

Other versions of the cartoon incorporate this more transformative metaphor. In one, representing "liberation," the fence has been torn down, giving all three fans an unobstructed view. In another, the three fans are participating in the game. Artists have reimagined this viral image in ways that highlight that the underlying trouble was not simply that people couldn't see over the fence or the unfair distribution of boxes, but the conditions that led to that inequitable distribution and the very presence of the fence.

Starfish and Babies

What can be confusing about the distinction between mitigative and transformative action is that the nibbling is often rewarded, especially when it's done in ways that are high on optics. Even people determined to protect existing distributions of access and opportunity can get on board with the nibbling, with the multicultural arts fairs and the diversity celebrations. In fact, they may have incentives to be pro-nibbling, to look like they support equity without having to truly invest in it.

This observation might explain why so many people love the starfish parable. You've probably heard it. A young woman is on the beach, alarmed that so many starfish have washed ashore and lay dying, drying out in the sun. She picks up starfish one by one and tosses them back into the ocean.

A passerby observes that thousands of starfish have washed ashore, far too many for the young woman to save. "You're never going to make a difference," the passerby says.

Then, picking up a starfish, the young woman responds, "I made a difference to *this* one!" as she tosses it back into the ocean.

As educators, we might be especially drawn to the starfish story. It's one of our popular tropes: *If I can make a difference for just one student, I will have done my job.* The starfish story abounds with warm fuzzies.

We support the young woman doing whatever she can to attend to as many starfish as possible so long as she's not inadvertently doing even more damage to them. This, in a way, is reminiscent of that "giving every student what they need" vision for equity. It feels immediate and manageable. And she's not wrong. It *does* matter to that starfish. It *does* matter to that student or family for whom we go to bat.

But there are limits to this starfish approach. The reality is, no serious organizational or societal change ever occurred this way. And really, is our goal to make a difference to just one student? It's a worthy goal, in a way. But it's not equity.

A few years ago, we were invited into a conversation with a school district's STEAM (science, technology, engineering, arts, and math) curriculum directors. As in many districts, they had struggled to quash gender disparities in course-taking. The further along students progressed in school and the more advanced the class, the smaller the proportion of young women taking math, science, and computer science courses. The disparity was especially dire in advanced high school computer science courses.

We asked the curriculum directors to share the most transformative initiative they had adopted to address this disparity. "It has to be the Women Gamers Club," the director in charge of computer science boasted. As academic clubs go, this one sounded exciting. Young women interested in gaming and other technology activities could gather free from the toxic masculinities often associated with gaming culture (Cote, 2020). They discussed sexism and racism in the tech world, met with a diverse array of women tech leaders, and used gaming skills to address gender inequities in their neighborhoods. According to one curriculum director, some members gained confidence enough to register for advanced computer science classes at the high school and, in a couple cases, at a local community college. All good stuff.

The Women Gamers Club created one transformed, temporary space for several young women in the district. It meant a lot to many of them. Still, from a transformative equity point of view, the club had no impact institutionally on gender inequities. It didn't appreciably alter the demographics of those advanced computer science courses. It certainly didn't address potential ways toxic masculinity might be showing up in computer science classes or in the school's institutional culture or in the attitudes or actions of young men in the school. It was a "starfish initiative" that helped a relatively small number of young women adapt to and maybe even push back against sexist conditions without leaders doing anything to address those conditions institutionally.

Hoping to nudge the directors toward adopting and acting on a more transformative view, we asked whether they had examined what sorts of institutional conditions might inform the course-taking disparities. We asked whether they assessed for troubling behaviors among young men that might have made young women hesitant to take advanced computer science courses. We asked how they helped teachers learn how to counteract societal messaging that might make girls much earlier in their educational lives feel like computer science was somebody else's pursuit. Obviously, as educators, we can't eliminate the impact of that messaging altogether, but we wondered how responsive they had been to it. What were they fundamentally changing to address the disparity? How had they reimagined curricula and pedagogies? What lessons were teachers and students learning about dismantling the culture of toxic masculinity in gaming and beyond? These are the sorts of questions educational leaders who embrace a transformative equity approach ask. These questions are informed by a deeper level of equity literacy.

In essence, district and school leaders had left those conditions unexplored. They offered young women a club instead of giving them access to the full slate of opportunity. The club changed nothing about the root causes of the disparities. It represented an adjustment to, rather than an abolishment of, the inequity. This is the hallmark of *mitigative* equity.

To be clear, we didn't for a moment believe the teachers or curriculum directors in that district were behaving maliciously. They weren't meeting in district offices discussing how to create the illusion of transformative equity action while offering only a mitigation. The problem, as far as we could tell, wasn't that they purposefully avoided deeper action but that it hadn't occurred to them that deeper action was necessary. Notably, it also hadn't occurred to them that the Women Gamers Club relied on a binary construction of gender that might have made it feel unwelcoming to people who don't associate with that construction. The district leaders didn't lack equity desire, but equity literacy.

We want to be equally clear that we loved the Women Gamers Club. Given the history of hostility in gaming culture toward people who are not white, cisgender, heterosexual men (Apperley & Gray, 2021), it's important to create spaces where girls and young women, as well as youth of color, LGBTQIA+ youth, and others can explore and express their gaming and other tech passions free from harassment and oppression. The trouble wasn't the presence of the Women Gamers Club but the absence of a more transformative equity commitment. It doesn't have to be an either/or. It can be a both/and so long as it really *is* a both/and.

This point brings us to a second parable. This time the young woman is sitting in her neighborhood park when she sees a baby floating down the river. She rushes to the riverbank, wades into the water, and carries the baby to safety. When she turns around, she sees another baby floating down the river. She saves that one too. The more babies she saves, the more she finds floating down the river.

Soon she begins asking passersby for help. Before long, dozens of people are wading into the water, carrying babies to safety. Once she knows enough people are in the park to save each baby, the young woman starts walking upriver.

"Where are you going?" her incredulous neighbors ask. "We have to save the babies!"

Hurrying along, she answers, "I'm on my way to figure out how all these babies are ending up in the river."

This is the transformative impulse, the systems-thinking impulse, of the equity leader. If we are serious about change, we work to cultivate this impulse in ourselves and one another. We need to ask what fundamentally is causing harm to the starfish or the babies. We need to question why there is a fence or whether the game is even worth watching. We can't mitigate our way to equity, so we need to ask transformative questions and then take transformative action.

Let's practice. Try to identify three examples of mitigative or "starfish" equity efforts in your school or district. Remember, these are programs, initiatives, or actions adopted in the name of equity that might help a limited number of students adjust to inequitable conditions or afford a small number from an underrepresented group access to an opportunity still denied a disproportionate number from that group, but that fail to attend to inequity's root causes.

What are the inequities your examples are mitigating? What are the root causes of the disparities that are left unaddressed? For each example, describe what a more transformational approach, one that addresses the root cause of the disparity or inequity, might look like.

Conclusion

Definitions of equity range widely, from softer, more mitigative under-standings often rooted in an appreciation for diversity and surface-level cultural awareness to deeper, more transformative approaches grounded in commitments to institutional change. We don't have to discard our softer approaches as long as our base approach, our con-stant drumbeat, is transformative.

Diversity is priceless. Inclusion is critical. But diversity and inclu-sion without equity are hollow. We reach meaningful diversity and inclusion through equity, not vice versa. In Chapter 2, we describe the key components of the equity literacy framework: the nuts and bolts that help us enact this transformative equity approach.

2

The Equity Literacy Framework

During our combined 40 or so years of working in and with schools, we have learned that the primary challenge in equity leadership usually does not involve a scarcity of equity strategies, programs, and practices. Rather, as we mentioned earlier, we've found that people who want to lead for equity but struggle to do so tend to rely too heavily on whatever shiny new strategy, program, or practice is making its way through education circles. The blockage isn't a lack of equity stuff. Rather, it's ideological: limitations to equity understandings that, in turn, misguide equity actions.

There's no shame in that. We all struggle with ideological blockages.

If we want to take mindful equity actions, we need something more than strategies. We need *equity literacy*: the knowledge and skills required to identify and eliminate inequity and to actively cultivate equity.

What Is Equity Literacy?

That "want but struggle to" bit was important as we developed the equity literacy framework, not with the goal of convincing people who tend to be dismissive of equity efforts to join the conversation, but rather for equity leaders who, like us, are desperate to do better. How can we create an approach that will help them, that will help *us*, maximize the integrity and transformative potential of our efforts?

Rather than a linear step-by-step protocol, we designed our response to that question around a series of evidence-informed, transformative principles for deep, meaningful equity efforts. We call them the basic principles of equity literacy. They make up the heart of this book.

We describe it as a *literacy* because, in our experience, the most effective equity leaders regularly and intuitively apply an equity lens to everything they do. When we're leading with equity literacy, we understand the distinction between mitigative and transformative equity leadership discussed in Chapter 1. We don't think of equity as a tool we occasionally pull out of a filing cabinet, or as an agenda item to discuss on Fridays, time permitting. We see it, instead, as an essential component of every aspect of education. As our friend, district administrator Daniel Spikes, reminds us, "Equity is the entire plate, not just another scoop of food." It should undergird our entire educational philosophy, our entire leadership approach, and our leadership actions. It's integral, not optional. It works best when it's second nature.

Of course, growing to a point where transformative equity leadership is second nature requires a lot of work, especially for those of us who do not personally experience the inequities we want to disrupt. Consider elite gymnasts completing complicated tumbles on a balance beam. They're not watching a YouTube video to learn how to do a backflip every time they want to do one. Through years of practice and determination, they've acquired the muscle memory to complete what once probably seemed impossible without having to pause every few seconds to remember how to do it. As equity leaders, we must invest that kind of time and effort to learn and practice equity literacy.

Making equity literacy second nature also requires a tremendous amount of humility. We must learn how to reestablish our balance when we trip. That's *when*, not *if*. Just like the world's best gymnasts, we *will* fall, and it won't be pretty. We can't avoid occasional equity face-plants. But we will get back up and consider what we could do differently and what understandings we need to do it. We have to work through inevitable struggles related to everything from our own understandings and ideologies to resistance from people angling to make equity the new bogeyman. We need to tap deep wells of fortitude to keep going even when, or especially when, we feel discouraged.

The Four Building Blocks of Equity Literacy for Leaders

At a more practical level, when we embrace it fully, equity literacy, the natural inclination toward equitable and just action, is constructed from four key building blocks: (1) equity desire, (2) equity knowledge, (3) equity skills, and (4) equity will.

Equity Desire

We start by asking ourselves: *What is the true extent of my desire for equity and justice?* As we've said, we know many leaders experience pressure to at least perform a desire for equity. But we need to challenge ourselves to achieve something more than optics. *How invested am I, really, in doing what it takes to lead for equity, in embracing and enacting the sorts of principles discussed in this book? Do I desire equity and justice for some people, such as students experiencing poverty, but feel less invested when it comes to, say, LGBQ+ people or people who do not conform to a binary construction of gender?*

We know the temptation might be to respond reactively: *Yes, of course I desire equity.* We'd feel tempted to respond reactively too, because that's how we want to see ourselves. It's how we want the world to see us. But the truth is, we've had to work tirelessly to face our own biases and fears about losing the advantages we have; we've had to reflect constantly, purposefully, to be honest about how deep our desire runs. It's not always easy or pleasant to do, but it is necessary.

We've also worked in and visited enough schools and districts, working with thousands of educational leaders, to know that it would be foolish to believe they all desire equity or that there aren't some leaders who desire it selectively, depending on which sort of injustice is on the table. But if we're invested in equity, we don't get to pick and choose who gets it. It's either equity or it's not.

So pause for a moment and reflect: Do you desire equity and justice? If not, the other building blocks won't help you. Do you desire a school or district free from *all* types of injustice? If not, what is getting in the way?

Try this exercise: Write down the form of oppression you feel least comfortable or confident discussing. Ask yourself, *How invested am I in abolishing this form of oppression?* Give yourself a couple minutes to write freely on this question. But before you answer, consider the sorts of actions you've adopted to abolish it and what risks you're willing to take. Equity is not a game of hypotheticals. We are equity leaders only to the extent we are determined to destroy the oppressions we feel least invested in destroying.

Equity Knowledge

Our desire for equity takes us only so far. We pose little threat to inequity if we skimp on the second building block: equity *knowledge*. If we don't understand how sexism operates, not just interpersonally but institutionally, or if we can't distinguish between mitigative and transformative approaches to gender equity, we're likely to perpetuate the conditions we want to eradicate. We're liable to become yet another educational leader investing our equity efforts in something less than equity, like a kindness initiative or an antibullying program. We might not realize that we need antiracism to achieve any real semblance of kindness, and not vice versa, and that antibullying efforts are no salve for institutionalized xenophobia. We need something more than the "shallow understanding from people of good will" that Martin Luther King Jr. bemoaned in his "Letter from Birmingham Jail."

Without deep, layered understandings, we cannot lead for equity and justice. The principles in this book are, in essence, baseline equity leadership knowledge: the basics we must understand to lead the way we want to lead.

Make a list of the various forms of inequity. There's racism, cisgenderism, ableism. What else? On a scale of 1 to 10, rate your knowledge about each one, then consider these questions: Is your knowledge personal and intimate, coming from lived experience? Is it deep, but mostly intellectualized? Shallow or superficial? Which form of inequity do you understand most thoroughly? Which do you least understand? How might you strengthen your understanding of the one you understand least? Deepening our understanding is the first step toward deepening our action.

Equity Skills

In the same way desire means little without knowledge, knowledge means little without the equity *skills* to apply it. We describe the most crucial of these skills, what we call the *five abilities of equity literacy*, later in this chapter. For now, suffice it to say that understanding how ableism or heteronormativity operates subtly in an elementary school is not the same as knowing how to eliminate them, how to engage people in conversations about them, or how to move people from a deficit view of them to an unwavering commitment to equity.

Let's say we have top-of-the-line equipment to detect when a flood is coming. We also have expert knowledge about how floods work and the nature and extent of damage floods can do. We have sandbags and access to high ground. We even have equipment to help rescue people from rising water. Let's say we have all of these resources, all of this knowledge and access, but we fail to enact proactive strategies to prevent flooding: better and more sustainable agricultural and construction techniques, perhaps, or climate change policies that would improve atmospheric conditions. We have a lot of optics, a lot of tools, and impressive knowledge of impending doom. But we don't have the ability to use the tools or engage the knowledge. That's a recipe for destruction, not equity.

Bringing this back into school, let's say we have PBIS and emotion regulation and mindfulness practices and SEL. We have several flood mitigations. Let's say we are so familiar with district data we can rattle off all the statistics related to racial disparities in discipline. But we lack the skill to name or address the root causes of the disparities, including institutionalized racism. Perhaps we misunderstand what the data tell us; so where we need antiracism, we're instead implementing mindfulness, trying to fix the wrong thing. That situation is the inverse of equity skill, the inverse of equity leadership.

Leading for equity requires us to have a toolbox full of abilities to strategically and effectively address inequities within our schools and districts, to address them deeply and transformatively. We assemble in our toolboxes the sorts of professional, technical, and facilitative skills that may not have been part of our administrative or teaching licensure programs. For most of us, they likely weren't. Here are a few of those skills, all of which we touch on in one way or another later in this book:

- How to collect, analyze, and interpret data through an equity lens, including data related to academic outcomes, discipline, assignment to gifted or special education programs, and more, and how to think critically about how data are collected and used
- How to reimagine what we consider to be data and to recognize that the stories and experiences of students, families, and staff members constitute data as important as anything we measure quantitatively
- How to facilitate meetings and other collaborative spaces to generate support and enthusiasm for transformative equity
- How to identify and hire people who bring with them a commitment to equity
- How to recognize subtle and not-so-subtle ideological blockages, such as deficit ideologies or savior mentalities, that pose as positivity but do tremendous damage to students, and how to bridge ourselves and our colleagues out of those blockages
- How to share critical feedback and hold staff accountable for the bias and inequity they perpetuate, and how to share positive feedback and support staff who are speaking and acting on behalf of equity
- How to *receive* critical feedback, recognizing it as a gift rather than an affront, and then to reconsider our practices and policies with that feedback in mind
- How to engage in both self- and community care to help equity leaders in our school or district survive the threat of burnout that often undermines the well-being of equity advocates

These aren't the only skills we need. But they're a pretty good start. If we're not screening for these skills as we hire people into our schools and districts, and cultivating them in ourselves, we are making equity efforts much harder than they need to be.

As you consider this list, reflect on your own skill level with each item. For which of these skills would you label yourself a novice, perhaps still developing expertise and confidence? How might you go about cultivating that skill in yourself? Which of these do you read and then think, "Hey, I'm pretty good at that, firing on all cylinders"? With whom can you share this skill? What is a skill you have that supports your equity leadership but doesn't appear on our list?

Equity Will

Finally, we need equity *will*: a commitment to act for equity and justice. Perhaps this seems obvious. As we stated earlier, equity requires action, not just pontification. The reality is, we know a lot of leaders who have equity desire, equity knowledge, and equity skills but struggle with equity will, especially in the face of intense and organized resistance to equity efforts. We know this kind of pushback is on the rise, but it's helpful to remember that it's nothing new.

Several years ago, while we were visiting a middle school, three 8th grade students stopped us in the hallway. Krissy, Jonathan, and Terrence explained how, months earlier, they had approached their principal, seeking permission to form a Gay-Straight Alliance (GSA). The principal responded enthusiastically. He instructed them to find an adult to sponsor the group. The GSA met once. Krissy, Jonathan, and Terrence were thrilled with the turnout.

Before their second meeting, the principal asked to meet with the students. They were devastated when he told them that he decided that they should change the GSA into a general diversity club. "He said he was worried some students and families would feel left out of the GSA," Jonathan explained.

We asked the students how they felt about the principal's suggestion. They were hurt and confused. They were outraged. "Anybody can join the GSA," Terrence shared. "We literally invited everyone." Krissy said, "The whole reason for starting the GSA was that *we* feel left out. We wanted a club where we could talk about things we can't talk about anywhere else in school."

Later that day, we shared the students' story with Thomas, the principal. "That's true," he responded. "That's pretty much what happened." We asked why he pressured the students to change their GSA into a generic diversity club. It turns out it came down to a question of equity will. Thomas had received phone calls from two parents who were irate that the school allowed students to create a GSA. "I don't want my children attending a school where that sort of thing is condoned," one parent insisted. That's all it took.

Perhaps, to some extent, this also came down to equity *skills*. At no point in any of the education degree or licensure programs we completed were we taught how to explain our equity commitments to irate equity-dismissive parents. Who doesn't stumble through situations they were never prepared to encounter?

Mostly, though, it was a question of equity will. Thomas didn't want the controversy. He knew how easily two irate parents, especially ones with powerful connections in the community, could foment a movement. We see this happening now with calls to ban critical race theory (CRT) and, really, anything related to antiracism and equity more broadly (whether they have anything to do with critical race theory or not). Thomas chose to acquiesce to two parents' heterosexism rather than protect Terrence, Krissy, and Jonathan's interests and the interests of all students who needed the space they had created.

We should note here that if students are forced into creating their own safe spaces, a bigger failure of equity leadership might be afoot. We'll address this point further in later chapters.

Our equity will, our commitment to embrace and enact transformative equity leadership, requires our willingness to reallocate discomfort off the shoulders of people already absorbing the most discomfort and onto the shoulders of the people—in this case, especially the adults—most perpetuating the discomfort. If we take some easier route, as Thomas did by placating a couple of parents committed to inequity, we are choosing to perpetuate, or even generate, inequity.

And yes, it is a choice. Any time we make a decision to allow oppression to persist in order to protect the interests of the people least interested in interrupting that oppression, whether heterosexist parents or teachers angling to opt out of their school's equity commitment, we compromise our equity will and leadership integrity, becoming enablers of the conditions that equity leaders ought to obliterate.

This is what Krissy, Jonathan, Terrence, and all the children in that middle school needed adults in their building to understand.

We know, believe us, that everything is layered, nothing is simple. We all have piles of spinning plates to balance, and some are wobbling precariously. It's not always easy to know which decisions, which actions, will move us furthest toward our equity commitments. We might even find ourselves grappling with competing needs, impossible to square. Perhaps Thomas was worried that if he took on those parents around this issue, it might put other equity efforts in peril. If that situation happened today, Thomas also might have had to contend with "don't say gay" laws popping up around the United States, meant not just to curb social justice–oriented teaching and learning but also to scare educators out of teaching the truth, teaching humanely. The potential for blowback is real. It's also increasingly well-organized and even well-funded. So our will has to be strong. (We discuss this topic in more detail in Chapter 8.) Adding insult to inequity injury, all of this is particularly threatening to leaders who experience the marginalization against which they're advocating, as Rita Kohli (2018) found when she interviewed educators of color fighting racism in their schools.

There's no getting around it: having the will to lead for transformative equity is not always easy. But it's easier than being a student who is experiencing inequity in a school where nobody has the courage and will to lead for transformative equity.

You might be wondering, what if Thomas had exercised equity will in this case? What would that have looked like?

There's no perfect prescription. Most important, though, he would have found a way to withstand the blowback from those parents rather than passing its impact onto Krissy, Jonathan, and Terrence. We, the adults with the power, should be the blowback cushions, not the students (Theoharis, 2007). He would have defended and protected the GSA. Then he would have addressed more seriously the conditions that necessitated the GSA, moving from the mitigative to the transformative. Why did middle school students have to create their own safe space? What does that say about ways we need to transform institutional culture, rethink hiring practices, and educate the educators?

To be sure, we won't get it right every time. As we said earlier, there's no equity perfection, so let's free ourselves of that notion. But we must have the will to move directly, unapologetically toward equity. Identify the inequity, eliminate the inequity, actively cultivate equity and justice. That, in the end, is the baseline role of the equity leader. As we work through the next several chapters, we will explore this role more deeply.

Recall a time you avoided taking equity action when you should have done so. What caused your tentativeness, and what sorts of inequity might you have perpetuated unintentionally as a result?

Now recall a time you took decisive action, a time when it felt like a risk to do so but you took the action anyway. What helped you take that action? What were the consequences?

The Five Abilities of Equity Literacy

Conversations about equity often begin with, and sometimes don't manage to veer very far from, reflection on personal bias. It's an important process for leaders: identifying our biases, determining their sources and impact, learning how to recognize when they pop up for us, working to eliminate them. If you've been heeding our prompts thus far, you'll notice we encourage this kind of reflection ourselves. Many powerful resources can help us with this sort of reflection, including Marceline DuBose and Tess M. Orseth's (2021) book, *No Stone Unturned: A Journal for Antiracist Equitable Pedagogy*.

As white educators committed to antiracism, for example, the two of us have attended many professional learning sessions over the years where skilled facilitators guided us through important reflection work related to whiteness and racism. They challenged us to examine our ideological clutter, such as the ways we've been socialized to interpret what's happening around us and act in ways that protect our advantages. They've also helped us examine how those ideologies can misguide us so that we risk perpetuating racist conditions we don't want to perpetuate. This inward-facing work is important, as far as it goes. It feels personally, individually rewarding.

This might be why common approaches for equity-related professional learning in education tend to emphasize individual reflection on personal bias and then maybe, eventually, get around to addressing institutional inequities. It's not uncommon for a school or district to hire professional development specialists to train staff and retain those specialists until they transition from asking *What is your personal racial bias?* to asking *How is racism operating in this school or district?* and then bring in somebody else to start over with *What is your personal racial bias?* It's an important question, for sure, but it's not the only important question. Nor, in our view, is it the most important question.

We need deeper, longer-term ideological work and the skills to examine the root causes of disparities within our systems. And we need to act for equity based on honest, critical feedback from people who are experiencing the oppression we're committed to destroying.

If our hope is to create and sustain equitable and just schools, the most important questions are *How is racism, and how are other forms of injustice, operating in this school or district?* and *What do we need to do to eradicate that racism and those other forms of injustice permanently, institutionally, sustainably?* The antibias process is valuable only to the extent it prepares us to reflect honestly on these sorts of questions. It's important to the extent it strengthens our equity literacy so that we can do the institutional work. But, as we mentioned earlier, we can embrace less intense biases interpersonally toward, for example, Indigenous, undocumented, or Muslim students while continuing to enact institutional policies and embracing institutional cultures that marginalize them.

That's why the equity literacy framework begins with these questions: *How are ableism, linguicism, and other forms of oppression operating here?* We can flip these questions, looking at them from the inverse angle: *How are nondisabled, first-language-English-speaking, Christian students and staff advantaged by our policies, practices, ideologies, and institutional cultures?* Then, *What do we need to do to permanently, institutionally, eradicate these inequities and oppressions, these systems of advantage and disadvantage?* If we can't answer these questions honestly and accurately, we can't be equity leaders.

We know that some educators might struggle just to understand what we mean when we ask these questions. If we don't have a deep and layered understanding of what, exactly, an injustice involves, if we think of it only as individual prejudices or interpersonal actions, for example, then we won't land on particularly useful answers to either question.

This is where equity literacy comes in. We start with that commitment to deep understanding (equity knowledge), then apply that deep understanding to inform transformative action (equity will). Each remaining chapter of this book covers one of the equity literacy principles that can help us make these connections to move from deep understanding to transformative action.

So yes, we need the reflection on personal bias, the inward-facing antibias work; but we also need to strengthen the abilities that will prepare us to do the outward-facing, institutional anti-oppression work, including navigating resistance to our equity efforts. Ultimately this is what will help us become annihilators of inequity and, just as important, cultivators of equity.

We call these abilities the *five abilities of equity literacy*. They are the abilities to (1) recognize inequity, (2) respond to inequity, (3) redress inequity, (4) actively cultivate equity, and (5) sustain equity (see Figure 2.1). We refer to these abilities throughout the rest of this book, which is why we want to close this chapter by describing them briefly.

FIGURE 2.1

The Five Abilities of Equity Literacy

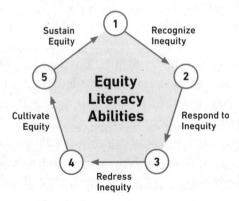

Recognizing Inequity

A few springs ago while visiting a high school, we noticed a yard sign in a grassy area just steps from the main entrance. It reminded students to bring their yearbook payments by that Friday, the final day to take advantage of the discounted early-bird rate. Over the years we've seen dozens of instances in which schools used early-bird rates for various things, from prom tickets to passes for sporting events. But for some reason it took us walking by that sign, equity radars on high alert, to catch the inequity.

As we've mentioned, we cannot eliminate an inequity we don't recognize. So the first ability of equity leadership is to learn how to recognize inequity. If we fail to develop and practice this ability, the other abilities don't matter; we're doomed to perpetuate inequity.

Here's an opportunity to practice your ability to *recognize*. From an equity point of view, why is the early-bird rate troubling? We understand the practical reasons early-bird rates are popular. But what makes them inequitable?

The day before we saw that sign, we had facilitated a focus group with economically marginalized students attending the high school, students who were eligible for the free-lunch program. They shared myriad concerns about learning opportunities at school that cost extra money they and their families didn't have. For example, the school offered a variety of senior trips during spring break, each of which cost several hundred dollars. "Senior trips are not for *us*," one of the students said. "A lot of stuff in this school isn't for us," another added.

They also shared examples of social opportunities they struggled to afford. One mentioned the day yearbooks are distributed as particularly humiliating.

The early-bird rate is an *equality* move. Any family who can pay early receives an equal discount. The early-bird rate is also an *inequity* move. The families most likely to be able to pay early are those with financial reserves, who don't need time to save for something like a yearbook. It all but guarantees that, on average, the families with the least amount of money will pay the highest price for the yearbook. We might call this situation a "perfect storm" inequity: it creates advantage for the families that already enjoy the most advantage while piling disadvantage onto the families most likely already struggling to manage accumulated disadvantage.

When we share this story, the most common response is something like "It never occurred to me that the early-bird rate is inequitable." This response is a matter of equity literacy, of equity knowledge. The problem isn't maliciousness on the parts of decision makers at the school or whichever staff member works on the yearbook, but a failure to recognize the implications of this practice. Equity literacy means preparing ourselves so that something like this *does* occur to us or at least ensuring that our team includes people whose inequity radars would pick this up. It means cultivating a culture in which pointing these things out is celebrated and appreciated, not scoffed at or shushed.

As we sharpen our abilities to recognize inequity, it's important to remember, again, that we tend to have an easier time recognizing the kinds of inequity that we experience. Conversely, we may struggle to recognize the kinds of inequity somebody else experiences, inequity from which our identities shield us. This is one way privilege operates even in the context of equity leadership.

For example, as cisgender people, the two of us don't have to recognize how cisgenderism or cisnormativity operates around us to navigate cisgenderist systems. Those of us who are cisgender reap the benefits of cisgender privilege whether we recognize or acknowledge that or not. One of those benefits is not having to spend an ounce of energy concerned about, dodging, or coping with the impacts of cisgenderism.

We might ask ourselves, if we are cisgender, *Would I recognize subtle presumptions of cisgenderness in early-literacy curriculum? If a library did not contain any books with characters who don't fit neatly into a gender binary, would I notice? If I'm in a school where no students or adults openly refuse to be defined within a gender binary, would I presume nobody in the school identifies outside the constraints of that binary, or would I be curious about the possibility that people have good reason not to be out as transgender, nonbinary, or genderqueer? Would I be able to spot the potential for cisgenderism in a dress code policy?*

As equity leaders, and as people trying to be decent human beings, we should learn how to answer these sorts of questions. We should learn to recognize inequity even in its subtlest forms. Doing so requires intentionality and a lot of equity curiosity because inequity isn't always loud and obvious to the people who aren't targeted by it. Transphobia, for example, doesn't always come in the form of some-body screaming transphobic slurs. It could be some teachers' unwill-ingness to use people's pronouns or our refusal to hold those teachers accountable when they don't. It could be curricular erasure or our failure to ensure honest, meaningful, and consistent representation of transgender people. It could be hesitation to protect transgender athletes who want to participate in school sports. It could be our hesi-tance to publicly, explicitly enact equity measures in the face of those "don't say gay" laws we mentioned earlier. It could even be related to something that is *not* there, something omitted, such as the absence of policies institutionalizing students' rights to use restrooms match-ing their gender identities or to respect students' pronouns without reporting it to their families. Whatever its form, our first responsibil-ity is to learn how to recognize inequity and to understand its accu-mulative impact.

Here's our *recognizing inequity* challenge: we must practice the recognizing until it becomes second nature, until it becomes a sort of literacy, and we need to practice most vigilantly on forms of inequity into which we're least tapped. Sometimes the temptation is to say, *I don't see any xenophobia or linguicism or Christian privilege here.* We should be careful not to mistake our inability to recognize subtle forms of bias and inequity for evidence they don't exist. In fact, it may be that people experiencing inequity are not sharing it because they don't trust us to respond in meaningful ways; it's not worth the risk to them to share it (Gorski, 2019).

Can we acknowledge that sometimes our inability to recognize inequity is evidence that we need to practice learning how to rec-ognize it rather than evidence it doesn't exist? We ask this question having learned from experience. Ramp up the humility. We're going to need it.

As we strengthen our ability to recognize inequity, we don't need to feel embarrassed or inadequate if initially we are clumsy with it. We're all tripping over ourselves to some extent because, as we've said, there's no blueprint. The tripping is to be expected. As long as we listen intently and respond openly to feedback, push forward, and remain vigilant about strengthening our equity abilities, we can see the tripping as part of our learning process, part of institutional progress.

Let's practice. Policy documents such as student conduct handbooks or district or board policy guides provide powerful opportunities to strengthen our *recognize* abilities. Find one from your school or district. Study it line by line with an equity lens. Look for policies that appear to be *equal* but could be *inequitable*. From a socioeconomic equity lens, that could include any policy that applies fees to learning experiences. Look for policies that could target or disproportionately affect students whose families are undocumented, disabled students, students in the foster care system, students who are unhoused, or any other group of students who may be marginalized within your sphere of influence.

If you want to delve even further into the heart of institutional culture, analyze school traditions. Whose cultural norms, talents, and interests are highlighted and normalized? Who is marginalized, erased, or tokenized? Who is an afterthought or an add-on? Whose needs do we accommodate rather than center our programs around? What traditions can we no longer justify if we consider them through an equity lens?

Responding to Inequity

Imagine this scenario: you're in a staff meeting discussing how to strengthen equity efforts related to students who are masters of languages other than English when a colleague says, "What they really need is for their families to value education more. If their community doesn't care, why would the students care?"

How do you respond right then, in the moment?

Failure to respond is not an option. Not for an equity leader. Equity cannot live where this kind of deficit ideology lives. We'll explore *deficit ideology* in greater detail later in the book. For now, consider what you would say, or perhaps ask, in response to your colleague.

This situation is an example of when we need the *respond* ability of equity literacy. We need the ability to respond effectively in the moment when a bias or an inequity reveals itself. A student shouts a sexist slur in the hallway; a member of the leadership team recommends a clearly inequitable policy or practice; a teacher casually shares ableist presumptions about a student. The first question is, *Do we recognize the equity problem in each of these scenarios?* The second is, *Do we have the knowledge, skills, and will to name it as an equity problem and to respond?*

Sometimes responding means educating. We like the strategy of asking questions: *What makes you presume they don't care? What are you seeing that leads you to that interpretation? Is there any other way to interpret what you're seeing that doesn't level blame onto families?*

Sometimes it means being able to explain why a policy, practice, or decision could have an inequitable impact. For example, *Sure, we might believe we're creating community when we ask students to leave cameras on during virtual learning. But that could have unintended consequences. For example, some students who are experiencing poverty might not feel comfortable inviting us into their homes, even electronically. Let's explore other possible reasons students might feel unsafe or uncomfortable always having their cameras on, and why for some students virtual learning presents all sorts of potential barriers, humiliations, and other challenges.*

Like all the other equity things, there's no blueprint, no one right way to respond. Some of us are better on the fly; some of us need time to think. Some people are skilled at using humor to disarm people, creating space to reveal the inequity and its impact. In some cases, however, levity can appear to the targets of injustice to be a failure to respond seriously. Responding later, especially if people don't know you are doing so, can look like implied support of whatever harm just occurred. Context matters. We might need to respond differently to different people, depending on what kind of feedback they're able to hear, our relationship with them, or who else is within earshot. And, of course, our contextualized identities might make some response strategies easier or more difficult, more rewarded or more punished.

We see this even in our own work together cofacilitating professional learning on equity. Paul is more introverted, Katy more extroverted. Katy was raised in the Midwest, where she was socialized to practice an Olympic-level passive aggressiveness, an urge she works hard to resist. Paul was socialized to intellectualize everything, a different avoidance strategy. In most situations, Paul, a cisgender man, can say things more bluntly without the level of blowback that Katy, a cisgender woman, might face if she says them with the same tone and vigor. As heterosexual white people, however, we're both at least somewhat protected in our directness. Neither of us has ever been labeled "angry" or accused of "having an agenda," as often happens to our LGBTQIA+ colleagues and our colleagues of color. And as people whose white cisgender bodies appear non-disabled and slender, we are generally welcomed into most school spaces, not treated as inconveniences to accommodate or people to fear.

That is a sort of currency both of us must be willing to spend. We call it *institutional likeability*. We're not actually more likeable than our colleagues who experience more forms of marginalization than we do, but we're granted a considerable benefit of the doubt often not extended to them. This protection from some types of blowback or invalidation means that we must leverage our privileged identities as much as we can in the service of equity and justice.

How have your identities and context informed how you respond to inequity? How does the type of inequity affect how you respond or the blowback you experience? How have your identities emboldened and equipped you to respond in creative, impactful ways?

Like the *recognize* ability, the *respond* ability requires practice. The more we practice, the more it becomes second nature, tempering our anxieties or discomfort when confronting inequity. We want to reach the point where it feels more uncomfortable *not* to respond than it does to respond. That's a sign we're growing our equity literacy.

Earlier in this chapter we quoted from Martin Luther King Jr.'s "Letter from Birmingham Jail." Later in the letter, he distinguished between what he called a "negative peace, which is the absence of tension" and "a positive peace, which is the presence of justice." The problem with the negative peace approach is that, for people experiencing inequity, the tension already exists: the racism or heterosexism or ableism. So if our approach is to resolve an interpersonal conflict while ignoring those fundamental tensions, all we're really doing is reproducing the inequity. Instead, we want to work toward the positive peace: the eradication of the racism, heterosexism, or ableism. Peace comes through equity and justice, not vice versa.

One last note on applying the *respond* ability. Responding also means extending care in the moment to people who have experienced inequity, harnessing institutional resources and commitments to address the harm they're experiencing in the immediate term. If students of color have been harmed by racist jokes or educators' insufficient responses to those jokes, we should be intentional about checking in with them and their families about how they're doing and what resolution they require. And we should be prepared for that resolution to involve not just interpersonal support, not just disciplinary action, but institutional changes. This is what the next ability, redressing inequity, is all about.

Let's practice *responding*. How would you respond to the following scenarios? Remember, we're not just asking how you'll resolve or calm the conflict. We're asking how you'll respond to them as incidents of inequity, as evidence of accumulative advantage and disadvantage. As we've said, there is not one right answer here, and who you are in relation to these scenarios may shape your range of potential responses. Here are the scenarios:

- **Scenario one:** During a casual conversation, your colleague recommends your school or district adopt a new online platform to communicate and share resources with families. The platform has great features. However, you recognize that although it will improve access for families who already enjoy the most access, it won't be easily accessible to the lowest-income families or families who primarily speak languages other than English at home. It might even result in those families having *less* access to important information than they did before. How do you respond?
- **Scenario two:** You notice a couple of students in the hallway mocking a classmate for her size. You watch as the students pass by a doorway, where a teacher rolls his eyes and shakes his head in disbelief but doesn't engage the students. How do you respond, both to the students and to your colleague?
- **Scenario three:** During a faculty meeting, a white male teacher keeps interrupting women while they're speaking, especially

women of color. Your sense is that he's not trying to be malicious and might not even realize what he's doing. Of course, his intent here is less important than his impact. It's apparent to many people in the room, but nobody is speaking up. How do you respond?

Redressing Inequity

Learning how to respond to inequity is important. But it's also inadequate if we're leading for transformative equity. When we're responding in the moment, we're being reactive; we're engaging after damage already has been done.

Over time, *responding* can feel like we're playing whack-an-inequity. It's equity triage. We're doing the best we can to attend to symptoms and repercussions of inequitable beliefs and actions, but we're not necessarily transforming anything. If we don't find a way to be more proactive and attentive to the root causes of inequity, we're going to spend a whole lot of time responding to their symptoms and repercussions, like the young woman tossing individual starfish back into the ocean while hundreds of others die on the shore.

What we want is *no* harm, *no* injustice. The only way to achieve that, or something close to it, is to address the underlying institutional conditions that allow inequitable incidents or ideologies to flourish.

One aspect of *redressing* inequity requires us to proactively identify and eliminate inequities. We don't wait, hoping nothing racist happens. Racism *is happening.* Heterosexism, ableism, and xenophobia *are happening.* So instead of waiting for "more proof" or for every person in the community to agree that there is a problem (which will never happen), we actively, honestly map out all the ways those things are happening.

This brings us back to the first kind of equity literacy questions, those related to *recognizing* inequity: *How is racism operating here? How are economic injustice, sizeism, Islamophobia, anti-Semitism, linguicism operating? How are they operating in the curriculum, in policies, in how we organize students academically, in who we hire? How do we eradicate these oppressions?* If we're waiting for people to lodge complaints and then only responding to those complaints, we're missing most of the problem.

Another important aspect of the *redressing* ability involves confronting the root causes of inequity, the root causes of disparities and disproportionalities. Obviously, if we recognize that a policy or practice is inequitable, we should change that policy or practice. Returning to examples we cited earlier, we should change practices such as requiring fees to access learning opportunities, rethink curricula that render some students invisible, adjust discipline policies that leave room for predictable racial bias.

But if we stop there, we're dealing only with symptoms. The deeper questions are, *What was the thinking that ever led us to charge fees to access learning opportunities? How did we ever adopt curricula that render some students invisible? Who assessed that curriculum and thought it was good for students? What institutional and ideological blockages resulted in these racist discipline outcomes?*

In the article "Language of Appeasement," Dafina-Lazarus Stewart (2017) demonstrates further how we can ask those deeper questions by prioritizing our commitments to equity and justice despite the allure of softer commitments to diversity and inclusion. Stewart compares the questions framed by a focus on diversity and inclusion with questions that center equity. For instance, "Diversity asks, 'Who's in the room?' Equity responds: 'Who is trying to get in the room but can't? Whose presence in the room is under constant threat of erasure?'" and "Inclusion asks, 'Has everyone's ideas been heard?' Justice responds, 'Whose ideas won't be taken as seriously because they aren't in the majority?'" (para. 10). These are great examples of *redress* questions, revealing the essence of equity so we can cultivate a more transformative version of it.

Because these questions get at the essence of equity rather than the symptoms of inequity, they might be harder to wrap our minds around. They force us into considering fundamental characteristics of our schools and districts, our vocational homes. As you work toward strengthening your *redress* ability, what interpersonal and institutional barriers make *redress* questions difficult to ask? What barriers make them difficult to answer? How might our equity leadership look different if we focused not just on the whack-an-equity triage of *responding*, but also on the deeper, root-cause undercurrents of inequity?

Let's return to our third scenario from the *respond* section. A white male teacher repeatedly interrupts women during a faculty meeting, a habit he enacts most often with women of color. We need to respond by naming the behavior, yes. Perhaps we have a conversation with him and require professional development on antisexism. We create conditions that increase the possibility that he stops that particular racist, sexist behavior. But with deep equity lenses, we realize there's more to do. For example, what is it about our institutional culture that kept other people in the meeting from being aware of, or feeling comfortable speaking up about, their colleague's behavior? What is it about institutional culture that may make it feel natural for that white male teacher to speak over women colleagues? Why has he been *allowed* to be unaware of doing so? Where is the accountability?

When we apply the *redress* lens, we might consider his lack of maliciousness—the fact that he probably didn't come into the meeting with the goal of marginalizing colleagues—as equally troubling a reality as if he were being malicious. The issue isn't the *intention*; the issue is the *impact* leadership and institutional culture are allowing him to have.

From a redress point of view, we also have to ask, *In what other ways is this sort of intersection of sexism and racism operating here? How is it operating in the curriculum, in pedagogy, in school culture and traditions?* We're not just playing whack-an-inequity. Instead, we're digging in deeply to rip racism and sexism out by their roots.

Let's practice redressing inequity. Identify an inequity to which you've responded but which you have not yet redressed. Create a mind map that addresses the following questions: *What are the root causes of the inequity? What aspects of institutional culture have allowed it to persist? To what other sorts of inequities might it be related? What would redressing inequity look like in this situation?*

Actively Cultivating Equity

In a way, the *redress* ability is a backward-facing ability. It prepares us to account for all the ways inequity has been operating in our school or district. We're mapping out the economic injustice, the xeno-phobia, the linguicism, so that we can eradicate them. This is essential equity work.

Equally essential, however, is the forward-facing ability to actively cultivate equity. In addition to responding to or redressing ineq-uity that already exists, we filter everything we do moving forward through an equity lens. We take *proactive* to another level, actively fos-tering justice in each decision we make. We commit to strengthening our equity literacy so that equity is our instinctual lens, our default; so that we naturally apply it to everything we do.

When we redress inequity, we might require ongoing professional learning on transformative equity for all staff to head off predictable bias in discipline practices or assessment. As an active cultivation, on the other hand, we might adopt hiring practices that ensure staff entering the school bring with them a commitment to equity and a well-tooled, or at least pliable, equity skillset. We might reimagine our discipline framework in a way that accounts for predictable racism, ableism, economic injustice, and other inequities from the beginning. Yes, we still need that ongoing professional learning. But we're also building institutional structures that *normalize* equity, that make it a core ethic of institutional culture rather than something we plug in when inequities are too obvious for us to ignore.

Beyond adopting equity-informed hiring practices that strengthen your school's or district's capacity to enact your transfor-mative equity vision, what can you do right now to transform your institution proactively?

If you're stumped, you might make a list of the institutional obsta-cles that most commonly undermine transformative equity efforts in your sphere of influence. What keeps those obstacles in place? What steps could you take *now* to remove those obstacles so that they no longer undermine equity efforts? If you find yourself thinking that the obstacle is something about *those kids* or *those parents*, challenge yourself to focus instead on aspects of institutional culture, practice, and ideology *within* your school or district.

The transformative approach gives us a pathway to deeper, more sustainable equity cultivation. The impacts of mitigative equity, like tossing the starfish back into the sea one by one, disappear quickly. An inequitable institution will always contort itself to preserve inequity unless we address the inequity's root causes. Redress, redress, redress. Cultivate, cultivate, cultivate. Reimagine, reshape, reconstruct.

One of the most powerful strategies for cultivating equity is assembling a staff stacked with people who already are committed to equity. Generate a list of interview questions that might assess a candidate's equity desire, knowledge, abilities, and will. Review advertisements for employment in your school or district through an equity lens and revisit the interview process itself. What could be changed or made more explicit that would attract equity-literate candidates?

Sustaining Equity

One day, on our way to a district office, we struck up a conversation with our taxi driver, Eric. When he learned where we were headed, he chuckled and asked if we worked for the district. No, we explained, we'd been hired by the district to help building and district leaders draft an action-centered antiracism plan. "I'm a proud Black man," he responded, "but that's *in spite of* that district." Turns out he had graduated from the district's only high school a decade or so earlier.

"I bet you will rattle some people," he said. "I'm guessing a lot of the folks there aren't excited you're coming."

Then he said something we've never quite managed to stop thinking about. "Well," he exclaimed, "if everybody likes you, you aren't doing antiracism hard enough."

True. It's important as equity leaders that we learn how to interpret blowback as evidence that we're building something real, doing something more than rearranging disparities. That's the philosophical end of it. The practical end of it, as we alluded to earlier, is that the blowback can be exhausting (Mayorga & Picower, 2018). It can threaten our job security or even our physical safety.

Let's be real: when we enact transformative equity, the blowback is coming. The question is not *Will there be blowback?* The questions are *when* and *in what form* and *for how long* and *how viciously?* Some of it will come from people who are misinformed and just need a conversation or two about what is really happening, like people who have seen nonsensical social media posts equating every equity thing under the sun with critical race theory. Other times it comes from people who knowingly ride the waves of mass misunderstanding, people bent on ensuring that existing systems of advantage and disadvantage persist, who worry we're encroaching on their advantage. If we're engaged in transformative equity, they are right to worry; we *are* encroaching on all unearned advantage.

No matter who the blowback comes from or what their intention is, it's important that we, as equity leaders, build a system of support around ourselves and prepare to withstand it, never wavering on equity. So check with your team. Do you have a clear, shared understanding of what equity is and isn't? Do you see equity as integral and nonnegotiable rather than optional? What is the plan for how to engage with blowback in ways that don't add unnecessary fuel to the fire? And most important, what is the plan for sustaining equity efforts despite the resistance and the pressures? Get specific and practice these plans with one another. As in a fire drill, it is easier to deal with the chaos, emotions, and pressures of the blowback when we've rehearsed what to do.

What we can't do is use the blowback to justify rolling back equity efforts, to soften our approach, or to undermine our commitments. This is why *sustaining* equity is closely tied to equity *will*. We return to the matter of blowback and will in great detail in Chapter 8.

Conclusion

The culture of change in schools tends to be oriented heavily toward strategies, practices, and programs. The belief seems to be that if we just find the right combination of practices and programs, we can solve equity problems and anything else. Experience tells us that although rigid strategies or predetermined practices can be helpful in some contexts, we as equity leaders need to be more flexible and nimble. We need the will to act for equity, but we also need the knowledge and skills to make our actions meaningful and transformative. And then we need to strengthen those equity abilities until they are second nature.

Next, we turn to the core principles that help us apply these equity literacy abilities. We start with the direct confrontation principle.

3
Offering More Than a Multicultural Arts Fair: The Direct Confrontation Principle

"I feel like a visitor at my own school," Samantha sighed. "That hasn't changed."

She was one of eight Black students participating in a focus group we facilitated at Blue Pasture School, part of a larger effort to examine the impact of its year-old diversity and inclusion initiative. The administrative team created the initiative, mostly cocurricular programs oriented toward diversity appreciation, after several Black families voiced concerns about racial bias at the school. The team spared little expense, investing substantial time and resources into the *food*, the *festivals*, and the diversity *fun*.

We asked the students their perceptions of the initiative and their school's commitments to equity. It turned out not all students were finding the *fun* in the diversity celebrations or at Blue Pasture more generally.

Sean lamented how he felt invisible but also hypervisible. "I'm *hyper*visible when teachers talk about slavery or Jim Crow and everybody looks at me, expecting I'll speak for all Black people," he explained. "I feel invisible the rest of the time." The initiative did little to address the racism he endured at school or the anxiety it caused him.

His classmate Terrence captured the group's sentiment: "The administrators have no idea what this school is like for us." We heard this message repeatedly from Blue Pasture students.

As our final question, we asked what the students wanted to share with school leaders. After a brief silence, Cynthia, who had been relatively quiet, pounded her fist on the table. "There's racism at this school," she shouted, "and nobody's doing anything about it!"

We scanned the room, curious about how Cynthia's classmates were reacting. We saw a chorus of nodding heads. The diversity and inclusion initiative was failing the very students whose concerns it was meant, at least ostensibly, to address.

Moments after we finished interviewing Cynthia and her classmates, an office administrator ushered us into a conference room adjacent to the principal's office. The school's power brokers, the assistant principals and department heads, sat around a long conference table. Jonathan, the principal, sat at the table's head. He tugged at his tie, which was decorated with cartoon sketches of diverse, smiling children.

Earlier that day, before school began, we observed Jonathan interacting with students. He seemed to care about them. He appeared affable. We hadn't heard a single negative word about Jonathan as a person from the Black students in our focus group or from anyone else.

Still, we knew from our conversations with various groups of students that Jonathan presided over a school where many people, including not just Black students but also other students of color, students from families experiencing poverty, immigrant students, transgender and nonbinary students, and LGBQ+ students, among others, were feeling all kinds of marginalized. In fact, the marginalization was not limited to students. Many Blue Pasture teachers and parents who shared these identities also felt the school wasn't doing enough to quell the bias and inequity bearing down on them.

We started the meeting by asking the administrative team about the diversity and inclusion initiative. "How do you feel your school's equity efforts are going?"

Jonathan leaned back in his chair.

Before we share how the Blue Pasture leadership team responded, we want to ask you to reflect on the same question. How do you feel *your* school or district's equity efforts are going? Make a list of the strategies, initiatives, programs, and practices your school, district, or department has adopted in the name of equity. What are their goals? Do they pose a threat to inequity? Are they designed to transform policies, practices, ideologies, and aspects of institutional culture that are doing harm to students, staff, and families? What percentage of them are directly focused on identifying and eliminating inequity?

These are the sorts of questions Blue Pasture leaders hadn't considered. Their hesitance undermined their equity impact.

"Diversity is our most important asset," Jonathan insisted, smiling. "That's what the diversity initiative is all about." We looked around the table at another display of nodding heads. "What we need to do here," he continued, "is to celebrate the joys of diversity."

The Equity Literacy Gap

Despite Jonathan's confidence, his response told a story about the most urgent equity gap at Blue Pasture and, really, at many schools. It wasn't a gap that could be fixed by celebrating diversity.

First, we noted the disparity between how the most marginalized students and the most powerful adults at Blue Pasture defined the problem that a diversity and inclusion initiative ought to address. We noted a troubling gap in perceptions about whether an initiative featuring student programming was a meaningful response to concerns about racism. We noted that the school invested resources in its initiative only after families raised these concerns; in equity literacy terms, it was very much a *response*, not a *redress,* and certainly not an *active cultivation* of racial equity.

So when Jonathan extolled the virtues of celebrating diversity, we responded as directly as possible. "We're concerned the leadership team is grappling with important ideological gaps," we told the assembled leaders. The trouble, a pattern we've mentioned before, was not that they refused to do *something* to address the biases and inequities students experienced at Blue Pasture. The trouble was that the *something* had no impact on the racism that students, parents, and even their own staff bore.

We shared what we had heard during the focus group. "We just met with a group of Black students. They told us that they're experiencing racism here and that the school isn't doing anything about it."

"They said *that*?" Jonathan asked, interrupting an assistant principal who had started defending the initiative.

"That's the gist, yes. We heard more or less the same story from all of the focus groups."

"Maybe it's time we rethink what we're doing," he said, in no small way modeling the kind of reflection and humility desperately needed within his team.

They did, indeed, need to rethink what they were doing. If they were as serious about equity as we believed them to be, then they needed to identify and directly confront all the ways racism and other forms of inequity were operating at Blue Pasture. They needed to cultivate an *actively* equitable institutional culture, built not simply around student programming, but around deep, consistent, and proactive efforts to identify all the manifestations of bias and inequity, to eliminate that inequity, and to reimagine every policy, practice, and bit of institutional culture with a commitment to equity and justice. That mandate was a far cry from the international nights and student clubs Blue Pasture had been offering as its antiracist solution.

The students described how teachers demonstrated low expectations for them, how the school responded inadequately to recent incidents of white students taunting Black students with racist slurs and jokes. In fact, as we've led focus groups across the United States and Canada, the concern we hear most often from Black and Brown students, LGBTQIA+ students, students experiencing poverty, and other students who are disproportionately marginalized at school is how unprepared adults in their schools are to deal with oppressive incidents as they arise and larger racist conditions. Celebrating diversity can't solve that issue at Blue Pasture or anywhere else.

So yes, Blue Pasture leadership needed to rethink the practical elements of their diversity and inclusion initiative. But they also needed to reflect on the sort of thinking that led them to confuse a *celebrating diversity* initiative with an *equity* initiative to begin with. What were the misunderstandings, or maybe even the strategic reframing, of the concerns shared by Black families that landed the school at diversity assemblies rather than a deep and layered commitment to antiracism as its primary response to institutional racism? Without this shift in paradigm, without the kind of ideological transformation we discussed in the Introduction, they were going to spend a lot more resources on a lot more programming that would do little to solve their racial equity problem.

To be clear, Blue Pasture was no cesspool of rabid racists, sinister sexists, or evil, plotting heterosexists. As we've mentioned, although such people certainly exist in education and surely existed at Blue Pasture, in our experience they are not in the numeric majority in most schools and districts. And yet, despite all the resources Blue Pasture poured into diversity and inclusion, despite the principal's kindness, racism persisted at the school. Whether the initiative was purposefully evasive or not, the result was a combination of disconnectedness, deteriorated trust, and alienation: not a great recipe for optimal academic achievement or engagement. The question was, what were Jonathan and his team going to do about *that*?

Here's the good news: As leaders, we can do something about it if we have the will to shift our perspectives. First, we can accept the responsibility to *directly confront* racism, sexism, ableism, cisgenderism, and other forms of inequity rather than carefully tiptoeing around them with fluffier responses like celebrating diversity. Identify the inequity, eliminate the inequity, actively cultivate equity. In Antonia Darder's (2011) words, "We must be courageously intolerant and uncompromising when it comes to human suffering and injustice" (p. 89). Meaningful programs and practices follow from there. That's the way forward, according to the *direct confrontation principle*.

This is not just pie-in-the-sky, wishful thinking. We know leaders who have courageously confronted and continue to confront inequity directly. In 2017, Monic Behnken ran on a platform of addressing racial disparities and became the second Black woman to sit on the school board in Ames, Iowa. Throughout her tenure, she was a tireless advocate, insistently sustaining a focus on equity and demanding action to match proclamations of equity support from district leaders and board colleagues. She never hesitated to name what was happening when district leaders prioritized saving face, smoothing things over, or avoiding controversy over racial equity. At her last meeting as a board member, she delivered a powerful farewell address in which she chastised the district for investing heavily in equity optics without fully embracing the transformational commitment equity requires (Behnken, 2021). Here, in part, is what she said:

> I do believe that the district wants to address the academic dispari-ties, but that will never happen until everyone in this room right now realizes they are part of the reason this exists. . . . There can be no change unless we acknowledge our reality. . . . I don't care how many books you buy . . . or awards you win. Until you wake up from your dream, nothing will change.

She advised the district to stop investing in equity if leaders weren't going to implement any of the recommendations described in reports and professional development. She admonished district leadership to start cleaning house, removing from the district adults who were caus-ing harm. She insisted they listen to the district's new equity office, respecting equity specialists' expertise as a matter of course, and not just when the media needed a statement. She suggested, as a reminder of the dissonance, that they print the district's disparity data and hang it next to the equity awards the district had won. Behnken could have been referring to many districts when she argued, "We are a district that wants things to be better, but for nothing to change."

We want things to be better, but for nothing to change. When it comes to equity, to what extent does that statement describe your school or district? Aside from an occasional program or initiative, aside from those starfish-type mitigations, are things changing fun-damentally? To be equity leaders, we must be curious about this: Are we clinging to magical thinking that somehow equity will material-ize without anything fundamentally changing? If so, who does that approach protect?

From *Celebrating Diversity* to *Equity Literacy* and Other Important Shifts

How are we rooting racism, ableism, and other inequities out of our schools? What efforts are we making to identify every way—big or small, intentional or not—that inequity is operating *right now* in our spheres of influence? What are we doing to transform policies, practices, institutional cultures, and ideologies that uphold systems of advantage and disadvantage to confront them directly rather than dance around them? As we discussed in the previous couple of chapters, this is our point of departure, the baseline principle, for equity literacy.

We cannot rely on food, festivals, fun, or multicultural arts fairs as our path to equity. We cannot rely on cultural competence or community dialogues or even social-emotional learning (SEL) as our way there. Try as we might to find them, there are no programs or initiatives capable of helping us fix conditions we are unwilling to name honestly and confront directly. It's not that cultural competence and diversity celebrations aren't important. It's not that SEL can't play some sort of role. They are, and it can. It's just that none of these initiatives prepares us to identify and eliminate inequity. None redistributes access and opportunity, which means none is, by itself, a meaningful approach for cultivating and sustaining equity.

People often ask us, "Isn't celebrating diversity a step toward equity, toward antiracism?" It's not. Every step toward antiracism eliminates racism or cultivates racial justice. Celebrating diversity doesn't do that, at least not on its own.

So again, *How does racism operate in this school? How does white supremacy operate?* Those are our first questions. *How does sexism operate here? And linguicism? And cisgenderism?* If we can't answer these questions, we have no shot at cultivating schools that are more equitable. Identify the inequity, learn how our systems and structures and policies and practices allowed the inequity to exist, eliminate the inequity, and reconfigure the systems and structures and policies and practices with an equity commitment. What we need more than the international food fair is the will to transform our policies, practices, institutional cultures, and, perhaps most important, the *ideologies* that inform our policies, practices, and institutional cultures, until we have driven inequities out of our schools.

From an equity literacy perspective, this distinction is essential. As we mentioned earlier, the most notable finding from the Blue Pasture focus groups was the gap between how the school community's most marginalized people and its most powerful person characterized the problem that a meaningful diversity, equity, or inclusion initiative ought to resolve.

"There's racism at this school, and nobody's doing anything about it." Notice the urgency and desperation in a perspective informed at least partially by the impact of compiling disadvantage and partially by the courage to demand justice. Our equity approaches should have the same urgency and courage for identifying and eliminating conditions that harm students and families.

"We must celebrate the joys of diversity." Notice the evasion, the dance of false positivity, the lack of urgency in a perspective informed at least in part through advantage, through the misunderstandings that unexamined privilege breeds, even in somebody like Jonathan, who does not wish to do harm.

Alarmingly, the problem of racism did not seem to be on the Blue Pasture administrators' radars despite the fact that parents and students had urged them to pay more pointed attention to *racial bias*. Instead of directly confronting that bias through staff professional development, changes in hiring practices, and a close examination of school policy and educator ideology, they chose an approach that left the racial bias untouched or that presumed it existed only in the minds of some bad apples. Worse, if it *was* on some of the leaders' radars, they did not feel comfortable enough to tell the truth about it in powerful company. So their approach was at best evasive and indirect. Either nobody was willing, or nobody knew how, to name and confront the racism directly.

This observation should inspire an important reflection for equity leaders: *Who do you have around you? Do they know they can challenge you on matters of equity and justice without you responding defensively?*

Who on your leadership team is willing to name something that might make you uneasy? What happens when they do?

As equity leaders, we must invite critical feedback related to equity and reward the people willing to risk offering it. In fact, in a healthy environment, it wouldn't be experienced as a risk at all but as an important part of institutional communication and culture. In a healthy equity institution, we embrace hard equity feedback as a gift, as a celebration of equity progress.

Eventually we posed some difficult equity questions to the Blue Pasture administrators: "For whom, exactly, is this diversity and inclusion initiative constructed? To whose interests is it really attending? What might you be hiding behind the food fairs and diversity assemblies?" These are the sorts of questions we should ask about all our equity efforts.

To their credit, Jonathan and his team received these questions gracefully and gratefully. They wanted to do better. Black students and many other groups of students insisted they do better. We had high expectations that they could do better if they could embrace the direct confrontation principle. *Identify the policies, practices, and aspects of institutional culture that perpetuate racism. Remake those policies and practices, and reconfigure that institutional culture, through a clear racial equity commitment.* (The next several chapters, describing the other basic equity literacy principles, offer guidance for how to do that.) *Critically examine the sorts of thinking and intentions that created the racist policies, practices, and culture and allowed them to persist. Move forward with an equity lens.*

There is no substitute for this process, no prepackaged program or initiative, no diversity assembly that can replace the honest and direct recognizing, responding to, redressing, and active cultivating. Of course, we could say the same about ability-based disparities and ableism, class-based disparities and economic injustice, and any other type of inequity.

What this means in a practical sense is that we should be careful not to invest our equity efforts and resources into initiatives and programs that never do this confronting, not because such initiatives and programs aren't important in a robust approach to education, but because they were never designed to identify and eliminate inequity or to actively cultivate equity. Here are some examples:

- Antibullying programs that frame oppression only in terms of interpersonal dynamics.
- Kindness or niceness initiatives that fail to address the ways institutional cultures often are unkind to, say, people who are undocumented immigrants from El Salvador, native Tigrinya speakers, Sikh students and families, or people experiencing poverty.
- Student "diversity" programming.
- Anything else that does not actively identify all the ways inequity is operating, not just between individual people, but in the policies, practices, ideologies, and institutional cultures of our schools.

So this is our equity leadership task: What are we doing *right now*, proactively, honestly, and directly, to identify and eliminate bias and inequity from our spheres of influence? How are we directly confronting inequity?

In the remainder of this chapter, we discuss what it means to directly confront inequity. We spend most of the chapter describing common barriers leaders experience that create pressures or temptations to avoid these direct confrontations. These include resting on the laurels of our good intentions for equity, waiting for an elusive consensus before addressing equity concerns, and misinterpreting and misnaming those concerns. More important, though, we explore what we need to do to break through those barriers.

Before we transition to that, we want to clarify that the term *direct confrontation* is not about a specific communication style or tactic. In a sense, it's much more practical than that. It's about being crystal clear about what the problems are that we're trying to solve and then making sure everything we're doing to solve them actually *can* solve them.

We know it has become much more complicated in some states or regional contexts to use terms such as *systemic racism* or *heterosexism*. Of course, we can't eliminate racism or heterosexism by pretending they don't exist. Restricting how we talk about these forms of oppression is one tactic that anti-equity advocates use to slow equity work. That said, there are many ways to name inequities and many approaches for shifting policies, practices, ideologies, and institutional cultures to directly confront the inequity in them.

This observation is not meant to let white, heterosexual, or other privilege-toting leaders off the hook. Rather, it's meant to challenge a tendency to circumnavigate the inequity, to nibble around the edges, to point our attention and resources elsewhere, or to soften our equity efforts so that they're more consumable to the people who are least interested in equity. Directly confronting inequity means being laser-focused on how it is operating and targeting the root causes that allow it to operate. If we're not doing that, we're falling short of equity leadership, no matter what else we're doing. If we *are* doing that, then we are truly leading for equity.

What Does It Mean to Confront Inequities Directly?

You might be thinking, "OK, so what does confronting look like? What, specifically, *should* we be doing?" We are getting to that.

First we want to acknowledge that we know some people find the word *confront* unsettling. Perhaps for you it connotes antagonism. When we use *confront* in this context, we're not suggesting we unleash our equity fury every time a colleague makes a deficit-oriented comment or takes what we perceive as some other equity misstep. Heck, we're all taking equity missteps. If that was the approach, all we'd see is fury, fury, fury, even among the most ardent equity advocates. We're certainly not suggesting we unleash our fury on a 2nd grader who repeats a sexist or heterosexist phrase heard at home.

When we talk about directly confronting inequities, we mean something more institutional: recognizing how inequity is operating around us and doing whatever we need to do *right now* to eliminate it rather than tiptoeing around it. Sure, we must address individual people's biased or inequity-laden views or actions if they demonstrate a lack of willingness to meet our equity expectations. Sometimes that means inviting students or colleagues into a conversation about what they believe, what concerns them, what they presume to be true. We can ask strategic questions and create opportunities to open a different, more equitable window of perspective. We can invite them to look with us through that other window: *I wonder if there's anything about how we're structuring family engagement opportunities that might make them less accessible to some families.* (More on this in Chapter 4, when we discuss the fix injustice, not kids principle.) We can name the damage they're doing without wielding the equity sledgehammer, at least until it becomes clear they are ignoring our feedback and continuing to do that damage despite being provided with the tools to do better.

Confrontation also means having some urgency—what we describe in Chapter 5 as *informed urgency*—around identifying and transforming policies, practices, ideologies, and aspects of institutional culture that perpetuate inequity. Go straight at the racism, the heterosexism, the xenophobia. Yank it out by its root causes, as we urged in Chapter 2. Graduate from baby steps to significant equity leaps (Gorski et al., 2022).

Have a community dialogue about it, cultivate buy-in. But don't mistake that dialogue for equity action. And don't let a lack of buy-in stop you. When it comes to equity leadership, the dialogue is not an equity action. It's what prepares us for the action. The action is eliminating inequity and actively cultivating equity. A community dialogue or book club doesn't do that.

Let's practice. Try to identify three examples of inequitable policies or practices operating in your school or district right now. How do they unfairly distribute access and opportunity? Whose interests are subjugated by each one and whose are privileged?

Remember, our examples don't have to be big, screaming, and intentional. Often inequity operates subtly, in the nooks and crannies of policies, practices, or aspects of institutional culture you might have inherited as a leader: a fee attached to an extracurricular activity, a deficit mentality that incorrectly presumes that some families value education less than others, a failure to account for bias while organizing students into academic tracks. As we suggested earlier, a great place to start is a student conduct or school policy handbook.

You might begin by identifying policies and procedures that could create disproportionate hardship for families and students experiencing poverty or for families and students who are learning English. We've examined hundreds of school policy handbooks and never struggled to find several examples we could characterize this way.

For example, consider after-school detention. It could be a significantly harsher punishment for families who don't have reliable transportation or for parents who can't easily take time off work to pick up their children who are held until after buses leave. Consider any policy that levies a fine or attaches a fee to a learning experience, or that punishes a child for unpaid fees. Or, to look at it a different way, consider the advantage accrued by students who can afford to pay for a parking spot at their high school, who can participate in extracurriculars that are scheduled before or after school because their families have reliable transportation, who easily can observe dress code rules because their families can afford to purchase multiple pairs of shoes and a steady stream of new clothes for them. As equity-literate leaders, we learn how to recognize the individual instances and accumulative impacts of these inequitable policies and practices from both the privilege lens and the oppression lens.

We've seen policies that lock students out of graduation ceremonies because their families can't pay for lost or damaged library books. We've seen children humiliated in the lunch line, handed cheese sandwiches in front of their peers because their families forgot or couldn't afford to add money to their lunch accounts. It's shocking that we still find these sorts of practices codified in school policy. They're inequitable, yes, but they're also inhuman. We can eliminate them *right now*. We *must*.

So when you identify your three examples, make sure to include at least one that piles on disadvantage in this way. What is an example of a policy or practice that creates intensified hardship for families already bearing the brunt of inequity?

What we're doing here is practicing the *recognize* ability of equity literacy, which we discussed in Chapter 2. Obviously we cannot confront an inequity we can't recognize. Once you have your list, choose one example to take through the rest of the exercise.

Our next questions: *How do we need to change this policy or practice right now to redistribute access and opportunity justly? What should we do differently?* This is the *respond* ability of equity literacy, directly addressing a specific, immediate equity concern.

Remember here that we're confronting the inequity, so our response should directly address what is inequitable about the policy or practice. We're not helping students cope with, or become more resilient against, the inequity. We're not merely softening the inequity's blow. We're intent on *eliminating* the inequity and then cultivating equitable policy, practice, ideology, and institutional culture in its place. We're eliminating that extracurricular fee; driving that deficit mentality out of ourselves and our schools; developing actively antiracist processes for organizing students in ways that maximize all students' learning opportunities, even if that means rethinking large-scale academic tracking altogether. What do you, as a leader, need to do to eliminate the inequity?

If we're serious about equity leadership, even this responding isn't enough. When we adopt a transformative approach to the direct confrontation principle, we also need to *redress* the inequity. Here are our questions: *What kind of biased or inequitable thinking landed us on this policy or practice to begin with? What aspects of institutional culture or ideology ever allowed it to exist in our school or district?* If we identify socioeconomic bias in tracking practices, let's say, or even in the ability grouping we do in individual classrooms, we ask ourselves, *How did it come to this?*

Similarly, we knew that attaching fees to extracurriculars would limit accessibility for students who already have the lowest levels of access to educational opportunity. *So what was the thinking that went into that decision?* If that didn't occur to whoever sat around a table and made that decision, well, that's an even bigger problem. *So what do we need to do to prepare ourselves so that next time it* will *occur to whoever is around that table?* This is our root-cause analysis, our redressing.

Then we dig deeper. *What other decisions have been influenced by the same thinking? Costly field-trip fees, perhaps, or decisions to schedule extracurriculars before or after school when the same students will enjoy the lowest levels of access?* Let's challenge ourselves to be honest and curious. How will you address those underlying conditions and causes? How will you transform them? How will you go straight at them rather than mitigate them or nibble around their edges?

We want to practice this thinking process until it becomes second nature. The second natured-ness is equity literacy.

As we discussed in Chapter 1, it's important to adjust policies and practices and even individual ideologies that are doing harm right now; we must confront them directly to mitigate the harm. But if we allow the bias-infused mental models that inform decisions to persist, they will continue to influence everything else we do. We have to confront the ideologies and aspects of institutional culture that resulted in the inequitable policies, practices, and pedagogies and that allowed them to persist. We must examine them, understand their nature and the damage they're doing, and transform them.

The shift from *respond* to *redress* is the key to sustainable institutional and individual change. It's the key to the direct confrontation principle. We're directly confronting the policy or practice and its root causes. We're going straight at the thing rather than finding some way around it. What is your plan of action?

Confronting Inequity and Cultivating Equity Without Consensus

Several years ago, during an event for school leaders, we met Heather, an elementary principal from the northeastern United States. Heather described what she called an "equity logjam" at her school. Over the prior decade, she explained, more and more families held their children out of school on Halloween. The trend reflected a growing population in the community of people belonging to a religious group that advises families not to celebrate the holiday. That year, nearly 15 percent of students did not attend school on Halloween.

"Historically, Halloween has been huge at our school," Heather told us. "Teachers really get into it. So I'm not sure what to do."

In our view, the equity solution here is simple. Those students' attendance is more important than observing Halloween in school.

Unfortunately, shifting educators' ideologies and schools' institutional cultures is not so simple.

When Heather floated the idea of ending or significantly limiting Halloween observations, a small but vocal group of teachers nearly rebelled. We asked how they argued for continuing Halloween observations when doing so made that day of school inaccessible for so many students. According to Heather, the resistant teachers argued that they shouldn't deny *most* students the opportunity to participate in their celebrations just because *some* students can't participate due to religious observances. In essence, they made an inverse-equity argument.

Over the next couple months, we coached Heather through the process of confronting this inequity and a variety of other equity-inertia challenges in her school. Her strategy, like her broader leadership approach, had been consensus-based. "How can we get everybody on board so we can move forward?" she often asked us. Every year she'd introduce the issue again. A few teachers would agree emphatically. A few teachers would disagree more emphatically. It was equity gridlock.

This is an important understanding when it comes to the direct confrontation principle and its messiness: *There is not going to be consensus.* We don't want to be hostile to or try to silence people who have questions and concerns. A strong equity commitment can withstand critical inquiry. We should invite novel ideas and tough questions. Leading for equity doesn't mean we have a secret handshake for those who get it and ridicule those who don't. We have the humility to know that we, too, don't always get it. So that sort of dialogue is important. Working toward shared understanding is crucial.

But sometimes, at some point, the people with the most power need to confront the inequity and make hard decisions even when many people *aren't* on board. We cannot wait for that elusive consensus. We need to spend our energy coping strategically with the blowback, with bridging people to our decision rather than allowing an inequity to fester. Either we cope with the blowback or we allow the inequity to persist, leaving the weight on students' and families' shoulders.

From an equity leadership perspective, there's only one real option here. Of course, this requires leaders who have the commitment, humility, and equity literacy to chart a course forward and the will to lead people where they sometimes don't want to go—at least not yet. Instead of moving slowly (or not at all) to create the illusion of universal buy-in, equity leaders create the change necessary *now* and bridge people to that change. We want to be diligent about seeking input, especially from people experiencing inequity, but we don't want to let people resistant to necessary change decide whether that change happens.

As it turned out, by describing the situation more clearly as an equity concern, Heather found that she created space for other equity advocates in her building to speak up more confidently. She garnered more vocal support. That helped. But eventually she needed to impose the policy change without consensus.

She didn't wag her finger at people who disagreed. She just emphasized the school's commitment to equity and introduced the new policy that disallowed observations of Halloween at the school. There were groans, she told us, and even an op-ed in the local newspaper suggesting she was robbing students of their childhoods. But again, those were a few loud voices. When she shared the announcement with families, she found that many who did observe Halloween at home, and especially several families experiencing poverty, were relieved they didn't have to send their children to school in costumes. Many others were relieved that their children wouldn't come home with plastic pumpkins full of candy before trick-or-treating even began.

Sure, some teachers complained. But within a couple years the complaints died down and everybody settled into the new, more equitable normal.

Identify the inequity, name it honestly, and then eliminate it. This is how we *respond to inequity* using the direct confrontation principle. If we, in essence, keep asking people for permission, there will always be enough pushback to freeze us in the inequity. Eventually, if we keep letting that happen, it's no longer an indictment of people who push back, but rather of our equity will.

Of course, depending on where we are and what the local or state politics look like, we might have to be strategic. As we mentioned earlier, the "don't say gay" and anti-CRT legislation emerging in some states can create situations in which withstanding the blowback is more difficult than engaging with a few frustrated staff members. We know principals and equity specialists who have lost their jobs for telling the truth about equity. We know educators who have been doxed, ravaged online, and physically threatened for little more than acknowledging the existence of LGBTQIA+ people or for hanging a Black Lives Matter flag in their classroom or school. Perhaps there is a time when morality requires some equity-committed leaders to take their stand, to be vulnerable to whatever repercussion may come. Of course, some of us are not in a position to do that, and that has to be OK too. Each of us must decide our best, most principled course of action. We need people to stay in the struggle even in places where the struggle feels at least temporarily fruitless. But we also don't want every equity leader to be chased out of schools and districts until there are no adults left who are willing to struggle for equity. There are positions in-between, ways we can lead for equity even where our equity efforts are attacked or even outlawed. We discuss those in Chapter 8.

Now for the *redress*. Let's return to this question: Why would we deny most students the opportunity to participate in Halloween traditions because a small number can't participate? This is common thinking, but it's also an ideological position that is incompatible with equity. It's the kind of thinking that impedes our abilities to identify and confront inequities because it's almost always an argument to protect somebody's privilege.

How would you respond to that question if one of your colleagues posed it?

The examples are plentiful. Try to recall examples of times when educators or educational leaders applied similar logic in schools you attended or schools where you've worked. Maybe there's a racist mascot: the Rebels with Confederate flags or the Warriors depicted by stereotype-laden images of Native or Indigenous people. *Why should we change our mascot just because some people don't like it? Isn't that unfair to everybody else?* Or maybe there's an expensive senior trip each spring. *Should we deny students who can afford the trip an opportunity to go because other students can't afford it?* Or maybe it's admissions procedures for independent schools. *Aren't you punishing students who work hard if anybody can be admitted to the school?* In our view, educators should not be in the business of reproducing the access and opportunity disparities and other forms of marginalization that exist outside school. Not if we're committed to equity.

So this is what directly confronting inequity looks like: We honestly, humbly map out the biases and inequities operating around us. When we identify an inequity, whether it's a racist policy, a practice that marginalizes students experiencing poverty, a cisgenderist ideological blockage, or something else, we go at it directly, even if some or many of the people around us aren't on board. We're guided by the needs and demands of the people who are being marginalized, not by the demands of people who would rather sidestep serious considerations for equity.

Then we examine what it was about our thinking or institutional culture that ever allowed that policy, practice, or ideological blockage to persist, and we go after that. We don't tiptoe around it or try to bury it beneath a program that was never designed to solve it. We educate about it, have a dialogue about it, but we don't sit back waiting for consensus. We, the leaders, take the blowback rather than passing the implications onto the people experiencing the inequity.

That's transformative equity at work.

Why Good Intentions Without Good Actions Aren't Enough

Returning to Blue Pasture, remember that the trouble wasn't the *presence* of diversity celebrations; rather, it was the focus on celebrating diversity in the *absence* of a more transformative commitment to antiracism. School leaders mistook celebrations of diversity for equity; celebrating diversity replaced the process of eliminating the racism Black families insisted be addressed. As we mentioned, the leaders who detoured into celebrating diversity were not rabid racists. Their biggest initial mistake was, perhaps, relying too much on what they presumed to be their good intentions. They saw themselves as good, kind people.

Unfortunately, goodness and kindness are not reliable purveyors of equity and justice. When we rely on good intentions, we always limit our equity impact.

Let's say we support a rally after students express concern about sexual assault. Or we arrange an assembly at which students watch an inspirational video about disability to help quell bullying. Or we respond to concerns about racist school cultures by hosting community dialogues while doing little to transform the policies, practices, and school culture norms bearing down on families of color. We're doing something in the way Blue Pasture administrators were doing something. But, as at Blue Pasture, that something is not really an institutionally transformative action.

This is not a question of intentions. It's a question of impact. What is our direct impact as equity leaders? Is it mitigative or transformative? Are we only responding or also redressing? Are we settling for what *we* might see as valiant equity or attending to the impact of inequity as demanded by the people experiencing it?

You might be thinking, *School leaders like Jonathan are doing their best. We all have good intentions.* We hear you. Jonathan and his team never met around the conference table swapping strategies for marginalizing students or families of color. However, racism and other forms of inequity do not depend on nefarious intentions to exist (Bonilla-Silva, 2006). And to his credit, Jonathan didn't want to rest on the laurels of his good intentions. He wanted to grow as an equity leader.

If we consider impact over intent, the reality is that Jonathan was, in fact, participating in the racism students of color were experiencing at Blue Pasture. He acknowledged that. We all participate in inequity, sometimes without even realizing it, because none of us is equity-perfect.

In the end, the students weren't interested in debating whether the racism or Jonathan's role perpetuating it was intentional or nefarious. Nor was Jonathan. The students were suffering and demanding racial equity. They needed him and his team to go right at the racism, to identify it and eliminate it. Without these good equity *actions*, their good equity intentions simply reproduced the racism (Castagno, 2019; Lewis & Diamond, 2015).

This situation is something we, as a community of educators, need to address in the bigger culture of education, at least in the United States. It often can feel as though good intentions, or the *optics* of good intentions, are rewarded more than good actions. Too often, damaging actions are excused with presumptions of good intentions. *She's a good teacher. She loves her students. She just didn't realize that she was doing something harmful.*

Recently a video of a math teacher went viral after a student recorded her doing her "soh-cah-toa" dance, which she performed while wearing a feather headdress. Her intent apparently was to teach sin, co-sin, and tangent. Her decision was rightly criticized as hurtful to Native and Indigenous students.

The defenses came quickly and forcefully: *But students love her! She has won teaching awards! She has been doing this for years, and no one has complained before!* All of that can be true, *and* it can be true that her pedagogical decision perpetuated racist stereotypes and cultural appropriation. People who have been harmed by those stereotypes or appropriations are justified in their outrage.

When those defensive responses become groupthink, it can be easy to fall into a good-intentions loop, relying on presumptions of goodness to help us avoid the hard work of imagining and applying equitable actions. That groupthink perspective can come across as self-congratulatory. *We're doing great! We feel good at the school, so it must be a great place to be. Anyone who says differently is an unfortunate outlier.*

Jonathan made this transition. He moved from a *celebrating diversity* emphasis to an *antiracist* emphasis. He created a professional learning plan that focused not just on individual bias but also on institutional equity. He wanted every educator in his building to understand racism more deeply so that they could respond to it and redress it more thoroughly. He had teams of people critically analyze school policy and patterns of how it was being applied. He scheduled ongoing focus groups, not just to hear about how students and families experienced the school but also about how they felt the school could strengthen its racial equity efforts. He hired support to help department chairs enact curriculum analysis and transformation through an equity lens.

His approach wasn't perfect. He needed a lot of nudging to dig deeper. But once he realized he needed good actions to confront inequity, not just good intentions, his entire approach to equity leadership changed. This shift created momentum in a much more equity-cultivating direction.

Directly confronting inequity is hard work. It can be embarrassing when we're confronting something we've perpetuated. It can be frustrating, exhausting, confusing. But if we want to lead transformatively for equity, if we want to create and sustain just schools, it's the only way forward. And it does get easier, as it did for Jonathan. It's like developing a set of equity literacy muscles instead of relying on knee-jerk reflexes that could be conditioned by privilege or fear, desperate to find an easy path forward where no easy path exists. If we want to stay in equity shape, we must exercise those equity muscles. That's one reason we've embedded equity literacy exercises throughout this book.

To be sure, we both have struggled, and continue to struggle, to remain focused on impact rather than intention despite having dedicated our lives to advocating and educating for equity and justice. No one is immune. Because we are committed to equity, we have learned, sometimes the hard way, to be constantly on the lookout for (1) how our intentions might be misguided and not as "good" as we think they are, (2) how even the best of our intentions may not align with our actions, and (3) how we can create or take advantage of opportunities to welcome feedback about this mismatch rather than deflect, disregard, or dismiss it. We welcome and solicit critical feedback, and we try, not always successfully, to respond with gratitude and humility. This is what Jonathan was learning how to do. This is what equity leaders do.

In *Is Everyone Really Equal? An Introduction to Key Concepts in Social Justice Education*, Özlem Sensoy and Robin DiAngelo (2012) describe common rebuttals people adopt when their criticisms of equity are questioned. These include *appealing to a universal humanity* ("All lives matter!"), *invalidating claims of oppression as oversensitivity* ("It's not *that* bad!"), and *dismissing evidence of inequity as the radical personal agenda of researchers* ("They just have an axe to grind!"). We should challenge ourselves not to become leaders who claim to be committed to diversity or even equity, but who, when push comes to shove, lean on these ways of thinking, sacrificing the possibility of clearer understanding if that understanding demands more direct, more transformative action.

Ask yourself these questions: *How do I feel when I receive critical feedback related to matters of equity? Do I find myself tempted to use these sorts of rebuttals? If so, how can I overcome that temptation, accept feedback as a gift, and continue to directly confront inequity?*

These questions are part of our direct confrontation challenge. We must learn how to catch ourselves when we're grasping so hard onto our philosophical goodness, or our presumptions of good intentions in those around us, that we refuse to acknowledge harm. When we're stuck in that place, or when we feel tempted to appease people who are stuck there, we render ourselves incapable of dealing directly and decisively with inequity.

We find it helpful to remember that even if our school or district is full of well-intended people, we can't presume the institution itself was created to be well-intended. In fact, if we look historically, we know that education systems in the United States, Canada, and elsewhere were not always, or even *usually*, created with good intentions when it comes to equity and justice (Sabzalian, 2019; Walters & Hayes, 1998). Many of us who work in those systems inherited conditions through which serious potential for damage thrives, even if we didn't create them ourselves. We find this in curricula, in tracking practices, in disciplinary measures that don't account for predictable bias. We inherited that potential for damage in policies, practices, traditions, organizational structures, and assessment approaches. So we must be vigilant, which means being willing to map out inequity and assuming the responsibility to eliminate it even if we didn't create it. We can't do that if we are hung up on our feelings when somebody points out there's more to do.

What is an example of an inequitable policy, practice, tradition, organizational structure, or aspect of institutional culture that you inherited when you took your current position? What have you done, or what can you do, to respond to and redress it?

If you retired tomorrow and somebody else was assigned to your job, what inequitable policy or practice would that person inherit?

How can you confront that inequity now, before it's passed off to somebody else, harming more students, staff, or families?

Naming the Problem, Extinguishing the Gaslight

As we mentioned earlier, to enact the direct confrontation principle, we need the skills, knowledge, and will to name inequity honestly. We don't need hyper-academic terminology to do this. We do need critical consciousness and courage.

Most of us embody at least one identity through which we experience inequity or oppression. This acknowledgment sharpens our abilities to recognize and name that specific type of inequity or oppression, sometimes as a matter of survival. However, as we mentioned earlier, when it comes to aspects of our identities that advantage us, most of us have work to do. That's not a criticism. It's an opportunity.

It's an opportunity, first, to *unlearn*. This is where humility is important, because unlearning requires us to identify aspects of our identity around which we experience privilege and then to assume we have much to learn about how oppression operates along that identity axis. One important way to do that is to seek out learning opportunities rooted in the voices, histories, and perspectives of people who bear the brunt of oppression along that axis, people whose oppression is tied to our privilege.

Unfortunately, education systems and other institutions generally do a bang-up job of erasing or distorting the voices, perspectives, and histories of all sorts of communities and liberation movements (An, 2016; Brazelton, 2021; Vickery & Rodríguez, 2021), so we need to be vigilant about the sources of our learning. We also need to be careful not to mindlessly pass that burden off onto our friends and colleagues who are experiencing the inequities we're learning about, overloading them with questions and requests for resources. We don't want to add to or exploit their emotional labor (Gorski & Erakat, 2019). Let's do our own work.

We also should remember that this miseducation is no accident (Au, 2010; Tuck & Gaztambide-Fernández, 2013). Misunderstandings about how equity and inequity operate are a feature of our school system and our society, and not a bug. We need to be intentional.

So let's practice acknowledging. What is one dimension of your identity around which you experience some level of unearned privilege or advantage in your life outside school? What are three ways inequity currently exists in your school or district that bestow that sort of unearned privilege on you or others? How might this affect your ability to effectively confront, or even to recognize, inequities?

This willingness to do our own work, to name our own privilege, is also an opportunity to strengthen our relationships with people who are tired of having to name things for us. Often the people doing the naming are also the people feeling the weight of the bias and inequity, which, again, is a good recipe for burnout. A useful measure of the depth of our commitment to equity leadership is how the people who have been doing the most insistent, boldest, most direct naming feel in our school or district. Too often they feel pushed to the margins of institutional culture. Leaders might shush them or tell them to quiet their politics (Gorski, 2019). Leaders might reframe their concerns to make them seem like idiosyncratic outliers.

In an institution truly committed to equity and justice, the strongest equity advocates should feel like the center of institutional culture. They should feel celebrated, appreciated, and recognized for their equity commitments. If the loudest voices for equity feel more marginalized in our school or district than the people dragging their heels on equity, it's time to reexamine our leadership approach.

Education scholars Frank Harris III and Luke Wood (2021) describe gaslighting as a process that "occurs when one begins to question their own sanity and reality because they are being manipulated by others. This type of psychological abuse causes people to second guess their experiences, emotions, knowledge, judgment, memories, and ultimately their humanity" (para. 2).

In a powerful account of how she was gaslit as a queer educator of color, scholar Boni Wozolek (2018) points out that gaslighting is an emotional and visceral process that is both interpersonal and systemic. "In short," she explains, "gaslighting is as much a product of privilege as it is about willfully using power to negatively impact victims. What makes gaslighting so hard to name for the victim is the combination of these factors that exist across layers of scale" (p. 334). In Wozolek's case, these layers of gaslighting included federal education policymaking, as when former Secretary of Education Betsy DeVos overturned policies that acknowledged and addressed transphobia. It also included streams of school-level incidents, such as administrators and colleagues repeatedly violating HR and board policies, dismissing her concerns, mocking her, threatening her, excluding her, applying or inventing rules only for her and the GSA she advised, surveilling her, and lying to her.

We can trace a long history of gaslighting related to equity concerns in schools, in responses to claims of discrimination or harassment, in debates about tracking, in all sorts of contexts in which people's concerns about injustice are ignored, dismissed, or addressed only in high-optics, low-impact ways. It's a popular tactic for people who feel threatened by a direct approach, or *any* approach, to equity. It's a distraction, a way to redirect the conversation so that now we're debating about whether, say, racism exists rather than identifying and eliminating racism. This is the epitome of *in*direct confrontation, which is no confrontation at all.

In fact, if we're allowing in our spheres of influence any sort of debate about *whether* racism exists, or *whether* we ought to eliminate cisgenderism, or *whether* it's important to talk about heterosexism, we're enabling a sort of collective gaslighting. People targeted by these oppressions should not be required to sit through a conversation about whether the oppressions exist and whether we should act on them. That is, in itself, oppressive.

Similarly, when we call racism something else to appease the people allowing it to fester, something that softens it, like *racial conflict* or *personal prejudice* or *unkindness,* we in essence gaslight people who experience racism. So again, we must be willing to name the oppression directly, knowing that doing so might make some people uncomfortable, including those who need to be made uneasy, while demonstrating to the people historically shouldering disproportionate unease that we're serious about eradicating injustice.

As we write this book, we find constant examples of this sort of gaslighting winding its way like an angry vine through the lives of many youth of color and youth who are undocumented, nonbinary or transgender, economically marginalized, or otherwise facing the lion's share of inequity. Legislators are passing laws to quiet honest conversations about racism and other equity concerns in schools. People are calling antiracism efforts "racism," which seems to mean that their version of antiracism is allowing racism to persist.

Equity leaders cannot be a party to this gaslighting. It's the opposite of direct confrontation.

Our temptation might be to simply try to diffuse the tension, avoid the controversy. Or maybe we search for a scripted response or choreographed program. Equity leaders avoid that temptation. The question for us is not whether tension exists, because tension exists everywhere injustice exists. Instead, it's *Do equity and justice exist?* Our effectiveness as leaders is measured by the answer to that question and how directly we respond to it.

Equity Is More Important Than Niceness or Kindness If We Can't Have Both

Recently, while we were visiting a school district, Sofia, a language arts teacher, pulled us aside. She was one of only a few Latina teachers in the district. "That's a problem," she insisted, "in a district where more than 30 percent of students are Latinos."

She confided how exhausted she was, how beaten down she felt, being one of the few people willing to advocate for that 30 percent. When we asked Sofia what kept her colleagues from speaking up, she answered, "Some of them just don't find it important. They think this diversity stuff is nonsense." She was quick to explain that this group comprised a small percentage of teachers at her school.

Then she described her frustration in a way that sounded familiar, based on what we have observed in many other districts, but that also was more direct than how we had heard anyone else frame it. "But for the ones who do find equity and inclusion important," she sighed, "the biggest barrier is niceness."

To be clear, we value empathy, compassion, and concern for others. We appreciate pleasant, upbeat vibes. Our concern is not the presence of niceness per se, but rather the presence of niceness or kindness as a substitute for equity, as a way around direct confrontations with inequity.

Several scholars have challenged us to consider the limitations of niceness, especially how focusing on "being nice" can maintain the power of dominant cultural, racial, ethnic, and religious communities (e.g., Low, 2009). For example, Enrique Alemán Jr. (2009) explores how calls for "decorum and respect" can prohibit "blatant and honest depictions of racialized oppression" (p. 306). Similarly, Richard Orozco (2019) describes students' criticisms of white teachers opting for the "niceness" of conflict avoidance rather than explicitly addressing racism. In *The Price of Nice*, Angelina E. Castagno (2019) explains how the pressure for everyone to "be nice" gives educators who would rather opt out of equity a convenient excuse to do so, and justification for punishing or silencing anyone who might, in Castagno's words, "attempt or even consider disrupting structures and ideologies of dominance" (p. xiv).

When we adhere to this brand of niceness—niceness without contextual awareness, niceness as compliance with deeply inequitable systems, as a means of avoiding conflict, as protection for people advantaged by inequity, as a substitute for equity—we risk undermining our equity efforts and replacing them with actions that are as oppressive as the problems we are trying to solve. Dena Simmons (2021) recently described SEL initiatives without an antiracist commitment as "white supremacy with a hug" (p. 31). We find this a useful way to think about niceness or kindness without a transformative equity commitment. It's white supremacy with a hug, heterosexism with a high-five, cisgenderism with a pat on the back, or ableism with a smile.

One concern about the increasingly trendy emphases on kindness and niceness, whether related to antibullying programs or office decor or bigger shifts to institutional culture, is that we end up burying deeper equity issues by implicitly suggesting that equity is simply a matter of individual relationships. *The path to equity is kindness, so we all just need to smile more often.* Imagine students whose families have for generations endured economic marginalization or racism, or both, being told that the solution to this injustice is simply being nicer, or that the situation will improve if white or wealthy students are kinder to them. Isn't it rational, even ethical, for people experiencing injustice to be angry about injustice? When was the last time you witnessed significant social progress on an equity issue simply because somebody asked for it nicely? And how is systemic and structural advantage disrupted by being nicer to someone without access to it?

Another concern about the focus on niceness is that, when we prioritize it over truth-telling, we limit the depth and sophistication, and certainly the directness, of our equity conversations and actions. Rather than creating institutional conditions in which people are hesitant to tell the truth or to name how their colleagues or institutions are harming students and families because they don't want to be labeled "unkind" or "mean," we should create conditions in which critical feedback is interpreted, as we mentioned earlier, as an invaluable gift, as a deeper form of kindness and love.

We could argue that, from an equity point of view, it's *un*kind to *not* point out when a person or institution has done damage, especially when it targets people who already experience disproportionate harm. Sure, we can point that out in a variety of ways, but we can't *not* point it out because we are worried that doing so is unkind. And if we're on the receiving end of that feedback, we can't focus more on *how* we are hearing about it than on the inequity itself.

Sofia was angry. "Latino students feel like this school isn't for them," she said. "They're nowhere to be found in the curriculum. Some teachers pronounce their names incorrectly. They hear racist jokes and comments from peers. And we, the teachers, can't even have a conversation about it or we're seen as unkind in a school culture that values being nice over being honest." She believed that some of her colleagues wanted to speak up but hesitated to break what she called the "kindness code."

When she approached her principal with this concern, he suggested she try to approach her colleagues with a "friendlier tone." She had. It didn't work. If anything, it undermined her urgency, and nothing changed.

This example points again to our need to create a school and district culture where telling the truth about inequity is seen as *kind* rather than *unkind*. We do that by modeling directness when it comes to equity and by demonstrating an unbending appreciation for people who say what needs to be said, no matter how they say it. Unfortunately, Sofia's principal made her feel as though it might be easier to go along with the inequity than to stand up for equity. But she was not about to go along with the inequity.

Who are the Sofias in your school or district? How are they treated when they speak directly to injustice? If we asked, would they say you have their backs? How do you acknowledge or even reward them for their directness?

Consider one more example. Robert was the principal of a high school that prided itself as being one of the best in the state. One weekend, a white student posted a photo of herself on social media in front of a Confederate flag, along with a racist message. When several fellow students raised concerns about her message and the symbolism of the flag, several other students replied defensively. During lunch, a Black student approached her to explain why the post was hurtful. The conversation escalated, and the students began to physically fight. Video of the incident caught the interest of a local news station.

Attempting to put out the fire, Robert announced over the PA system, "We just need to be kinder to one another." Many Black students expressed frustration with Robert's message, which did not acknowledge the harm they experienced or the courage of their classmate who confronted it.

Robert struggled at first to understand why his call for kindness was inadequate. He attributed the incident to social media, to the fact that the young woman who posted the message had not grown up in the district and, in his words, to the Black students' "angry overreaction" to the post. He responded to racism by expressing a desire for everyone to get along, to be kind to one another, to extend grace, while characterizing the post and the fight as isolated incidents. Meanwhile, he avoided a head-on examination of racism, including the ways the school systematically marginalized youth of color.

Robert's belief in kindness was sincere. He confided in us, "I was responding the most productive way I knew how." We believed him. But productive for whom? The Black students weren't asking for kindness, and their efforts to kindly address the situation were ignored. They wanted justice. They wanted somebody to honestly name and grapple with the harm they endured. They wanted accountability.

To his credit, Robert, like most school leaders with whom we work, was open to rethinking his interpretation of the events. The most important shift he made was acknowledging that, in fact, these were not isolated incidents, that they were just unique expressions of longstanding racial inequities at the school. But he also came to understand that he needed to address racism directly, *as racism*. He can philosophically support the young woman's right to express her views while also being very clear that he and the school find those views reprehensible.

"I get now that the fight wasn't just about that one incident," he later told us. "So my response shouldn't have been just about that one incident. I minimized the experiences of students of color."

This distinction is important when it comes to the direct confrontation principle. We made this point previously, but it bears repeating. The issue in this case was racism, not personality clashes or social media. Maybe those elements exacerbated the problem, but they aren't the root of the problem. It bubbled up through individual racist actions: a racist post and a slew of racist responses supporting the racist post. As he came to acknowledge, Robert could have, and *should* have, named and taken action on the racism (*respond*). He should have addressed it, not just as an individual act but as part of a set of conditions with which Black students and other students of color had to contend (*redress*), and then reemphasized institutional efforts to ensure a racially just school (*actively cultivate*).

In this case, we would argue that the bubbling over is an illustration not of Black students' failure to be kind, but of the school's failure to protect them from racism. How was encouraging kindness going to accomplish that?

Robert missed an opportunity to cultivate trust with many of the Black students when he stepped gingerly around the racism rather than naming and addressing it directly. That too was a racist act, an act with racist impact, whether Robert was intentionally evasive or not. We were impressed by his willingness to own that and his determination to do better. We're all going to trip. It's not our level of equity perfection that makes us formidable equity leaders, but rather our willingness to own our stumbles and our determination to do better.

With the direct confrontation principle in mind, how might you have responded differently to this series of incidents? What would *redressing* the inequity look like in this scenario, so that we're not just reacting to incidents but understanding and addressing them in relation to bigger sets of conditions, directly confronting the racism?

Can you recall a time when you misdiagnosed inequity in this manner? What would you do differently now?

Yes, kindness matters. But *kindness* is not *equity*. And equity matters more than kindness if we must choose between them. After all, what twisted kind of kindness is *not* rooted in equity? What mangled version of kindness allows sexism or heterosexism as its backdrop?

To be clear, we're not suggesting that directly confronting inequity is "anti-nice" or unkind. We can't imagine a more genuine kindness than eliminating inequity and other causes of harm.

Conclusion

Educational outcomes disparities across race, whether test score gaps, differences in graduation rates, or differences in rates of registration for advanced academic classes, *are racism*. Socioeconomic disproportionalities in assignment to special education or in school discipline *are economic injustice*. They are symptoms of a combination of unjust conditions in and out of schools, ranging from employment discrimination to school segregation to curricular erasure to teacher bias. We cannot cultivate equity without addressing these conditions directly, without learning how to recognize even their subtlest manifestations in classrooms and schools. We can't redress a problem we refuse to understand. And no amount of celebrating diversity excuses us from the responsibility for doing so. The only path to equity involves, first and foremost, a direct confrontation with inequity.

More generally, the goal of equity requires us to understand and directly confront *all* inequities. That means our equity strategies should begin with identifying how inequity operates in our classrooms, schools, and districts. Remember, at their roots, inequities are unfair distributions of access and opportunity. They are systems of advantage and disadvantage generally following predictable patterns. So we must take careful, precise stock of how access and opportunity are distributed across race, ethnicity, religion, gender identity, sexual orientation, socioeconomic status, size, language, disability, and other dimensions of difference.

Let's challenge ourselves not to choose the path of least resistance, such as calling for kindness instead of antiracism or investing in an antibullying program while allowing ableism to fester. We must be willing to name conditions honestly and confront them directly. This is the direct confrontation principle: we focus most forthrightly on *equity*, directly confronting and eliminating all the ways inequity operates in our classrooms and schools.

Equity, not just celebrating diversity. Equity, not just cultural competence. *Equity*. The most important questions are not *How diverse are we?* or *Do we celebrate diversity adequately?* but rather *How equitable and just are we?* and *How can we become more equitable and just?*

Figure 3.1 highlights some of the key points presented in this chapter. It summarizes the direct confrontation principle by illustrating, from a leader's point of view, the difference between mitigative equity and transformative equity in terms of actions and attitudes.

FIGURE 3.1

The Direct Confrontation Principle: Comparing Leaders' Mindsets Related to Mitigative Versus Transformative Equity

Mitigative Equity	Transformative Equity
Most of my energies are focused on addressing symptoms of inequity.	Although I recognize and respond to symptoms, my primary goal is redressing root causes of inequity.
I try to steer away from conflict or discomfort when addressing inequities.	I am willing and able to name inequities frankly with a variety of audiences.
I am committed to equity, but my priority is to approach it in a way that does not elicit controversy.	My priority is equity, so I am willing to take risks and make controversial decisions if it advances that priority.
Stakeholders need to trust that I am doing the right thing behind the scenes.	I am transparent about my goals, plans, and accountability measures with all stakeholders.
I am committed to making sure the reputation of our school is a good one; bad press or a public focus on our problems just undermines our efforts.	I embrace critical feedback and trust that our reputation will best be built by stakeholders witnessing how we recognize, respond to, and redress inequities in our school.

4

Ditching Deficit Ideology, Quitting Grit: The Fix Injustice, Not Kids Principle

This is a fact: On average, parents and other caregivers who are experiencing poverty are less likely than their middle class peers to visit their children's schools for family engagement opportunities (Child Trends, 2013). They are less likely to attend parent-teacher conferences, volunteer at school, and make it to school events. This fact has been measured a hundred different ways. There are exceptions, of course, but as a general pattern we know this to be true.

Just in case we don't know it to be true, think tanks, nonprofits, and popular-press authors have produced a flood of articles and reports reminding us that it's true. They often argue enthusiastically that closing the family involvement gap is the key to abolishing disparities in educational outcome (Global Family Research Project, 2018; Thomas Fordham Institute, 2021).

It turns out, despite the national obsession, that the disparity in parent involvement does not appear to be the most formidable cause of outcome disparities or the key to eliminating them. In fact, research findings on this topic are notably inconsistent, sometimes showing positive effects of parental involvement on school achievement and sometimes finding no impact at all (Fan & Chen, 2001; McNeal, 2012).

We're not saying it's not important for other reasons: families' sense of connectedness to the school, for example, or educators' sense of connectedness to families. But the intense emphasis on families visiting their children's schools and other forms of engagement is, according to a growing body of research, way out of proportional whack and, in some cases, a troubling distraction from more important concerns, including teacher and institutional impacts.

As we see it, this conclusion raises a couple of questions with which we, as equity leaders, ought to grapple. First, why do rates of at-school family engagement differ across socioeconomic status? If we hope to build more solid family-school relationships, we need to understand *why* some families are less likely than others to visit their children's schools. We need to identify, clearly and *accurately*, the conditions that underlie this disparity.

Second, what accounts for the popular misperception that gaps in family engagement largely explain educational outcome disparities? What sorts of realities are hiding behind this misperception? And why, despite all the evidence otherwise, do so many educators, education writers, and others continue to cling so tightly to the family involvement trope?

We'll return to the second question later in this chapter. Let's start with the first question. What is the first thing that comes to mind when you consider why parents from families experiencing poverty are, on average, less likely than their wealthier peers to visit their children's schools for family engagement opportunities?

Keep your response handy. We'll return to it momentarily.

Again, the facts are not in dispute. Parents experiencing poverty are, by almost every measure, less likely than their wealthier peers to visit their children's schools. What might be in dispute, though, is how we *interpret* the facts and to what we *attribute* the disparities. If we interpret the facts improperly, we become incapable of addressing the disparities in meaningful ways. In other words, interpret wrongly and we position ourselves as more of a threat to *equity* than a threat to *inequity*.

Ideological Lines and the Possibility or Impossibility of Equity

In the Introduction to this book, we briefly discussed the importance of ideology. Ideology drives our perceptions and interpretations. Our interpretations, the way we make sense of a set of circumstances or define a problem, determine the solutions we are capable of imagining. The solutions we pursue determine the extent to which we position ourselves to cultivate and sustain equity or inequity. It all begins with ideology.

When we ask why parents experiencing poverty are less likely than their wealthier peers to visit their children's schools (or some other question that elicits ideological reflection about issues such as poverty), educators tend to make sense of the disparity along one of two big ideological lines. Along one line are educators who embrace what people who study such things often call *deficit ideology* (Gorski, 2016; Johnson & Johnson, 2021). These educators believe, for example, that people experiencing poverty are the agents, the *causes*, of their own economic conditions. As a result, they primarily attribute educational disparities across class lines, and poverty itself, to what they *wrongfully* presume are moral, intellectual, dispositional, or even spiritual deficiencies in people experiencing poverty or in high-poverty communities more broadly. For example, they might believe, despite decades of research demonstrating otherwise (Johnson et al., 2016; Robinson & Volpé, 2015), that people experiencing poverty do not value education the way other people do. Their impulse is to identify the source of outcome disparities as existing within, rather than as pressing upon, people from economically or otherwise marginalized communities. This perspective is the inverse of an equity perspective. More important, it's factually inaccurate.

This ideological view works the same way across race, gender, and other identities. If we tend to look at circumstances or outcome disparities as results of inherent deficiencies that we associate with individuals' or groups' identities—*girls are less likely to take advanced science courses because they are not as good as boys in science,* or *Black students are more likely than white students to be suspended from school because they misbehave more often,* for example—we are trapped in a deficit ideology. We are unlikely to imagine effective, equity-based responses to these disparities because we are not accounting for the conditions, biases, and inequities that actually do cause them. We'll explore those conditions, biases, and inequities a little later.

Along the other ideological line are educators who tend to believe that these disparities are unjust but logical outcomes of bigger societal disparities, especially inequitable access to resources and opportunities both in and out of schools. Embracing a *structural ideology,* they tend to see individuals experiencing poverty as *targets* rather than *causes* of gaps in both *material conditions* (related to who has access to financial and various other material resources) and *experiential conditions* (related to who has access to various sorts of experiences and influence). With this ideological view, people who embrace the reality of structural ideology recognize how inequities based on race, class, gender identity, sexual orientation, language, and other identities cause educational disparities.

Their impulse upon noticing disparities in at-school family involvement, for instance, is to wonder what sorts of challenges and barriers might limit economically marginalized families' access to involvement (Hornsby & Blackwell, 2018). Their next impulse is to wonder how school policies and practices, and perhaps even their own ideologies, might perpetuate those challenges and barriers. Their equity action, then, is to remove or at least mitigate those barriers by, in equity literacy terms, recognizing, responding to, and redressing bias and injustice.

Whereas a leader with a deficit ideology might wonder, *How can I convince these families that they should value their children's education enough to take advantage of these opportunities?* (imagining there's something to fix about *these families*), a leader embracing a more structural or equity view might wonder, *Am I scheduling opportunities for family engagement in ways that make them accessible to families who work multiple jobs, who don't have paid leave, who have limited transportation and childcare options?* In the latter case, the impulse is to identify and eliminate inequity rather than to adjust something about the people experiencing the inequity.

These might sound like equally credible points of view. They aren't. Not from an equity perspective. Nor is there a useful middle ground. Deficit ideology obscures inequity by locating fault within what people *falsely* assume to be "deficient" mindsets, cultures, or dispositions of individuals and communities who are racially, economically, or otherwise marginalized. So deficit ideologues tend to think in terms of "fixing" people who are marginalized (Davis & Museus, 2019). *We have to convince lower-income parents that they should care more about their children's education,* the deficit ideologue might reason, as we mentioned earlier. Or, *We need to adjust the behaviors of students of color to close discipline disparities.* Or, *We need to help young women interested in STEM to be more resilient so they can handle the rigor of advanced science courses.* All these responses are paths that lead deeper into inequity (see Figure 4.1).

FIGURE 4.1

Equity Problems and Solutions Through the Lenses of Three Ideologies

	Deficit Ideology	Grit Ideology	Structural Ideology
What is the problem?	The cultures, mindsets, behaviors, emotions, or actions of people who are marginalized or who are the targets of a disparity	Insufficient resilience or stick-to-it-iveness in the face of disadvantage	Inequity, structures of advantage and disadvantage, injustice
What is the solution?	Adjustments to the cultures, mindsets, behaviors, emotions, or actions of people who are marginalized in order to eliminate a disparity	Increased grit and resilience by people who are marginalized	Equity and justice

As we noted earlier, there is no evidence, not even a little, that parents from families experiencing poverty are less likely than wealthier parents to visit their children's school because they value education less. To embrace this perspective, we must ignore decades' worth of studies showing no such gap exists (see Gorski, 2018). Similarly, we must ignore piles of research detailing sexism in STEM contexts to presume that women are inherently less STEM-capable than men (McGuire et al., 2020) and loads of evidence about racist discipline practices that undermine the presumption that Black students are more likely to be suspended because they misbehave more often than their peers (Carter et al., 2017). How can we expect to make effective and equitable decisions on policy and practice when we formulate them on these sorts of misperceptions?

The presumptions of deficit ideology explain why schools often spend energy and resources solving problems that do not exist—problems conceived not around reality and evidence, but around stereotypes and biases. "Families experiencing poverty do not value education" is *a problem that does not exist*. So why would we spend resources trying to solve it? Deficit ideology always detours us away from the equity path, not least by misallocating precious resources.

A structural ideology, on the other hand, is rooted in reality. It ignites our curiosity about barriers, challenges, biases, and inequities. Consider these questions, the sorts that a structural ideology encourages us to ask: *What are the barriers and challenges that might make it more difficult for families experiencing poverty to visit their children's school? What are the barriers and challenges they experience outside school that might limit their at-school involvement? What are the barriers and challenges we unintentionally uphold within classrooms and schools that could inhibit their engagement? What are the* actual *causes of educational outcome disparities, and what are we doing about those?* Bridging us to the prioritization principle we discuss in Chapter 6, we might ask, *How can we provide opportunities for engagement that prioritize access for the families that historically have been denied access?*

These are the sorts of questions equity leaders ask but that leaders clinging to deficit ideology rarely consider. These are the questions we never think to ask when we fixate on what we misperceive is wrong with *those people.* That's why the *fix injustice, not kids principle* is so crucial to effective equity leadership.

The simple reality is, there is no path to equity through a deficit ideology. The two are incompatible. We can achieve equity only through a structural ideology, by recognizing and removing challenges and barriers and their underlying inequities; by adjusting our institutional cultures to be actively antiracist, antiheterosexist, antioppressive; by eliminating injustice.

On a practical level, equity initiatives should *never* focus on adjusting anything about people who are marginalized: changing their cultures, modifying their mindsets, strengthening their grit, or moderating their emotions. Equity efforts focus instead on eliminating the conditions that marginalize people. This is where the fix injustice, not kids principle interacts with the direct confrontation principle. We cannot effectively confront an inequity we misunderstand or fail to see because it's obscured by a deficit ideology.

If we hope to apply this principle, we must grasp an important distinction. It is popular in education circles to associate efforts to dislodge deficit ideology with efforts to embrace an assets-based mindset, focusing on what a student does well. We agree that it's important not only to recognize but also to cultivate the assets and gifts in each student, colleague, family, and community; to embrace a "funds of knowledge" approach (Moll et al., 1992) and to acknowledge and value everybody's cultural capital (Yosso, 2005), including students' knowledge about and experiences with trauma (Zipin, 2009).

However, it's also important to remember that the opposite of a deficit ideology is not an assets-based view. We can recognize gifts students bring and acknowledge their funds of knowledge while also implementing policies or practices that marginalize them. Instead, the opposite of a deficit ideology is an unbending commitment to identifying and eliminating all the mechanisms that marginalize people. Without a structural ideology and its deep understandings of the realities of inequity, we remain incapable of identifying inequity and, as a result, of eliminating it.

Several years ago, while visiting Low Lands High School, we met Samuel, a student who had just returned to school after a long suspension. "I'm one of only a few Native students in this district," he told us. Then he described the relentless racial microaggressions he had withstood since kindergarten. "Teachers here are clueless about my experience and culture. I have to hear them say racist things, and they never respond when other students say racist things."

Samuel told us about a small group of white students who had been especially ruthless and relentless, often calling him and the other Native students the N-word. "They've been doing this since elementary school," he said, "over and over and over." He had reported their racist taunts a few times over the years, but "whoever I told always said they couldn't do anything unless somebody caught them in the act."

When we visited Low Lands, Samuel was in 11th grade. A couple of weeks before, one of those white students who had been tormenting him since elementary school called him the N-word. After 11 years of taunts and no real response from the school or district, Samuel no longer could contain his hurt and anger. He punched that white student in the face.

We certainly don't advocate violence. But wasn't what Samuel experienced, 11 years of oppressive torment and 11 years of his district's inaction, also violence? At some point, wasn't Samuel's reaction unsurprising, perhaps even justified? Sure, we can apply a rule. We can say Samuel's reaction broke a policy prohibiting physical violence. But can't we also look at this a different way? Couldn't we even say that it's impressive—but also horribly oppressive, given his district's inaction—that Samuel withstood 11 years of that racism before he met violence with violence? What frequency or level of abuse do we expect Samuel to withstand from classmates, from institutional inaction, and from unresponsive adults before unloading?

Samuel was suspended and ordered into mindfulness and emotion-regulation lessons, he told us. "They taught me to sing a song to myself when I feel angry, or to take some deep breaths." What problem was the school solving there? What problem was it ignoring? From an equity view, the root issue was the school's failure to protect Samuel from racism. The problem was that adults repeatedly invalidated his reports of racist taunting. The problem was the fact that some students found it entirely normal to use the N-word at Low Lands. The school's response resolved none of this. Instead, it punished Samuel for an outcome of its own inaction.

Sure, mindfulness strategies can be useful life skills if applied in meaningful, contextualized ways (Venet, 2021). But providing coping mechanisms to help students overcome rightful anger or frustration—well, that's just another way we marginalize youth. Dena Simmons (2019) asks, "Why teach relationship skills if the lessons do not reflect on the interpersonal conflicts that result from racism? Why discuss self- and social awareness without considering power and privilege, even if that means examining controversial topics like white supremacy?" (para. 6).

Samuel's experience exemplifies classic deficit ideology. The school identified Samuel and his anger as the problem that needed to be resolved, as the thing to punish. Meanwhile, leadership failed to address the racist conditions that elicited Samuel's reaction.

So how do we dislodge deficit ideology and embrace structural ideology? We begin by cultivating in ourselves and one another what we call the *structural impulse* so that we're instinctively asking the right equity questions: *What are the challenges and barriers? What are the inequities and injustices? What are the characteristics of institutional culture that have enabled these inequities and injustices to persist?* And we learn to catch ourselves when we begin to slide toward a deficit view.

This shift takes practice, even for those of us who have been working at it for a long time. Later in this chapter we offer some strategies for cultivating this structural impulse.

The Practical Benefits of Ditching Deficit Ideology and Adopting Structural Ideology

We realize that all this talk about deficit ideology and structural impulses can sound a bit heady, disconnected from the day-to-day practical realities of classrooms and schools. Considered a different way, however, the fix injustice, not kids principle might be the most practical principle in this book. Embracing a structural ideology prepares us in a very grounded way to do everything more equitably, from making instructional decisions to interpreting data to adjusting policy. By embracing a structural ideology and rejecting a deficit ideology, by rooting deficit ideology out of our schools and one another, we also prepare ourselves to cultivate more trusting, meaningful relationships with the most marginalized families, with students and parents who, unfortunately, sometimes are accustomed to uneasy, inequity-ridden, or even hostile relationships with schools. Even when we try to hide our deficit views, students and families can spot them.

Returning to the issue of at-school family involvement, parents experiencing poverty generally identify two sets of barriers that impede their abilities to visit their children's schools at the same rates as their wealthier peers. The first set consists of material barriers. Some work multiple jobs, including evening jobs, often with inconsistent hours, making it difficult to attend late afternoon or evening events. Because these are usually hourly-wage jobs, they rarely have paid leave, which makes it difficult to take time off work to attend school events or even to pick up their children if they become sick during the school day (Gupta et al., 2018). Families experiencing poverty often struggle to afford transportation or childcare if either is necessary in order to visit their children's school.

Note that none of this has anything to do with how families value education or how hard they work, whether they have a growth mindset, or whether they have sufficient grit. All these conditions are trackable primarily to wealth and income inequality, the scarcity of living-wage work, and other bigger social conditions. If we want to take a more micro view, they are trackable to how we, the people working in schools, tend to organize family involvement opportunities, often without considering this context and the barriers we create for families experiencing poverty.

Harkening to the prioritization principle, which we will discuss in more detail in Chapter 5, some schools have adjusted the way they do family involvement by prioritizing access for families that historically have had the least access. But if, due to deficit ideology, it doesn't occur to us to consider this context, it's easy to presume people aren't showing up because of *their* mindset or value system. In that case, it wouldn't occur to us that our most important solution is to destroy barriers and elevate access.

That's unfortunate, you might be thinking, *but it's also well outside our spheres of influence as educators.* Fair point. We would argue, though, that people can at least influence these forces; we can choose to be part of larger equity movements. In the short term, however, we get it. Although we cannot individually afford to purchase a functioning mode of transportation for all families or wave a magic equity wand and *poof!* create legislation to fully fund public transportation and make childcare a human right (which it ought to be), we absolutely *can* adjust the way we conceive of and design these opportunities to make them more accessible to everyone. Some schools work with bus services, organize ride shares, or provide onsite childcare. Others find ways to be creative with when and where family meetings and school events are scheduled.

The second set of barriers to at-school family involvement is relational. These barriers are characterized by the kinds of interactions families experiencing poverty sometimes have with educators when they do visit their children's schools, including interactions that may mirror the harmful experiences some had when they were students. They might report feeling that their children's teachers condescend to them, presume they do not value their children's education, or treat them as though they do not have their children's best interests at heart (Gorski, 2018), all of which we should expect if they are interacting with educators who embrace a deficit ideology. Notably, studies detailing the experiences of families of color, families who are masters of languages other than English, and families whose identities might otherwise ignite educators' implicit or explicit bias have revealed similar relationship-crushing teacher-parent and teacher-student dynamics (e.g., Lechuga-Peña & Brisson, 2018).

This is a problem whose solution is smack dab in the middle of our spheres of influence. We can do more than *mitigate* its impact; we can *eliminate* it. We can commit to changing the ways we relate to families. As leaders we can cultivate a structural ideology and challenge every instance of deficit ideology, attempting to shift the institutional culture from the deficit to the structural at every turn. We can invest in professional development and practice engaging more equitably with families.

But again, these actions may not occur to us if we harbor a deficit ideology, which obscures this way of thinking. If that's the case, we undermine the possibility that we will land on a solution that requires us to adjust *our* mindsets, dispositions, and behaviors rather than those of parents or students. In a practical way, the deficit ideology makes us incapable of fostering the equity we desire.

Moreover, illustrating the idea of transformative equity we shared in Chapter 1, we have found that even if we attempt to nip this problem in the proverbial bud, educators with a deficit ideology often struggle to implement structural responses. So the intervention can't just be a practical shift. It must include the work that will bridge them to a structural ideology. People who locate the source of the problem as *existing within* rather than as *pressing upon* a marginalized group require a significant ideological reckoning before they can effectively implement solutions that might rub against their perspectives.

This is why we argue that equity-related professional development should focus first on ideological shifts, not on silver bullet strategies. In the end, no combination of curricular or pedagogical strategies can turn a classroom or school led by an educator with a deficit view of families experiencing poverty or families of color or any other families into an equitable learning space for students and their families.

Choosing the Structural Approach

To be clear, we are not referring here to purposefully racist, xenophobic people plotting to oppress families experiencing poverty, families of color, or other families. Of course, we would be foolish to presume that the extended community of educators is free of people doing intentionally bigoted things: teachers dressing up like a border wall for Halloween, a middle school social studies teacher secretly hosting a white nationalist podcast. The bigger problem, as we see it, is the racism, xenophobia, ableism, and other forms of inequity that are

perpetuated more quietly and insidiously, perhaps even unintentionally, through deficit ideologies and other ideological blockages.

In some ways, it's easier to ferret out the explicit bigots than to
identify the more subtle, insidious ways deficit ideology persists in
schools. The latter might have even harsher consequences for students
because it hides in the shadows of our ideologies and institutional cultures. It quietly insinuates itself into every practice, policy decision,
and interaction.

So if we are choosing to cling stubbornly onto a deficit view
despite this evidence—and it is, in fact, *a choice*—then can we honestly call our own participation in perpetuating inequitable conditions unintentional? If we embrace a view rooted in inequity-laced
misunderstanding, our interpretations and actions will be laced with
inequity. At some point, if we're clinging to a deficit ideology, we're
choosing inequity.

We must choose, instead, to drive deficit ideology out of our classrooms and schools, out of ourselves, and out of one another, and to
embrace a structural ideology. As a practical, high-impact strategy,
we can make this choice *right now*. If you are a leader hoping to make
equity headway, you *must* make this choice. *As a school we are embracing a structural ideology. We will identify and eliminate inequity in all
its forms. We are rejecting a deficit ideology. We will drive the deficit
narrative out of our spheres of influence.* Equity cannot live where deficit ideology lives.

Later we describe how structural ideology positions us and our
schools for equity and how to cultivate the structural impulse in ourselves and one another. To help get us there, we begin by exploring
how to recognize deficit ideology and the deficit impulse, using several
examples from our experiences working in and with schools.

Ditching Deficit Views

Earlier we asked you to reflect on this question: *Why are parents who
are experiencing poverty less likely than their wealthier peers to visit
their children's schools for family engagement opportunities?* As you

probably understand by now, if your impulse was to attribute the disparity to the values, mindsets, supposed grit shortages, or dispositions of *those parents,* you embrace a deficit ideology to at least some degree when it comes to poverty and educational disparities. Unfortunately, you have a lot of company.

Understanding the roots of deficit ideology requires us to understand that it is in many ways a symptom of socialization. The myth of meritocracy, ideals of rugged individualism, the old *pull-yourself-up-by-your-bootstraps* mentality: all this feeds a deficit view because it suggests that everything is determined by how hard somebody works and discounts the devastating systems of advantage and disadvantage linked to inequity. If you were raised in the United States, chances are these ideals were communicated to you in a variety of implicit and explicit ways. *If we work hard, play by the rules, and value education, we can achieve whatever we want to achieve.* The function of these ideals historically has been to trap us into individualistic thinking while dissuading us from systems-level thinking, to train our scorn and judgments down the power-and-privilege continuum at "deficient" individuals who couldn't quite manage to take full advantage of their "equal opportunity." When we embrace this view, we're unlikely to recognize the realities of inequity.

Yes, all factors being equal, hard work makes a difference. But all factors *aren't* equal. Some students contend with structural racism in and out of school. Some do not have access to preventive healthcare. Some expend significant energy coping with heterosexism or cisgenderism, the worst of it often happening in school hallways. Some students need to work to support their families. These conditions are all related to systems-level deficiencies; they have nothing to do with individuals' intelligence, work ethic, or desire to learn. They certainly don't suggest a shortage of resilience or grit. And even the hardest-working students are unlikely to completely erase their impact.

If we struggle to work these realities into how we understand educational disparities, we have little chance of shedding the deficit view. As a result, we're less likely to question how the opportunity continuum and existing systems came to be and who benefits from them. This might be especially true if we are the ones benefiting from them.

Our first step toward cultivating a structural ideology in ourselves and our schools, then, is to learn how to recognize deficit ideology in all its forms. We can begin by examining how to spot the ways deficit ideology creeps into our own thoughts and actions.

This examining and spotting is no easy task. Often our ideologies operate in subtle ways that we might not even notice if we aren't attending to them purposefully. Complicating matters, as we mentioned earlier, we can appreciate diversity and even believe we want the best for each student while still grasping onto harmful ideological beliefs. So let's begin by finding the humility to look closely and learn how to interpret our observations differently. This is one of the best ways to strengthen our equity literacy.

With this goal in mind, let's parse out the following three interlocking ways of thinking and interpreting that are indicative of deficit ideology:

- Presuming a level playing field of equal access and opportunity where one does not exist
- Failing or refusing to acknowledge inequities and how they influence educational experiences and outcomes
- Basing interpretations of and responses to educational disparities on stereotypes and presumptions

As you read through the following descriptions of each one, you will see how they build on one another, leading us to troublingly common, ineffectual, often oppressive educational "equity" practices.

The (Un)Level Playing Field

A few years ago, we were taking a break during a workshop for student support personnel at a high school when a student named Gregory approached us.

Gregory, a sophomore, confided in us that he is gay, but also that he's not "out" at school, at home, or anywhere else. Not officially, anyway. Despite never coming out at school, students who presumed he was gay bullied him, often calling him heterosexist names and sometimes even shoving or physically threatening him. This usually happened between classes, when the hallways were so chaotic that classmates could abuse him without adults noticing. Because he was not out, and because he had witnessed teachers failing to respond in any significant way to heterosexist comments from his classmates throughout his school career, he felt unsafe reporting the emotional and physical violence to anyone at school.

Instead, he looked for places to hide for a few minutes between classes until the crowds thinned. Once he felt safer, he headed to class. Unfortunately, this often meant that he arrived a few seconds late.

Eventually he had accumulated enough tardies that he was subject to predetermined punishments. The next tardy meant a call home. That terrified Gregory. A few more and he could be punished with after-school or in-school detention. The more tardies, the harsher the punishment: this policy was codified in the student conduct handbook.

From an institutional perspective, the injustice here is clear. In essence, Gregory was being punished for the school's failure to protect him from heterosexism.

You might be wondering, "How can the school protect him if he doesn't report the abuse?" That is the deficit impulse speaking. Homophobia and heterosexism exist in every school, including yours, as they exist in most every context. Even if your school has a Gay-Straight Alliance; even if you have a Pride Day, a Day of Silence, or an antibullying initiative; even if several lesbian, gay, bisexual, and trans-gender teachers and students, or people who reject sexual orientation and gender identity labels altogether, are open and out at your school, there are those, like Gregory, who cannot or choose not to be open or out. Heterosexist name calling, comments, and jokes generally flood the hallways of middle and high schools. If we're waiting for people to report it, we're being too passive. Equity is active, not passive.

No student should need to ask to be protected from oppression. It is not Gregory's responsibility to protect himself from these conditions, especially if doing so might compromise his safety in other ways. In his case, Gregory was especially worried that his parents would learn about his sexual orientation. He believed they would kick him out of their house if they knew he was gay. We, the educators, are responsible for recognizing that oppression exists and doing everything we can to eliminate it. We can't do that if we're so stuck ideologically that we are incapable of seeing the whole inequity picture.

Deficit ideology operated in multiple ways in this scenario, the combination of which made matters considerably worse for Gregory and probably for other LGBTQIA+ students in his school. First, according to Gregory, when teachers asked him why he was late and he hesitated, with good reason, to tell them the truth, they seemed to just presume he was lollygagging, lazy, lying, or inattentive. "Everyone else manages to arrive on time, so why can't you?" one teacher scolded him as she recorded his tardiness. This teacher presumed a level playing field that did not exist; after all, "everyone else" did not need to dodge the threat of violence with every trip through school hallways. This teacher also destroyed any possibility that Gregory would feel comfortable confiding in her.

Certainly, we understand that she could not have known Gregory's specific circumstances. The teacher's perspective was based, perhaps, on her best read of the situation, given the information she had. Or perhaps it was based on her frustration with the disruption that can happen when a student regularly walks into class late. Still, the lateness was not Gregory's fault. The disruption was a symptom of the school's failure, not Gregory's.

What we learn from this scenario is the damage being done to Gregory, a student already carrying the weight of inequity and violence, when the impulse of at least some of his teachers, whether out of frustration or ostensible efficiency or whatever, was to presume that the rules affected all students equally. The problem is the deficit impulse, the presumption that there was something wrong with Gregory. There wasn't. But he was the one being punished. That outcome represents a breakdown of institutional equity. As leaders, we can't allow that sort of thing to happen.

As we strengthen our equity literacy, we learn to create space in our mental models, curiosity space, that will help us avoid this sort of deficit impulse. We can practice this right now. What are three examples of legitimate reasons a student might be perpetually late to class? More specifically, what are reasons a student might not feel safe sharing with us? What are three reasons a student might be late that could be associated with ways that student is marginalized within school?

In the end, Gregory explained, he did tell his principal why he had been arriving late to class, hoping to avoid the predetermined punishment. The principal's initial response, another layer of deficit ideology, was not to apologize for allowing heterosexism to persist in the school, but instead to chide Gregory for not coming to him sooner.

Meanwhile, Gregory was forced to out himself to someone in whom he had not intended to confide, potentially making himself vulnerable to a school leader who already wasn't doing enough to eliminate the heterosexist *experience gap* with which Gregory contended. This forced revelation constituted injustice. And it was perpetrated not by hateful heterosexists, but by educators whose ideological limitations interfered with their abilities to imagine Gregory's reality. So although they were not rabid heterosexists, their ideologies and resulting actions and inactions enabled heterosexism.

This story exemplifies what happens when we lack the structural impulse: we, too, might have been unwilling or unable to consider the possibility that Gregory's lateness could reflect our own equity failures rather than Gregory's failure. As long as heterosexism, racism, ableism, sexism, or any form of oppression is tucked behind deficit ideology, students like Gregory will struggle on an uneven playing field of *our* making and be blamed for it as though it's of *their* making. *Those people* don't value education. *Those students* aren't engaged learners. *That student* isn't attentive enough to make it to class on time. Few things are as inequitable as that ideological position.

What Happens When We Don't Acknowledge Inequities

Let's try another equity literacy exercise. Can you imagine a situation in which a student who regularly does not turn in homework, let's say a student experiencing poverty, might be behaving *responsibly* by choosing not to do her homework?

If we tend toward deficit ideology, we might struggle, at least initially, to allow for the possibility that somebody could be coping with life barriers such that she could make a rational, reasonable decision not to do what we, as enthusiastic educators, hoped she would do. Perhaps she's caring for younger siblings, helping them with their homework, and needing to share time on a computer. Perhaps she's caring for elders in her family who do not have adequate healthcare. Perhaps, due to the scarcity of living-wage jobs for working-age adults, she's working after school to help her family survive. Perhaps she's balancing all three of these responsibilities simultaneously.

When we embrace a structural ideology, we can see how this unfortunate situation is rooted in inequity and economic injustice, in the scarcity of living-wage work, in decades-long wage stagnation (Mishel et al., 2015), and other barriers families may face, rather than presuming that it reflects character flaws, community dysfunction, or a lack of grit. Before we jump to a deficit presumption, we can learn, again, to be curious, creating space in our minds for more compassionate understandings that acknowledge the inequities and barriers bearing down on families. This is the structural impulse.

As educators, we can't necessarily eliminate all these economic injustices, but we can create and implement policies and practices and adopt dispositions that are responsive to them. That way we're not piling on by creating and enforcing policies that punish students for the results of the inequities they're already facing. Shaming students or reducing their grades for conditions connected to ways they're already marginalized is perfectly anti-equity.

We're reminded of how often some teachers insistently tell us stories about students of color, most commonly Black students, who, in their view, simply refuse to engage, refuse offers of help, refuse their attempts to cultivate trusting relationships. The impulse for some of these teachers is to point to these refusals as proof that the students simply lack the desire to learn. *They don't want to engage with me,* they might presume.

When we reach out to these students to try to understand their reluctance, when we *listen* with a structural view rather than *presume* with a deficit view, it does not take long to understand what's really happening. In many cases, the students' refusals are not really refusals but temporary defense mechanisms. They often are reasonable responses to the racial biases and inequities they've experienced throughout their lives from white teachers and white administrators and white people in all sorts of authority positions.

For some Black and Brown students, cross-racial trust is risky business. They have observed and experienced teachers punishing them and their classmates of color more harshly than white students. They have observed how other white authority figures, from police officers to store managers, treat them and their friends. In our focus groups with students of color across the United States and Canada, they almost universally express disappointment about how white adults in their schools respond inadequately to racist comments and actions by their white classmates—an issue that, as you've probably noticed in our examples from student focus groups, comes up over and over again. At some point, it is reasonable for some students to respond to these conditions by constructing an emotional wall between themselves and white educators until those educators *earn* their trust. The issue is racism in and out of schools, not students' attitudes, and certainly not their abilities to regulate their emotions.

We can start to strengthen this sort of structural equity lens by cultivating in ourselves and one another the structural impulse. When our first impulse is *What are the challenges and barriers?* instead of *What do I need to fix about this student so that she complies with the rules?* we are in a much better position to cultivate equity. If we cannot answer this question—*What are the challenges and barriers?*—we simply cannot create equitable homework policies or equitable student engagement practices or equitable anything. We can create and enforce *equal* homework policies: rules that apply equally to all students whether they work after school, take care of younger siblings, and provide care for elders in their homes or not. But equal is not always equitable. And vice versa.

Of course, we do understand that all students across the spectrum of socioeconomic status or gender identity or race can face all sorts of challenges and barriers, from depression to violence at home to bullying. Sometimes middle class families struggle to afford high-quality preventive healthcare. Many young white boys struggle emotionally in a misogynist, patriarchal world that tells them to repress their feelings. That's a problem, and equity-literate educators find ways to support those students. That said, we find that people who are uneasy with the ideological work necessary to embrace equity literacy tend to point this out with great enthusiasm. *Everyone has challenges and barriers. That's no excuse.*

The *no excuses* rhetoric is, itself, indicative of deficit ideology, often masking inequitable conditions. Sure, all youth have challenges. Economically marginalized youth are subject to all those challenges *plus* the challenges associated with poverty. These might include big out-of-school injustices limiting access to preventive healthcare and healthy food or in-school inequities such as low expectations and class-biased tracking practices. Youth of color who also are experiencing poverty might contend with all of that *on top of* the ravages of systemic racism. And so on.

We can choose to make sure our equity approach minimizes the pile on that happens when we enact policies and practices that add to or deepen the impacts of all those challenges and barriers. But we can't do that with strategies and initiatives that ignore those challenges and barriers or that hide them behind "no excuses" rhetoric or presumptions that an equal playing field already exists.

Note that we aren't advising you to lower standards or expectations. We wouldn't advise the teacher to let go of any expectation that Gregory is capable of making it to class on time. That solution enables the inequity to persist. Gregory deserves a full class period just like everyone else. We just want a solution that attends to the root cause of Gregory being repeatedly cheated out of access to that full class period rather than reactive rule-flinging.

The adults in the school must be attentive to the structural conditions contributing to the situation and then be creative and courageous about what *they* need to do to ensure him the promise of full access. For the student taking care of her family and working after school, the equitable action isn't to relieve her of learning the content. We would want, instead, to figure out ways to support her learning that don't ignore or exacerbate the inequitable conditions she's contending with outside school.

As a leader, how might you do that?

Misinterpreting Disparities Through Presumptions and Stereotypes

We cannot stress enough the importance of the first ability of equity literacy, recognizing inequity, with regard to the fix injustice, not kids principle. To illustrate this point, let's return to the topic of discipline disparities. Across the United States, Black and Brown students are being suspended or expelled from school at significantly higher rates than their white classmates (Girvan et al., 2019), a trend related to what often is called the school-to-prison pipeline or nexus (Stovall, 2018). They are more likely to be referred for behavioral incidents, more likely to receive *any* punishment for those incidents, and more subject to the *harshest* punishments. As another quick equity literacy exercise, consider *why* this is the case. *Why* are they more likely than white students to be referred for behavior and then suspended or expelled?

Let's try looking at this from a slightly different angle. One way to assess our perceptions of why this is happening is by looking at our responses to it. So if we examine the most popular responses to this disproportionality in referral and punishment, what can we glean about the conditions to which we, as educators, tend to attribute it?

In our experience, schools and districts grappling with racial discipline disproportionality most commonly embrace one of two basic approaches for solving it. The first involves strategies and initiatives designed, in large part, to adjust students' emotions or behaviors. The second is based on attempts to decrease suspensions and expulsions or to eliminate them altogether, at least temporarily, without addressing the underlying causes. It's notable and, in our opinion, no mistake that a slew of shiny new behavior intervention frameworks, including Positive Behavioral Interventions and Supports (PBIS), sprang into popularity right around the time more districts were either choosing or being legally forced to take a closer look at their disparate suspension and expulsion rates. Simultaneously spiking in trendiness are programs we discussed earlier in this book, from mindfulness and SEL initiatives to emotion-regulation exercises that are designed or, more accurately, *repurposed* to regulate the emotions, mindsets, and behaviors of students. These initiatives appear to be especially popular in schools with high proportions of students of color and students experiencing poverty. All of this raises the deficit ideology red flag.

This is not to say that attention to students' social-emotional well-being is undesirable, that PBIS is inherently a corrupt framework, or that mindfulness has no potential role in schools. Some students, and educators for that matter, benefit from social-emotional supports and mindfulness practices (Bazzano et al., 2018). However, it *is* to say that these sorts of interventions reflect a dangerous brand of deficit ideology when they are used as core approaches for eliminating the referral, suspension, and expulsion disparities or as central *equity* approaches, and when implemented with the goal of adjusting the behaviors, mindsets, or attitudes of students who are economically, racially, or otherwise marginalized. Most troubling, they presume that the source of disproportionality lies in those behaviors, mindsets, and attitudes.

The presumption might make sense if evidence suggested that, say, racial disproportionality in referrals and punishments resulted primarily from students of color misbehaving more than their white classmates. But, as we established earlier, it doesn't. The trouble from both an evidence-based-practice perspective and an equity perspective is that the most significant cause of this disparity appears to be racial bias in educators (Riddle & Sinclair, 2019; Santiago-Rosario et al., 2021), not behavioral differences in students.

In many of the schools with which we've worked that have collected data on the matter, the referrals can be tracked largely to a few teachers who account for a big portion of the total, and then to layer upon layer of big and small, implicit and explicit interpretations and actions by other educators and whoever is doling out the most serious punishments. In other words, in these schools, it's a few especially biased educators doing a lot of disproportionate referring and almost everybody else doing a little.

Research is showing that, on average, white teachers interpret the behaviors of students of color more harshly than the same behaviors in white students. So they are more likely to refer them for minor infractions and especially for vague, subjective infractions such as "disrespect" or "insubordination" (Bryan, 2017; Milner, 2013; Wegmann & Smith, 2019). When interpretive processes are filtered through even the smallest remnants of racism, the accumulative results are doomed to be racist. It's important to remember that all it takes is everybody contributing a little; the accumulative repercussion of those little bits of disproportionality could be a big, decisive disparity. One thing we, as leaders, can do right now if we're not already doing it is to begin tracking these sorts of patterns so that we know where we most urgently need equity interventions.

So why do we find so few schools whose *primary* strategy for eliminating this disparity is rooting out the racism that is causing it? Why do we find this approach so scarce when it's the *only* approach that can work?

The growing, although still too rare, conversation on implicit bias within individual educators has helped. If we want to locate deficit ideology, we can follow the stereotypes because deficit ideology at the individual level is rooted in biases and stereotypes. If we already believe Black and Brown students are prone to behavior problems, it might not occur to us that there could be some other, more accurate explanation for the disproportionate behavior consequences or, to be more specific, consequences for the *perceived* behavior. It's either that or we're consciously complicit. In a way, by attributing this to ideological blockages, we're extending a considerable benefit of the doubt.

If we want to eliminate this disproportionality in referral and punishment, our primary path is this: identify the racism, eliminate the racism. You might be thinking, *OK, then how do we do that?* If we are grasping onto a deficit ideology, we can't do that. The impulse to want to jump to practical strategies before addressing the ideological roots that keep landing us on bad strategies is part of what keeps us stuck in the deficit ideology trap. That's why the ideological shift is more practical than any practical strategy constructed before the ideological shift.

Equity cannot live if we grasp onto the presumption, conscious or not, that *of course* those students *are suspended and expelled more often, because they misbehave more.* And *of course* those parents *don't show up as often for family engagement; they don't value education.* And those parents *just don't want to learn English*. And the students who don't want to learn *make it hard to teach the students who do want to learn*. And girls *are just less interested than boys in STEM subjects*. And any other explanation for outcome disparities that blames people who hold the short end of the access-and-opportunity stick for *our* inability or lack of willingness to create equitable learning spaces.

Bridging People from a Deficit to a Structural Ideology

Let's get back to that question about what we can do about this. If we want to root out the oppressive actions, we first must contend with the oppressive ideology underlying those actions. We can begin by developing our abilities to bridge people from deficit views to a structural lens.

What are the challenges and barriers? How is inequity operating? These questions characterize the impulse we want to cultivate in ourselves and one another. It's the impulse we want to normalize within our institutional cultures. It is especially important that equity leaders, positional or otherwise, learn how to cultivate and then model this impulse. Remember, any lingering deficit ideology destroys our potential to build and sustain equitable classrooms and schools.

At the most basic level, we cultivate the structural impulse by naming deficit ideology. In whatever form it appears, every time it appears, we refuse to let it survive. We need people to understand from what and to what we are bridging them. We can do this by providing opportunities for people to practice looking at things through a different lens.

Leading this sort of ideological shift can be difficult, especially where deficit ideology has a strong hold on institutional culture. But it is possible. We've seen it happen.

Every time somebody subtly or explicitly directs blame at youth or families from communities that are racially, economically, or otherwise marginalized, or attributes any disparity to a perceived deficiency in their mindsets, cultures, attitudes, grittiness, behaviors, or values, we name it as deficit ideology and use it as an opportunity to practice embracing a structural view. We don't have to shame or wag our finger at anyone. But we can't let it slide. Then we can offer a different ideological window, redirecting the conversation toward a structural view.

We find "I wonder" statements useful in this regard. Let's say a colleague, frustrated by the parents of his most economically marginalized students missing a family engagement opportunity, remarks, "Those parents never show up for anything. They obviously don't value their children's education." We bridge our colleague to a structural view: *I see you're frustrated and appreciate your concern for students. I wonder what we can do differently to help facilitate their involvement. I wonder what sorts of barriers families might be experiencing that make involvement challenging for them. I wonder what barriers we're unintentionally creating by how we schedule and structure these opportunities.*

The important thing here is giving people with a deficit view a structural window. Sure, some are so stuck in their view that they will decline our invitation to look through that window. That's why, in addition to implementing these individual interventions, we can unequivocally embrace, normalize, and reward a structural perspective. *We reject these deficit views. This is who we are as a school. We do not blame children or families. We focus on what we can do better to eliminate the barriers in our spheres of influence and at least mitigate the barriers outside our spheres. We are in the business of creating equitable opportunity for all families.*

Another strategy is to always refocus the conversation on what *we* as a school or district can do differently. Whenever somebody talks about what this or that group of people can do differently, remind them that they're slipping into deficit ideology. *Our concern is what we can do differently to remove barriers, eliminate access and opportunity disparities, and sustain an equitable school. So let's talk about that. What can we do differently? How can we embrace a more transformative approach to equity?*

When we discuss disparities in academic achievement, discipline referrals, graduation rates, or anything else, *What are the challenges and barriers? What can we do differently to eliminate them?*

Conclusion

As we stated earlier, equity cannot live where deficit ideology lives because the function of deficit ideology is to obscure inequity. So we can't be passive. There is no inherently, universally right way to respond. But not responding means condoning.

We recommend that leaders start by practicing the equity ability of recognizing deficit ideology. Get a sense of how prevalent it is in day-to-day chatter in your sphere of influence, in school policies, and elsewhere. It might be useful to gather an equity-skilled team that can help identify the ways deficit ideology operates in our schools or districts and help us practice responding to it. We even can practice "listening" for it in our own thoughts, examining it in our own ideologies. As soon as we find ourselves responding to disparities by thinking *these students* this or *those families* that, we should consider what we might be missing. Remember, equity leadership never involves adjusting anything about people who are alienated, marginalized, or oppressed. It always involves eliminating conditions that alienate, marginalize, and oppress: the things that need fixing.

Figure 4.2 highlights some of the key points presented in this chapter. It summarizes the fix injustice, not kids principle by illustrating, from a leader's point of view, the difference between mitigative equity and transformative equity in terms of actions and attitudes.

FIGURE 4.2

The Fix Injustice, Not Kids Principle: Comparing Leaders' Mindsets Related to Mitigative Versus Transformative Equity

Mitigative Equity	Transformative Equity
I support students and families however I can as they learn how to fit in at our school.	I examine all of the systems, structures, policies, and practices that may be barriers to students and families feeling that they are a part of the school.
The best way to help students is to consider their individual needs and stories.	I closely monitor patterns and trends of inequity as I consider each student's contextualized individual experience.
I take care of incidents as they arise, with consequences for people who have acted in racist, sexist, or otherwise discriminatory ways.	My response to flare-ups of racism, sexism, and other forms of discrimination in school includes individual consequences as well as an examination of the underlying systems that enable the harmful behavior.
I have an open-door policy and get frustrated when students or staff don't report their experiences with inequity.	I proactively and regularly seek critical feedback and provide avenues, and presume that just because I haven't heard about an inequity doesn't mean it isn't happening.

5

Emphasizing,
Not Just Equalizing:
The Prioritization Principle

A few years ago, we sat in a conference room with an enthusiastic and angry crowd of students from Gracelynn High School. They had been organizing, blasting the school on social media for refusing to respond more adequately to the racism, cisgenderism, and heterosexism they withstood at school. Students of color were furious about racist discipline practices. Transgender students were incredulous at leadership's failure to insist that staff use their correct names and pronouns.

When we discussed these concerns with Gracelynn's leadership team, they responded defensively. That's never a good sign for equity leadership, which should always be curious about how inequity might be operating rather than reactively self-protective. They began rattling off all the school was doing in the name of equity: hosting a Black History Week, adhering "Safe Space" stickers to a scattering of office and classroom doors, providing annual antibias training for staff. "We have many equity initiatives. More than most schools," the discipline coordinator insisted.

During focus groups we facilitated with Gracelynn students, they acknowledged the school's efforts but felt those efforts fell considerably short of responding substantially to their concerns. The students demanded big institutional changes, such as a curricular overhaul and a transparent accountability system for people who repeatedly behaved in racist, heterosexist, or cisgenderist ways. Leadership responded with a hodgepodge of minor diversity initiatives.

Sound familiar? It's the same frustration we hear over and over again.

During a focus group of LGBTQIA+ students, one participant, Derrick, asked, "A 'safe' classroom or two is nice, but what about all the other spaces?"

Leadership needed to scale up its efforts. When we asked the principal, Liz, whether she felt ready to do that, she wavered. "We have to meet people where they are," she worried, "or they'll stop engaging altogether."

Liz was committed philosophically to equity, but she struggled to understand inequity's scope or the level of change required to transform Gracelynn into a just learning and working environment. "It's about baby steps," she kept insisting. What that meant in practical terms was that she appeared more concerned, and *acted* more concerned, about how resistant staff and families might feel about the school's equity efforts than about how to stop marginalizing its students. This approach wasn't fooling the students, and they weren't shy about letting her and other adults at their school know about it.

To be fair, like all leaders, Liz contended with a long list of challenges. She was new to Gracelynn. She had inherited a small but vocal group of teachers who vigorously resisted any serious equity effort. She also had inherited a small and even more vocal and well-organized group of privilege-wielding parents. They showed up at school board meetings to protest even the most mitigative equity initiative. On top of these challenges, Liz worried that staff already felt overextended.

"The apple cart is teetering," she told us, "and any way I move, I risk knocking it over."

We do have to be strategic, of course. Like Liz, we all are juggling numerous balls. But as we've mentioned previously, being strategic can't mean that we proceed as though we're more focused on avoiding controversy with people who are hostile to equity than we are on transforming conditions that are harming people who are suffering the impact of inequity. It can't mean that we prioritize the demands of people who would rather we ignore racism, heterosexism, and cisgenderism altogether over the demands of people who deserve to attend school or come to work without spending their energy dodging racism and hetero- and cis-normativity.

Instead, being strategic means that we embrace unbending goals of equity and justice, prioritizing the best interests, desires, joys, and demands of the people who have been cheated out of equitable and just educational experiences. Then we proceed toward those goals while also accounting for the barriers and resistance. We plan for the barriers and resistance but never use them as reasons for slowing our pace or rolling back our commitments. We begin to see the resistance as the natural result of progress, not as a reason to soften our equity efforts and commitments.

If we're honest, we should ask ourselves which people we mean when we talk about *meeting people where they are*. What would our equity approach look like if we met people who bear the weight of institutionalized ableism, sexism, or economic injustice where *they* are? What if Liz heeded students' demands for something more meaningful, more transformative, than baby steps?

This approach is the *prioritization principle* in action. Equity leaders prioritize the best interests, joys, desires, demands, and needs of the people who schools historically have failed to prioritize.

When we say "prioritize the interests," we don't just mean we should ask people what they are interested in and prioritize that. We mean we need to reimagine policies, curricula, institutional culture, and everything else, not just in ways that squeeze transgender or economically marginalized people into our existing ways of doing things, but that transform our ways of doing things so that students who bear the brunt of inequity no longer need to do all the squeezing. This requires us to make decisions that specifically benefit and advantage the people who historically have derived the least benefit and advantage from school.

Imagine three schools whose leaders are planning an event to teach newly arrived Spanish-speaking families how FAFSA (Free Application for Federal Student Aid) works. The first school holds the meeting in English, making it difficult for many attending families to fully participate. The second school hosts the meeting in English but provides translated materials and an interpreter. This is an equity improvement over the first school, right? Unfortunately, this approach represents only mitigative equitable access. The school is doing a bit of tweaking to make an inaccessible event minimally accessible. At the third school, leaders host the event in Spanish, providing interpretation services for people who don't speak Spanish. The power dynamic has shifted; what is normally in the margins has been relocated to the center.

What would a decision to host the meeting in this way communicate to the families the school hopes to support? How might it strengthen relationships? What sorts of inequities is it disrupting? This is one example of how we might enact the prioritization principle, at least in the context of this one event.

Digging a little deeper, how could leaders' choices about *where* to hold the meeting prioritize families' needs? What about *when* the meeting is scheduled? What might leadership consider about the process of planning this meeting, about who is involved in making these decisions? We might even reconsider how leadership determined that this event would be helpful to families in the first place. How did they know some other focus might not be more helpful?

Needless to say, the prioritization principle can be difficult to apply, in terms of both its logistical complications and the resistance it often reveals. We explore a couple of these difficulties at the end of this chapter. But if we genuinely embrace transformative equity, we simply can't prioritize our own needs or the comfort of people who have enjoyed systemic advantage over our responsibility to eliminate inequity. In fact, when we do so, we embrace the opposite of equity leadership, what we sometimes call the "pacing for privilege equity detour."

Pacing for Justice, Not Privilege

The prioritization principle requires, first and foremost, that we move institutional equity efforts at the pace of the people who most desperately need us to do better, not of those who would rather we not move at all. We call this commitment "informed urgency." That "informed" modifier is important; we're distinguishing between reckless action without deep understandings of how inequity and equity operate in our institutions and deliberate, strategic, *deeply informed* action. Our experience is that if we act with abandon, without deep understanding, our equity efforts can do more harm than good. The other principles we discuss in this book offer guidance for that deep understanding.

When we make the mistake Liz was making, when we pace our equity efforts to placate the people who are resistant to equity, we're taking that *pacing for privilege* detour (Gorski, 2019). Pacing for privilege stops transformative equity in its tracks. So instead of looking at the most resistant people and asking, *What are they ready for?* equity leaders prioritize the people experiencing the most inequity and ask, *At what pace of change do* they *need us to move? What do* they *demand we do better?* That's the pace at which institutional change for equity ought to happen.

Returning to Gracelynn, we worked with Liz to proceed more substantively and strategically with informed urgency. We recommended, as we do with many leaders, that she begin by cultivating a support system. We asked her to identify staff, parents, and students who were ready to step up immediately, or who had been stepping up and were waiting for her to join them. Start with them, we suggested; make them the center of institutional culture and make sure they know that when they speak up, you'll have their backs. Work with them to establish a shared vision of transformative equity so that they can help roll that vision out schoolwide. We coached her to talk with them about how they could support her equity leadership, which they were more willing to do now that she was acknowledging their contributions at Gracelynn, prioritizing their pace, and demanding more of all staff.

Of course, we didn't want Liz to *stop* with this group, another common misstep. Equity can't be optional. If all we do is provide professional learning or a book group to the same few people who choose to show up, we're still stuck on baby steps. The purpose of cultivating this group is to support the larger rollout—the bigger goal toward which we're moving.

We also coached her, as we always do, to frame equity as a lens and an underlying commitment to just action that informs every aspect of school. It's important to avoid framing equity as another program or initiative. Educators are drowning in programs and initiatives. We want equity to be woven into the fabric of institutional culture.

When Liz shared how difficult it was to move past the baby steps and embrace deeper equity change, we empathized but challenged her to never lower her expectations for her equity leadership. Certainly, we agreed, leading for equity *is* hard. But, as we've mentioned before, it's not as hard as being a student who is experiencing inequity in a school where nobody is leading for equity. So again, who are we prioritizing?

Here is an important equity literacy exercise. Make a list of the three biggest challenges you face when it comes to leading for equity. Reflect on how you might strategically work through each challenge while sustaining your commitment to transformative equity. Make sure your strategy does not include weakening your equity efforts or slowing the pace of change. The question we're exploring here is *How do we maintain our transformative intentions despite the challenges?*

Liz heeded our advice. She fortified her confidence and support and then began making more substantive changes. She led a review of school policy and an overhaul of the curriculum with equity as a pillar. She gathered and incorporated student and community feedback. The anti-equity contingent remained ruthless, hollering at school board meetings and shaming Liz for doing what was right. But in follow-up focus groups, students started reporting for the first time that their school was becoming more equitable. This, and not the emails and calls of angry anti-equity parents, became her measuring stick for progress. She had embraced the prioritization principle.

We can't be equity leaders if we hedge our bets in the face of privilege-wielding stakeholders who urge baby steps (or backward steps), trying to slow progress. It's important to remember that many people and many communities have endured generations of inequity, discrimination, exploitation, and violence, fighting for justice all the way through. During an interview late in his life, which was included in Karen Thorsen and Douglas Dempsey's 1989 documentary, *James Baldwin: The Price of a Ticket*, Baldwin asked,

> What is it you want me to reconcile myself to? I was born almost 60 years ago. I'm not going to live another 60 years. You always told me "It takes time." It's taken my father's time, my mother's time, my

uncle's time, my brothers' and my sisters' time, my nieces' and my nephews' time. How much time do you want for your progress?

When we say "Change takes time" or insist on taking baby steps, when we pace for privilege rather than for justice, this is what we become a party to: inequity by inaction. At some point, when we bow to the pressure of people who prefer we avoid instituting equity altogether or substantially slow its pace, we become the avoiders. We become complicit. We can do better. Figure 5.1 outlines specific examples of how to distinguish pacing for privilege from pacing for justice.

What is one equity change you know you should make but have been hesitant to make? Who is benefiting from and prioritized by your hesitance? What supports might you need to stop hesitating and make the necessary change?

FIGURE 5.1

Characteristics of Pacing for Privilege and Pacing for Justice

Pacing for Privilege	Pacing for Justice
Requiring everyone to attend the same basic, introductory professional development year after year or offering slapdash workshops that contradict one another	Providing differentiated, sustained, transformative professional development that helps staff develop the five abilities of equity literacy and understand the importance of institutional, not just individual, change
Shushing, silencing, or shaming educators advocating for equity when they speak out, or insisting they slow down	Making the most vehement equity advocates the center of institutional culture
Making a commitment to equity optional, for those who are interested or "ready"	Incentivizing equity growth, rewarding people's risk taking to disrupt inequities, and holding people who choose not to embrace an equity commitment accountable
Hiring and promoting people who appreciate diversity but struggle to discuss equity	Hiring, promoting, and providing resources to educators who have significant equity-related expertise and skills
Relegating equity to one person or committee or treating it as a standalone issue or line item on an agenda	Infusing equity into all decision-making processes

Honest Self-Reflection, Serious Institutional Rethinking

These are critical self-accountability questions for the equity leader: Who are we coddling, and why? What sorts of inequities are we permitting, and why? How might we be undermining our efforts toward transformative equity, imagining that, over time, inequitable conditions will just take care of themselves?

Remember: Every action we take and every action we don't take communicates what we value and prioritize. Every choice we make must be made with equity in mind.

The prioritization principle also requires a rigorous accounting of the ways schools prioritize the needs and comforts, and the access, of the most advantaged people: those who already have the most access and opportunity. We need to be honest about who we have been prioritizing; we must acknowledge how the needs, best interests, joys, and points of connection for white students, cisgender students, Christian students, students from wealthy families, students with access to privilege, have been so overwhelmingly normalized in schools that it can be difficult to recognize all the ways we prioritize them.

Remember, the advantage can be subtle, buried in unquestioned practices, traditions, or old policies. So we have to look in the nooks and crannies of institutional culture and not just at big, obvious inequities. Once we start making a list of the forms this normalization takes, it's hard to stop: the fees we charge for students to park at their high schools, the ways the curriculum promotes the myth of meritocracy or uncritically celebrates colonialism, heteronormativity in language arts classes. It's everywhere.

For example, many public school districts and independent schools construct their calendars largely, if not entirely, around Christian holidays. This is an old practice that is so normalized a lot of Christian people might struggle to imagine any other possible way to organize the school year. Sure, we might offer "excused absences" for students from other faith communities if they miss school for religious observances. But their tradeoff is losing instructional time. There is no tradeoff for staying home to observe Christmas. That's structural advantage; it's an example of a system that prioritizes the interests of privilege.

Perhaps we've adjusted the optics. We might use phrases like "spring break" rather than "Easter vacation." But what are we changing *institutionally*? Maybe teachers have started calling their activities "winter crafts" while using the same Christian iconography, like presents, Christmas trees, and ornaments (Rodríguez & Swalwell, 2022). How does this mitigative change contribute *substantively* to equity? Adjusting the terminology and the optics is the epitome of performative equity: we change the label, but we continue embracing the same inequitable structures and practices.

These examples are only the tip of the proverbial iceberg when it comes to how Christian families' interests, schedules, needs, and joys are prioritized in many schools and districts, not to mention societally (Joshi, 2020). The reality is, despite the optics, we are still prioritizing these families' best interests, needs, and joys, which already are *overwhelmingly* prioritized in virtually every aspect of school and society. In fact, the change in terminology (e.g., "winter concert") only masks the structural advantage. From an equity literacy point of view, that's an equity regression.

Sometimes, it's difficult to notice these conditions on our own, especially if we are the beneficiaries of the privilege we're trying to upend. One way to learn how to recognize these dynamics is to be in deep, trusting relationships with people experiencing harm, relationships built on *a lot* of listening. By "listening," we mean the kind of profound listening that is intent on hearing and *believing* tough truths. If we're going to apply the prioritization principle effectively, we must invite people to tell us when we're wrong about our assumptions or beliefs. But we should be careful not to over-rely on people experiencing the harm to be our perpetual instructors in the harm. In the end, it's up to us to learn how to recognize and correct it.

Let's practice. Think about a tough equity truth you've learned from a student, family, or community member, something that pushed against what you thought you understood about your equity priorities or efforts. How did learning that truth change your leadership approach or help you imagine a new solution to a persisting equity problem?

Everything is complex, of course. Sometimes our equity ideal butts up against unjust realities. These realities aren't always easily remedied in institutions that exist within unjust communities and societies. We don't expect that overnight you will be able to reshape your academic calendar or start scheduling school events every Wednesday evening. But we do expect that you can, or will learn how to, recognize how the accumulative impact of this sort of privilege-prioritizing sustains disadvantage, and perhaps even disconnection, for students, families, and staff who presently do not reap the benefits of being prioritized.

We must acknowledge that "this is the way we've always done things" and "most people are happy with how this works" are non-sensical reasons to continue doing things how we've been doing them, especially from an equity point of view. Noting that an unjust reality is not easily remedied doesn't let us off the hook for remedying it. It just reminds us that we should proceed strategically.

Practice recognizing who your school's or district's institutional culture, curricula, student-sorting mechanisms, and other processes and conditions prioritize. Ask yourself, *To whose demands do we respond most quickly and vehemently? Whose demands are most likely to be put on hold?*

Then ask, *What is the worst that could happen if priorities were reshuffled? What steps could be taken to buffer the repercussions?*

Considering Equity Context

If we hope to apply the prioritization principle effectively, we need a solid understanding of what Bettina Love (2019) calls "the sociopolitical landscape of [our] students' communities [understood] through a historical, intersectional lens" (p. 12). If we don't know what harms they have experienced both in and out of schools and continue to experience now, we limit our abilities to respond to and redress what we ought to be responding to and redressing.

For example, our efforts to support students of color will be stymied if we fail to understand the experiences of communities our schools serve, if we are unaware of how white supremacy and anti-Blackness and racism and xenophobia have harmed, and continue to harm, students and their families. As Love (2019) explains,

> Education research is crowded with studies that acknowledge dark children's pain but never the source of their pain, the legacy that pain has left, or how that pain can be healed. . . . [Professional development workshops] rarely discuss the topics of redlining, housing discrimination, White flight, gentrification, police brutality, racial health disparities, and high unemployment, problems that are not due to low levels of education but to the racism discussed. (p. 12)

In a recent study, for example, researchers who followed the lives of 101 Black adolescents found that they experienced racial discrimination on average more than five times each day (English et al., 2020). Notably, although the researchers accounted for a variety of direct and indirect experiences, they did not account for insidious racist conditions that are built into everyday systems, such as racially biased school tracking practices or racist housing practices. So participants withstood an average of more than five racist incidents per day *in addition to* those conditions.

Those incidents did not all occur in school. (The authors of the study did not provide detailed contextual information of that kind, other than specifying that participants experienced racial discrimination both online and offline.) But the stuff that didn't occur at school is still important context. As educational leaders, we might not be able to eliminate anti-Black racism in, say, healthcare systems. We might not be able to stop shopkeepers from following Black students around their stores. Perhaps we can't eliminate the health impacts of environmental injustice, such as higher rates of asthma among the predominately economically marginalized Black and Brown students who live in areas with greater levels of air pollution (Lovinsky-Desir et al., 2019). But we must understand these manifestations of racism as part of the context of students' and families' experiences. Consider, for example, how racism that Black and Brown students may endure outside school could influence how they experience school. And remember, we're not just talking about specific racist incidents. Consider the impact of insidious systemic racism in healthcare, housing, employment, policing, and other systems. For example, how often are we telling students to mindlessly respect and defer to adults in our buildings when, in some cases, those students have good reason to withhold respect until it is earned?

You might consider questions such as these: *How might racism in housing or policing affect our students' experiences at school? How might ableism in broader society affect students' school experiences? What can we do to be responsive to these oppressions even if we're not in a position as educators to eliminate them? How might we expand our spheres of influence to help eliminate them?*

This is one way the prioritization principle deepens the distinction between equity and equality and between mitigative and transformative equity. We're not just leaving the historical impacts of those systems of advantage and disadvantage in place, then trying to move forward from there. We're reimagining our policies, practices, and institutional cultures with the history of inequity's impacts in mind. Context is crucial.

Take stock of how well you know your community's history with regard to racism, cisgenderism, economic injustice, and other forms of oppression. Some of us might be plugged into that because we've been subject to one or more of those oppressions ourselves. But remember, we often struggle the most to recognize the kinds of oppression that harm somebody else and create advantage for us. What do you know about the injustices students, staff, and families are experiencing in the community, in society at large? If we don't have a deep sense of this reality, we can't be responsive to it.

As you learn more about these histories, pay special attention to the sorts of resistance and organizing in which families and youth from the same communities have been engaged, sometimes for generations, and how or whether schools have responded or partnered with them. Again, if we're prioritizing the needs of people who have been harmed by inequities in schools, then we should ensure we're aware of what students and families are experiencing, and who and what has stood in the way of their efforts to make the situation better, including educators and schools.

Flipping Priorities by *Responding to* and *Redressing* Inequity

The prioritization principle works in two layers, and it doesn't work at all if we neglect either of them. In the parlance of equity literacy, the first layer represents the *responding to inequity* component of the principle: repairing harm to individual people who have withstood specific instances of bias or inequity, prioritizing their immediate needs, best interests, and ideas for what constitutes a just resolution. The other layer, the one in which we enact deeper, more transformative equity leadership, is institutional and sometimes even systemic in nature. It requires efforts to redress inequity, reimagining what schools can and should be. When we embrace this layer of the prioritization principle, we commit to flipping the opportunity and access allocations of our schools and districts.

The Responding Layer: Repairing Harm in the Immediate Term

Many existing equity-proximal frameworks provide guidance for how to respond to harm in the immediate term. We have witnessed in some schools the positive influence of restorative justice, a framework for building more effective discipline practices, addressing harmful behaviors, and resolving conflict in humane, community-enriching ways (Evans & Vaandering, 2016; Winn & Winn, 2021). In the end, though, our equity efforts should focus not merely on resolving conflict; we should focus, instead, on eliminating injustice if we hope to prioritize the needs of people most affected by inequity.

This goal, eliminating injustice, is why some educators have raised important questions about the kinds of practices commonly adopted in the name of restorative justice (Lustick, 2021; Romano & Almengor, 2021), such as responding to oppressive acts by bringing the person who has been harmed together with the person doing harm in order to repair the harm, while ignoring the institutional conditions that perpetuate the harm. (Most restorative justice experts would say this is a misapplication of the model, which raises other questions about why it's such a popular application.) This meeting of the harmer and the harmed might make sense if the harm revolves around property damage or general community disruption. It can be a powerful practice as we build relationships of care and concern. But if we fail to attend to power dynamics or to acknowledge the relationship between, say, an individual act of racism and institutional racism in a school where the racism is not merely interpersonal, then we are perpetuating a significant equity shortcoming. Restoring some semblance of community between the harmer who weaponizes race and the racially harmed is a devastatingly low bar of a goal. It might even be a racism-sustaining goal.

Moreover, *restorative* is a somewhat shaky word from an equity and systems point of view. If what students ultimately need is to not experience ableism at school and all we're offering is an intervention with one person who has harmed a student with an ableist slur while ignoring all the other ableism, we really haven't restored much of anything. Similarly, in a school that has never been equitable for immigrant students, what exactly are we restoring with restorative practices when somebody has been harmed by xenophobia? We can't restore what never existed.

From an institutional point of view, where inequity exists, harm is always happening. So our questions when it comes to the prioritization principle are these: Who gets to decide what the dissolution of that harm, what the resolution or accountability, looks like or when we've accomplished it? More practically, how are we taking direction and cues from people who are being marginalized with regard to what equity would look like for them, or the best way to achieve it?

Addressing these questions means engaging with students and their families, with local communities, to hear their stories, demands, and visions for equity and justice. Some schools do this formally, using listening circles or community discussion events in which we invite people to share their stories, experiences, and ideas while we listen, validate, and learn. In other instances, this listening might happen in the moment or soon after a blatantly oppressive incident has occurred. Digging a little deeper, understanding that inequity is *always* operating, we can make these conversations an everyday part of our relationship building with students, families, and colleagues without waiting for an oppressive incident to occur.

The Redressing Layer: Checking Our Long-Term Priorities

The redressing layer of the prioritization principle begins with a way of thinking. We want to shake free from the tendency to be so mindlessly immersed in what *is* that we struggle to imagine what *could be*. As Bettina Love (2019) reminds us, we should embrace "what seems impossible: education for collective dignity and human power for justice" (p. 12). The prioritization principle pushes us toward the transformative approach because it urges us to focus our equity efforts on the best interests of people to whom we've failed to adequately attend. It is actively antiracist, actively antisexist, actively equitable and just.

How utterly different might our school or district be if we chose to strengthen our equity literacy and embrace a transformative, institutional approach to equity? If we can't imagine this without giving in to the "what about" anxieties—*What about state anti-CRT laws that limit our options on how or whether we teach about racism? What about the controversy that will ensue if we hold teachers accountable when they refuse to use students' correct names and pronouns? What about the families that expect that we'll continue sponsoring this spring break trip even though so many students are denied access because their families can't afford the fees?*—then we've stripped the prioritization principle of its power. Its primary longer-term function is to help us reimagine *everything* about education using a clear, focused equity lens. Its primary value is in helping us understand the scope and depth of change required to implement and sustain transformative equity leadership.

Once we understand this goal, we can work with the people most harmed by what exists now to imagine and construct something better. We don't want to pass the labor of making it better onto people who are marginalized; that, again, is our labor as leaders. But we do want to cocreate our visions out of their expertise and demands.

Let's practice. Imagine if school systems prioritized the interests, needs, demands, desires, and joys of students, families, and staff of color in every way in which, and for as long as, they have prioritized the interests, needs, desires, and joys of white students, families, and staff. We're not talking about pasting a few "No Place for Hate" posters in hallways or initiating a diversity club. We're talking about reshaping everything: how we choose curricula, what we determine to be required or elective, how we create policy, how we decide who we hire, how and what we assess. *Everything.* We're not nibbling around the edges. We're going right at the heart of the thing.

We can start the reimagining as an exercise in equity literacy, letting go of the "what abouts." How would you need to think differently about who you hire as teachers or as student services personnel? What would need to change about the curriculum, not just creating a couple narrow pathways of connection for students of color, not just adding a couple readings by authors of color, but *prioritizing* their pathways of connection, *prioritizing* Black and Brown students' engagement and joy? How would we reshape institutional culture, not just to vaguely "include" Indigenous people, but to align it with their diverse voices, experiences, joys, and concerns? What would that look like in your school or district? How would you have to adjust your leadership approach to accomplish and then sustain this vision?

Imagine if school systems prioritized the interests, needs, desires, and joys of LGBTQIA+ students and staff, set aside the "what abouts," the "but this is how we've always done its." What would our systems look like?

We've explored several examples related to policy and practice, so let's consider something different: the architecture of schools. Thanks to disability rights activists in the 1960s and 1970s (Patterson, 2012), many of whom were LGBTQIA+ people of color and youth, the U.S. government required public spaces such as schools to incorporate ramps, elevators, and chair lifts for people using wheelchairs and people with other mobility needs. Although those hard-fought accommodations may seem "normal" now, there are still many ways in which approaches to school design prioritize comfort and accessibility for people without those needs.

The way we in education often talk about *accommodations* and *assistive technology* demonstrates how this works. Schools are built mostly to accommodate students who don't have disabilities. Sure, we adjust schools to accommodate students with mobility-related and other disabilities. But a truer form of equity would mean that we build and equip schools so that they don't have to be adjusted; we wouldn't have to make up for disparities in systemic access with "accommodations" that fell outside "normal" practices because schools and classrooms would be constructed from the beginning to accommodate *all* students.

Imagine how schools might be built differently if school designers prioritized the needs of deaf students, for example (Martins & Gaudiot, 2012). They might attend to sight lines, acoustics, and other factors in dramatically different ways. Notably, hearing students would not be *dis*advantaged if school design prioritized access for deaf students in this fashion. They would just attend schools where the needs of students who have been systematically disadvantaged were normalized the way hearing students have always been normalized.

Although this form of prioritization might seem radical to some leaders, it reflects the basic tenets of universal design: considering the needs of students who face the most significant challenges when designing learning that is accessible, engaging, and validating. And, of course, it's no more radical than what many schools have been doing, which is to align policies, practices, curricula, and everything else to privilege.

As we attempt to apply this *redress* dimension of the prioritization principle, a few basic commitments will help.

Commitment one: Make equity advocates the center of school culture. A truism that the equity crowd often discusses is that in many schools it's easier to be a racist than an outspoken antiracist. In other words, often the people who speak up most vehemently about inequity face more hostility from colleagues and more shushing from school leaders than the people who mindlessly, or even deliberately, perpetuate inequity. We've mentioned this a couple of times: it can be especially true for people who speak up about the sorts of inequities they themselves experience. For example, when compared with their white colleagues, teachers of color who speak up about racial inequities often face elevated levels of hostility and marginalization simply for telling the antiracist truth (Kohli, 2018, 2021; Magwood, 2021).

Sometimes, taking an impassioned stand for equity is seen as deviant. Meanwhile, when people drag their heels on racial equity, they might be seen as moving through *a developmental process* (Mayorga & Picower, 2018). Alfreda Jarue, a high school student, broke down this phenomenon in a chapter she and several of her peers coauthored about the demands and frustrations of student activists (Chen et al., 2021). "It has become so normalized to the point that it's okay for a white kid to go through an 'insensitive racist phase' where they think saying the 'n' word is okay or say insensitive things to the LGBTQ+ community," she noted. "But some of them don't grow out of that phase. . . ." (p. 220). She continued, "The white coddling thing? That needs to stop" (p. 224).

In an equity-healthy school, one that prioritizes the best interests of people who have been denied equitable access and opportunity, those most adamant about equity should feel like the *center* of institutional culture. We might even say that any staff who are unwilling to commit to a deep equity vision despite our efforts to provide them with the knowledge and resources to do so should begin to feel as though *they* are out of place. As we've said, we don't need to wag our fingers at them or call them names. Instead, we establish our expectations and begin to shift institutional culture in ways that champion the equity champions. The institution is moving whether everyone is on board or not. Because the culture is changing toward equity, the people most resistant to equity will naturally begin to feel like, *Hey, maybe this place isn't for me.*

OK, you might be thinking, *I get prioritization and urgency. But we do need to at least try to get everybody on board, right?* Sure. Equity leaders shouldn't be arrogant know-it-alls or solitary heroes. The prioritization principle does, however, require us to respond to the urgency of the moment while simultaneously providing resources and support so that staff have multiple different entry points to get up to speed. There *must* be space to honor and engage people's genuine questions and concerns, even if it means routing them to another time and place where they can't do harm, such as a private conversation.

We recently observed a leader rise to the occasion of one of those tough truths. During a conversation with a superintendent we'll call Gloria, she asked us to help her troubleshoot a situation in one of her schools. The school's principal was known to ignore, if not openly resist, LGBTQIA+ students' efforts to draw attention to the heterosexism and cisgenderism they experienced at school. For months, Gloria wrestled with how best to accelerate equity efforts while navigating pressure to not rock the boat. She met with the principal several times. She required him to attend professional development about equity for LGBTQIA+ students. But nothing seemed to move the needle.

We urged Gloria toward informed urgency. "As you wait for something to click with him that might never click, whose interests are you prioritizing?" we asked. Gloria fell silent, a look of steady resolve coming over her face. "How many hurt kids are too many?" she wondered aloud. We watched the prioritization principle lock into place. The next time we spoke with her, she asked if we could help her spread the word about a job opening for a principal. "I couldn't let one more student be hurt in my school," she told us. "Enough is enough."

She tried and tried, and eventually all the trying without any real progress to show for it meant that she became a party to the inequity. She stepped up and made an equity decision. It wasn't easy, but that's the nature of transformative equity leadership.

We don't stop building bridges; we give people chances to get on board. But we're not giving people who repeatedly refuse to engage the power to undermine our efforts. We do not need to prioritize their needs or pace. The next couple of commitments speak to what this looks like in practice.

Commitment two: Establish equity as an imperative, not an option. Equity is integral, not optional. As we've mentioned, we often recommend that school leaders begin their equity efforts by cultivating a support system among people who already are advocating for equity in their schools. As you create your equity team, be sure to tap the people most knowledgeable and engaged when it comes to equity. The equity team should not spend time debating whether white privilege exists or whether its work should address cisgenderism. Provide that team with advanced professional learning opportunities, cultivating the sort of deep, transformative vision for equity we've been describing in this book. As we advised Liz, they can be your system of support as you roll out your equity vision and expectations.

But we can't stop there. The point of that step is to help us take the next step, which is establishing equity as an institutional commitment. We prioritize the needs, joys, and best interests of the people who have not enjoyed equitable access and opportunity when we take that next step.

So, after we build that support system, we provide *required* and *ongoing* professional learning rather than optional workshops or book groups. We also make sure we incorporate an assessment of equity practice in job performance reviews. And we apply equity as a lens in every conversation.

Taking these actions doesn't mean we stop talking about, say, social-emotional learning and talk only about equity; instead, it means we apply our equity lens to our SEL curriculum and everything else. *Let's explore how this practice we're considering adopting might affect our most economically marginalized students. How might we reimagine this policy in ways that prioritize the joys and engagement of the families whom we've most failed to prioritize? What would this discipline framework look like if we filtered it through a commitment to racial equity?*

These shouldn't be occasional conversations. They should be everyday conversations, normalized and demystified. Nobody gets to opt out. This is how we redefine equity as an imperative aspect of our school or district.

Commitment three: Reward equity efforts. How do you compensate the people in your sphere of influence who are leading the equity charge? How do you reward their persistence, especially if they have carried the equity mantle even when you were more hesitant about it? How do you demonstrate that you appreciate their equity labor in concrete, material ways?

This undertaking is one of our hills: employees should be compensated for equity efforts that transcend their job descriptions. Too often, school leaders exploit the labor of people with the most equity-related expertise and passion, who disproportionately are people who experience inequity themselves. We might assign them to every equity-related task force or workgroup or use them to ensure at least the illusion of inclusion on committees. But this kind of service requires real time and effort, intellectual as well as emotional labor, especially if one or two people are trying to inject a consistent equity view within a group of people bent on minimizing that view.

Maybe we reduce other parts of their workloads or offer the sorts of stipends often provided to coaches and other educators who take on additional responsibilities (Gorski et al., 2022). If we choose *not* to do so, we're making a clear statement about what we deem important.

The other side of the rewarding-equity coin is the will to resist pressure from people who don't have the best interests of all students at heart, people angling to retain disproportionate access and to roll back or soften equity efforts. We find it helpful to practice responding to parents or other community members who might pressure us to stop talking about heterosexism or cisgenderism, or who suggest we're the racists for naming and trying to eliminate racism. In Figure 5.2, we provide a few examples of the ways we might respond to various scenarios.

FIGURE 5.2

Suggested Responses to People Who Resist Equity Efforts

Scenario	Response
A white parent insists that elementary school–aged students are too young to learn about racism.	I appreciate your willingness to share your concern with me. We certainly want to be careful to make any conversation age-relevant. We also know that even at preschool ages, children of color witness and experience racism. So it's important to start talking about this at the youngest ages. And we are committed to preparing teachers to do so in the most honest, engaging way possible for the students they're teaching. Luckily, there are many great research-based resources to support educators that we rely on in these efforts.
	What concerns you about your child having conversations about the racism their classmates and their families experience? What potential benefits can you imagine from engaging students in this learning, and what might reassure you that those benefits are happening? What are you worried might happen that could do harm to your child if they learn about racism in schools?

Continued

FIGURE 5.2

Suggested Responses to People Who Resist Equity Efforts (*continued*)

Scenario	Response
A school board member complains after learning that your school library includes books with LGBTQIA+ characters.	I know that some people might see these books as controversial. But we don't see them that way. Lesbian, gay, bisexual, transgender, and nonbinary people exist. They exist in our larger community and in this school. Our professional responsibility as educators is to make sure that all students know they and their families belong here and feel like they can be completely themselves. This is one small step toward that for a group of students who often are alienated and don't see their experiences, families, and questions reflected in the curriculum. We also are committed to making sure that *all* students have opportunities to learn, not only about the existence of LGBTQIA+ people, but about how they navigate and resist oppression. We know that bullying against LGBTQIA+ students and incidents of self-harm decrease when students have access to these books. Students' health and safety is of utmost importance to us as leaders in the district, and I operate under the assumption that the board wants us to use tools proven to reduce bullying at school. Of course, I am always open to concerns and questions, but it goes against my values as a leader to decrease students' access to any kind of learning, especially when it's the kind of learning that helps them to be more humane and whole.
	What concerns you about having books that reflect the lives of our students and their families in the curriculum? What potential benefits can you imagine from having those books available to students, and what would help reassure you that those benefits are happening? What are you worried might happen with these books that could do harm to your child?
A white community member accuses you of "spreading critical race theory" after you seek financial support from the school board for staff development related to equity.	Thank you for sharing your concern. We know there is a lot of misinformation circulating about critical race theory. To us, the question is not whether or not we embrace critical race theory. Our concern is whether or not we embrace what evidence shows are the most useful approaches to prepare us to eliminate harm happening in our schools and to ensure that we give all students the opportunity to achieve to their fullest capabilities. We owe this to our students: we will use whatever has a strong track record of helping us do better when it comes to equity.
	What would you like me to keep in mind as I lead our staff in improving their ability to reach and teach all students? What type of resources would be helpful for community members interested in learning more about how racism operates in our schools and community?

Scenario	Response
A devout Christian staff member expresses outrage with your decision not to allow Christmas decorations in the public school.	It can be difficult to let go of something we really enjoy and look forward to every year. But we can't let our enjoyment of something be more important than kids' sense of belonging. As the adults in the building, what we do and say sends powerful messages about who belongs and what it means to belong here. Not only are we a public school with a constitutional obligation to separate church and state, but we have students and staff who are not Christian. As a leader in this school, I am committed to finding ways to build community that do not rely on any group being the unquestioned norm.
	What was it you loved about the Christmas decorations, and what ideas can we come up with for how to scratch that itch without excluding or marginalizing kids and families who are members of our community? What is a way we can be festive or make this time of year special that does not rely on the traditions of one religious community?

As a final scenario, let's say a parent approaches you, angry that teachers in your school are engaging students in conversations about racism or xenophobia. "How dare you allow that sort of indoctrination at this school!" the parent says. "You're making my child feel guilty about being white and American." How would you respond?

Before you answer that question, we suggest that you respond *positively*. Don't allow yourself to be drawn into a debate. As our colleague Marceline DuBose says, know your values. Be firm. What would you say? How often and in what ways do you prepare your leadership team and staff for these kinds of interactions? They're going to happen, so we ought to be ready.

Commitment four: Hire with equity in mind. The first level of equity accountability lies in the hiring process. Educational leaders who are committed to equity hire people who are committed to equity. We can't expect equity perfection from applicants, of course. We're all on a path. But we prioritize the needs, joys, and best interests of students who have been denied equitable access and opportunity when we hire people who are committed to and prepared to enact equity.

When interviewing prospective employees, we recommend asking equity-related questions that excavate their ideologies. As we discussed in Chapter 1, ideology drives practice. It's easier for interviewees who haven't really enacted an equity commitment to fudge their way through questions that are merely philosophical (e.g., *Do you feel that diversity is important?*) than it is for them to fudge their way through ideological questions. We find *why* questions to be particularly useful in this regard, especially when they revolve around disparities. *Why do academic disparities exist? What causes them?* Interviewees with an equity mindset should be tapped into the fact that these disparities are structural and institutional in nature; they're the result primarily of bias and inequity.

We should be cautious about interviewees who tend to respond to these sorts of questions with a deficit view (e.g., "Families experiencing poverty don't value education the way other families do"). At the very least, this kind of response is an important data point about the sorts of ideological interventions we need to adopt before we put new hires in front of students. On the other hand, if an applicant consistently demonstrates a deficit view, it can suggest a serious ideological blockage and warrant moving on to the next candidate. It's a lot easier to shift somebody's practice given an *equity*-embracing ideology than it is to shift somebody's *inequity*-embracing ideology.

Once we have a sense of where somebody is ideologically, we can pivot to questions that are more practical: *What would you do, and what have you done, to disrupt these disparities? What should schools do, and what institutional supports do you need, in order to help?* Take a moment to generate a list of other questions that might help you assess applicants' ideological stances related to equity and their track records of putting those stances into effective practice.

Of course, none of this is particularly useful if the people conducting interviews and making hiring decisions don't have the knowledge and skills to interpret applicants' responses to these sorts of questions. Remember, the most stellar equity advocates who have applied for a job, perhaps especially people who know what it feels like to be marginalized at school, *are also interviewing us.* They're looking for red or green flags in the questions we ask and what signals we're sending about how we value and enact equity. So make sure the people doing the interviewing are able to articulate your equity vision and interpret interviewees' responses to equity questions.

Here are a few additional interview questions that we often recommend to schools and districts. Note that the dimensions of inequity addressed in each one are interchangeable:

- Why are Black students more likely than white students to be suspended or expelled from school? How have you attempted to address this disproportionality? What can schools do differently to disrupt it?
- What is an example of a classroom or school policy that looks equal but might have an inequitable impact? How would you change that policy to be equitable?
- Describe a time you realized you were perpetuating an inequity. How did you realize it? What were you misunderstanding? What did you do to prepare yourself to stop perpetuating it?
- In your opinion, what is the relationship—or what *should be* the relationship—between trauma-informed education and equity?
- What are three common ways heterosexism operates in schools? Why do you think they are so common? What can educators and schools do differently to eliminate them?

Overcoming the Challenges of Implementing the Prioritization Principle

As we mentioned earlier, the prioritization principle can be difficult to apply, in terms of both its logistical complications and the resistance it can reveal. Of all the principles we cover in this book, this one elicits the most anxiety when we present it to educators. So even as we encourage equity leaders to apply the prioritization principle diligently, we want to be upfront about the challenges it presents and provide suggestions for navigating them.

Locus of Control

Something particularly difficult about applying the prioritization principle is that a considerable portion of the marginalization people experience happens *outside* schools, outside our spheres of individual influence. Not all of it, of course. We have plenty of work to do in schools. The point is that none of us can single-handedly eliminate systemic xenophobia and its impacts. None of us can unilaterally change immigration policy or eradicate anti-immigrant bigotry from national political discourses. Nor can any of us end poverty by ourselves. Even at the institutional level, schools can't afford to pay for high-quality preventive healthcare for all families, even as equity-literate leaders can point to inequitable healthcare access as one of the core barriers for students in their care.

Although we can't eliminate big, societal-level structural injustice in our roles as educators, we *can* be proactive and responsive to these oppressions in school. We can refuse to be silent about them, refuse to pretend they don't underlie students' and families' struggles. And we can find ways, big and small, to leverage the agency we do have to make sure we don't replicate or exacerbate societal-level inequities in schools and districts. Being clear-eyed about that and prioritizing the needs, joys, demands, and best interests of people experiencing inequities are vital to this commitment.

This is where mitigative equity can be useful. Perhaps we can't eliminate poverty, but we can be responsive to its impact. We can make sure our policies don't recreate that impact. We can create policies and adopt institutional cultures that mitigate it. Eliminate all those fees. Rethink homework policies. Drive deficit ideology out of institutional culture. Prioritize the best interests of students experiencing poverty in school. Because we can't control everything, we should ensure that everything we can control is as equitable as possible.

We can adopt these practices right now. What's one policy, practice, or aspect of institutional culture in your sphere of influence that could exacerbate the impacts of societal-level economic injustice or heterosexism? How can you adjust it to mitigate those impacts instead?

One Size Fits Few

We are complex combinations of identities; nobody is a member of just one identity group. Some of us have multiple identities through which we experience interlocking oppressions that bleed into one another. Some of us—white men or cisgender heterosexual people or white cisgender heterosexual men, for example—embody multiple privileged identities that provide access to interlocking systems of advantage. In fact, both of these can be true for individual people simultaneously. That's some serious complexity.

Given all the interlocking, when we prioritize, say, LGBTQIA+ students, we want to make sure we're not subjugating the needs of, say, Black and Brown students; after all, there are LGBTQIA+ Black and Brown youth. Moreover, the heterosexism, cisgenderism, and racism they're experiencing interacts with ableism, sexism, and myriad other forms of injustice (Stewart & Nicolazzo, 2018). It's one big intersectional mess of advantage and disadvantage, privilege and oppression.

It can be useful to foreground a particular group's needs or experiences, to consider school from the perspective of students who are masters of languages other than English or who cope with mental illness, for example, and to specifically discuss how to prioritize them. It's important that we do deep dives on every form of oppression, from anti-Black racism to fatphobia to Islamophobia. But we are better positioned to be transformative equity leaders when we account for the broad and intersecting range of experiences.

Remember, no demographic group is a monolith. One size fits few. When prioritizing the needs and concerns of any group that is marginalized in our school or district, it's important to understand that needs and best interests and sources of joy and harm could vary significantly. We exacerbate harm when we presume consensus or homogeneity within a group.

Legal Threats

As the adage goes, when people are accustomed to advantage, or when they feel entitled to it, equity can feel like a loss. Sometimes that feeling can result in angry blog posts or vitriolic comments at school board meetings claiming reverse racism or suggesting school leaders are antiwhite or anti-Christian, or maybe even anti-American or unpatriotic. But the blowback can be even more disruptive. In some places, parent and community groups, some of which are funded by national political interests, are leveling lawsuits against school districts (Marcelo, 2022; Schwartz, 2022). These groups appear to claim, in essence, that attention to equity is inequitable. That's the "reverse racism" argument: anything we do in the name of antiracism is racism against white people, even if it's simply creating equitable access for people of color, and even if it's expanding learning for white students.

From an equity point of view, the argument is nonsensical, we know. But when we acknowledge that there's no path to equity without the prioritization principle, people looking for an angle to undermine our efforts—policymakers, news commentators, parent organizers—might interpret it as us acknowledging that what we're doing is discrimination, which is the opposite of what we're doing. Of course, generally these are people who do not acknowledge the generations of discrimination and inequity to which we are responding through our equity efforts.

Certainly, dealing with this sort of legal threat is not easy. We know we must forge ahead regardless. But we must forge ahead strategically, accounting for the possibility of these threats, especially if we're in states with anti-CRT or "don't say gay" legislation. We know everyone's context is different, and each of us must make decisions related to whatever contextual factors swirl around us while also prioritizing equity. One way we can do this is to have our proverbial ducks in a row, to gather the resources we need ahead of time to demonstrate how what we're doing aligns with standards or district goals.

Conclusion

What the prioritization principle demands of us, especially those of us who are systematically advantaged, is to take stock of our priorities and demonstrate a willingness and ability to help build something different, no matter what blowback it might elicit. It means never, ever prioritizing the comfort or safety of the people who are most resistant to equity-related change at the expense of the people who are most desperate for us to do better or who vehemently demand we do better.

Sometimes equity leadership means reallocating comfort and safety. It means taking risks and being prepared for the consequences.

Either we face the consequences, or we leave the most marginalized members of our community to continue facing them. Who are we going to prioritize?

Figure 5.3 highlights some of the key points presented in this chapter. It summarizes the prioritization principle by illustrating, from a leader's point of view, the difference between mitigative equity and transformative equity in terms of actions and attitudes.

FIGURE 5.3

The Prioritization Principle: Comparing Leaders' Mindsets Related to Mitigative Versus Transformative Equity

Mitigative Equity	Transformative Equity
I try to consider everyone's needs to determine what is the best next step.	In consideration of the community, I prioritize the needs and concerns of those most harmed by inequity over those who are deeply invested in perpetuating inequity.
I slow down or stop efforts when they kick up too much resistance.	I pace for change, working on a timeline that is based on the needs of the most marginalized stakeholders.
I need to get everyone on board before making any substantial changes.	I need to offer opportunities for everyone to get on board as we make substantial changes.
I'm vaguely aware of broad-stroke histories and current events affecting students and families.	I'm deeply cognizant of the micro- and macro-context in which the school exists.
I am friendly with stakeholders who experience various forms of marginalization and inequity and trust that they know my intentions are good.	I've built relationships of trust with stakeholders who experience various forms of marginalization and inequity because I listen to, believe, validate, and act on their concerns.
I get frustrated with external constraints that keep me from leading for equity.	I consider external constraints to strategize about how to navigate or remove them, and not as reasons to stop leading for equity.

6

Expanding Access to Something Inequitable Is Not Equity: The Just Access Principle

A few years ago, just before we facilitated a focus group of Black students attending a predominately white high school, the principal pulled us aside. She shared that one of the participants, a senior named Tanya, was on pace to graduate as valedictorian.

"I know you've heard rough stories from some of our Black students," the principal shared, "but I bet you'll hear something different from Tanya. She has a perfect GPA. She's involved in everything. She's student government president. By all outward appearances, she has thrived in this district."

Tanya remained quiet through 45 minutes of a 50-minute focus group. Then, when we asked the participants a question about how connected they felt to their school, she said, "I know people look at me like I'm well-adjusted, like I have a lot of school spirit. I'm graduating as valedictorian. I'm uber-involved."

She went on to explain how her "actual experience" did not conform with all outward appearances. "I've faced racism in this district since I was in elementary school," Tanya said. "I had to fight to get into advanced classes. I've sat through history classes, including AP and honors classes, where teachers lied to me about my history and then tested me to make sure I learned the lies. I've watched teachers refuse to respond when white students say blatantly racist things. I stayed involved because I knew I had to do way more than most students just to be seen as equal."

"The truth," she continued, "is that I can't wait to graduate from this school in a couple months. And when I do, I will *never* come back here."

Does that sound like equity?

We've worked with numerous leaders who are enthusiastic about dismantling inequitable systems, who are knee-deep in disaggregated data, looking for patterns and trends. We've worked with principals who make bold moves and adopt important equity metrics for their schools. Some are applying the principles we've outlined thus far but still miss a significant piece of the equity literacy puzzle if they don't consider whether their goals and metrics are themselves rooted in transformative equity.

Here's the rub: students can have roughly equitable opportunities and, like Tanya, can even achieve impressive outcomes but still not experience their schools equitably.

As leaders, we should be careful not to limit our equity thinking to inputs and outputs; we must ensure that the things that happen in the space between inputs and outputs—the pedagogies, the engagement, the experiences—are equitable too. Students who are experiencing poverty can be active in extracurriculars and win academic accolades but still experience painful class bias and feel fatigued from navigating barriers related to their financial status. Immigrant students can demonstrate brilliance in advanced coursework while also experiencing xenophobia, curricular erasure, and cruel jokes about their ancestry. Equitable outcomes, inequitable systems.

This is the essence of the *just access principle*: The question is not only whether we provide equitable access to this or that opportunity, this or that program, this or that class. It's not just about tracking the equity health of our institution with output data such as graduation rates. Instead, it's about whether *what we are providing access to* is itself equitable. In other words, the issue is not just *access*, but *equitable and just access*.

Rethinking What Constitutes Equity Success

If we're committed to transformative equity, we make it a regular practice to examine the harm that can be done *within* the experiences we're trying so hard to ensure students can access equitably. We critically examine the opportunities through which we're trying to maximize student success. We ask ourselves, *From an equity point of view, are our goals sufficient?* If those goals are simply to raise test scores without considering students' school experiences, then we're only affecting the illusion of equity.

Consider tracking. Perhaps providing historically underrepresented students with more access to gifted or advanced programs is a step forward. But that's just *access*. On the other hand, *equitable* access, *just* access, means we're assessing whether those students are equally as invisible in the curricula of those upper-track courses as they were in other academic tracks. *Just* access means transforming entire systems of programs and curricula and selection processes. It means recognizing that academic tracking systems are riddled with predictable bias (Lofton, 2021), so equity may require eliminating them altogether. As we mentioned earlier, when it comes to transformative equity, everything must be on the table.

Assessing Equity Beyond Academic Success

Do we consider it a success when girls or gender-nonbinary students excel in history classes that tokenize them or that render them invisible? When LGBTQIA+ students receive stellar grades in health classes that marginalize or stigmatize their concerns and questions, we might see them as achieving academically. But that's not equity if we don't confront the damage the curriculum is doing. When we notice that Asian American or Pacific Islander students graduate at high rates in the aggregate, we might feed into the "model minority" myth by saying, *Hey, we're doing really well with this demographic.* But that's not equity. We should disaggregate this broad ethnic category to recognize the vastly different experiences of diverse students within it. We also should reckon with the possibility that, even when students do exceed stereotype-laden expectations, they might have to do so while dodging incessant microaggressions and navigating the pressure to buy into the model minority myth (Hartlep, 2021). Although the news might look good, if we dig a little deeper, we may find that we are generating new layers of inequity with these shallow conceptions of achievement.

We might ask ourselves, *What does it cost students to participate in and "succeed" in this sort of dehumanizing learning? What do they have to concede, to what must they acquiesce, to play the game of school? If we're requiring them to deny, ignore, or hide important elements of who they are so they might appear to belong or succeed, can we consider seemingly equitable "outcomes" to be indicative of equity?*

In fact, increased opportunity and improved outcomes in situations such as these could actually represent *greater inequity* for students if the opportunity and outcomes place them in conditions that remain inequitable or intensify inequity and harm. We could be adding an additional burden for students to bear, especially if they feel pressure, like Tanya, to *appear* "well-adjusted."

As an example, Gabriel Rodriguez and Monica González Ybarra (2020) have explored how "Latinx youth . . . perceive their schools prepared them and impacted their engagement for civic life" (p. 922). They describe these youth navigating predominately white suburban schools. In particular, they examine how students develop *facultad*, or instincts for avoiding common dangers such as outright hostility, intimidation, and exclusion from staff and classmates. Students' strategies for survival include literally silencing themselves as a form of protection and self-preservation; avoiding certain spaces, people, and events; and tiptoeing around conversations, just to name a few. In other ethnographic work, Rodriguez (2020) relays story after story of students who were academically successful but did not feel a sense of belonging at their schools. Here's one example:

> [The Latinx students] technically could go and sit in the commons, and indeed some had done so, but when they did, some white students stared at them and asked what they were doing there. The impact also was felt in the hallway outside of the commons. Joaquín, a senior in honors classes, shared that he walked as fast as he could because he felt white students were judging him. (p. 22)

Another honors student athlete, Camilla, shared, "It's not that we don't understand the content, it's the environment that we're placed in" (p. 27).

Equity means we don't require students to demonstrate *facultad* or resilience just so they can succeed academically while attempting to survive other aspects of school. Instead, we transform the conditions and hold ourselves as professional educators accountable for removing the barriers, biases, oppressions, and inequities they face.

Here's another example. During a recent conversation with an AP history class at a high school in the Mid-Atlantic, Shaima, a student who described herself as "first-generation Pakistani American," said, "I feel like I'm crossing a border every time I come to school and every time I come to this class." As equity leaders, we must account for the exhaustion, fear, and frustration experienced by youth who are marginalized *and* appear to be performing well academically despite contending with racism, xenophobia, linguicism, and other forms of oppression, possibly from teachers or classmates or policies or a combination of these. Shaima's school experience can't be described as equitable, even though she was graduating near the top of her class, took several honors and AP classes, and avoided the principal's office. No matter how they're doing on quantitative measures, if students feel like they're crossing a cultural border to go to school, we're failing at equity.

Who are the Shaimas or Camillas or Joaquíns in your school or district? Who are the students who may be faring well on traditional academic measures but still might feel marginalized, as though they cross a border when they enter your school? Who are the students who have managed to appear well-adjusted while still facing significant bias and inequity? What do you need to change about institutional culture and practices so that students like Shaima, Camilla, and Joaquín aren't forced to spend their energy learning how to survive in your school, regardless of how they appear to be achieving?

We also need to be careful to make sure we are not drawing comparisons between, say, students who are experiencing poverty who are doing well on traditional achievement measures and those who are struggling on those measures, using the former to justify equity inaction or to evoke deficit ideology pertaining to the latter. Focus, instead, on what is inequitable, on what is harming, or has the potential to harm, all students who are experiencing poverty. In the same way, it might be easy to look at a district full of leaders of color and assume it is an equity oasis. *We have a Black principal. Doesn't that prove anybody who works hard enough has access to career advancement here?* If we want to know whether that is actually the case, we would need to know what sorts of racism that principal endures. We certainly can't assume that being a principal protects somebody from racism or sexism or other forms of oppression. To the contrary, in our own circles of colleagues and collaborators, many people of color who are in school or district leadership positions have experienced elevated forms and levels of racism since being promoted to those positions. That is the precise opposite of racial equity.

Miseducating Privilege

Incidentally, in a different way, these sorts of conditions also can be damaging for students with dominant identities, students the system ostensibly serves. What do students learn from schools that consistently center, normalize, and even idealize them? What do they learn about themselves? About others? We can't strengthen their capacity for solidarity or community if they're immersed in schools that obscure or justify inequity, that are designed around their cultural norms and lived realities, that constantly give them the benefit of the doubt (Swalwell, 2015).

During a focus group of white students at a school that had tapped us to help assess its racial equity efforts, we asked, "Where in your education at this school have you learned about racism?" Sam, a senior at the school, a white student, spoke up. He was about to graduate with a GPA above 4.0. He had been accepted to an Ivy League university. Here's how he responded:

> The Industrial Revolution or the Revolutionary War was primarily white people; you can't really incorporate Black people into that time period just because that's not how it was. So, you can't really change the curriculum because that would just be like changing history. You have to keep history the same.... I think the curriculum is fine.

Sam's response should worry all of us when we imagine the impact he might have in the world. But more than that, we're concerned about the impact school prepared him to have. He graduated near the top of his class and somehow came out of that experience with dangerous misunderstandings, *racist* misunderstandings of history. In a very real sense, he too was failed by his schools.

What do you see in his remark that demonstrates how school failed him?

The first thing we noticed was that he conceptualized learning about racism as learning about Black people during particular points in history rather than the mechanics of white supremacy. He conceptualized race as a Black/white binary. He understood the Revolutionary War and Industrial Revolution eras as being disconnected from Black people when, in fact, these eras were deeply influenced by Black communities and other people of color—their oppression, but also their contributions, their resistance, their art and invention and community. Perhaps most troubling, Sam contended that learning a more inclusive, more *accurate* account of these eras would be tantamount to "changing history" rather than correcting decades of racist, exclusionary erasure from historical narratives. He was quick to reject a more accurate and complex understanding because he presumed his understanding was accurate. And he was notably confident about the legitimacy of his inaccurate view. This is a big mess of curricular failure.

As a student, Sam never triggered any red flags; nobody saw him as "at risk." But his response indicates a serious equity problem at his school. The trouble is, in most schools, nobody would assess for this sort of misunderstanding. In most schools, nobody would recognize this as a problem, except perhaps some especially equity-conscious teachers. The just access principle demands we see this situation as our failure and correct it.

How many Sams do we send out into the world with accolades, high marks, and glowing recommendations? What are the consequences for Shaima and Camilla and Joaquín when we do that?

In sum, when we fail to enact the just access principle, we risk exacerbating equity crises by retraumatizing marginalized youth as well as reproducing systems of advantage for people who are privileged under the cloak of equity. The just access principle helps us avoid the trap of presuming that what we're doing is equity-great when actually it might be equity-marginal or even *inequity*-producing.

Take a moment to consider the ways your school or district strengthens students' skills and knowledge related to equity literacy. As members of a diverse democracy with devastating inequities, what do students need to know and be able to do? Are the adults in your school or district prepared to help them know and do it?

The Danger of a Good Reputation

Notably, we often find that the leaders who struggle most to turn a critical eye on what, exactly, constitutes equitable access are those whose schools and districts enjoy mighty reputations among traditional power brokers: the "best in the state" types of schools, the ones whose aggregate achievement data suggest that most students are performing well. We've witnessed this particularly in some "elite" independent schools where some staff may feel that students of color, students experiencing poverty, and other students who traditionally have been excluded from their campuses are fortunate to be there at all. It's as though the implicit sensemaking is that *"those students" are winning simply because we allow them to be here* no matter what their experience is or how they're being educated (Sánchez Loza, 2021).

In these contexts—in *all* contexts, really—we need to make sure that stark disparities are not written off as outliers, or of little concern, simply because they reflect the experience of a small number of students. We've struggled at times to convince stakeholders who enjoy structural advantage in schools with impressive aggregate outcomes, along with significant disparities in disaggregated outcome and experience, that equity is not about the aggregate. It's about eliminating the causes of disparities, regardless of what overall percentage of students or staff or families are suffering those disparities.

The equity greatness of a school is not measured by aggregate outcomes or the experience of a majority, especially if that majority represents communities with structural advantage. For us, an equity-great school is one that deals frankly and directly with the inequities within it. It's one that courageously applies the principles we've described, one that is unwilling to gloss over patterns of experiences as though they are outliers or fringe concerns. It's one where the students, staff, and families who are most marginalized in other parts of their lives feel a deep sense of belonging and experience the school in a healthy, just, equitable way.

Who raves about your school, and who doesn't? Are there predictable demographic patterns?

Consider, as a leader, how you discuss your school or district in public. Particularly, how do you promote your school or district, and how do you use equity, diversity, or inclusion to do so? Do you frame your reputation in ways that account for the extent to which, and the manner in which, inequities are responded to and redressed, and how equity is actively cultivated and sustained? If not, how might you incorporate these considerations into the way you discuss your school or district?

Before we explore more detailed examples of why the just access principle is so important and how it operates, we want to acknowledge, again, the intense pressures we know educational leaders—at least those of us in administrative roles—may feel to use input and output data as the only, or at least the primary, metrics for equity. It's hard not to prioritize the metrics upon which our job performances might be evaluated. It's also hard not to get swept up in the test score obsession that was reintroduced by No Child Left Behind and has never quite let up since.

We have vivid memories of attending a national educational equity conference 20 or so years ago and hearing a heralded keynoter frame his entire talk on racial equity around raising test scores. Not eliminating racism, not curbing the resegregation of schools, not examining racial disparities in discipline, not attending to curricular erasure, but *raising test scores.* Just a few years earlier, the message at that conference was, in essence, *identify the racism, eliminate the racism.* From an equity point of view, that keynote address was about as complete a reversal of an equity goal, from eliminating racism to raising test scores, as we could imagine.

Twenty years later, we're still wading through the muck of that equity-as-raising-test-scores discourse. And where has that approach left us? The disparities remain, and the focus on test scores has obscured the causes of the disparities: racism, heterosexism, and other forms of oppression that can't be solved by raising test scores.

We explore the collection, interpretation, and use of data in more detail in Chapter 7. Suffice it to say for now that we understand the challenge facing us as we try to buck or balance those raising-test-scores pressures. But we also know that this is the nature of the *transformative* in *transformative equity leadership*. We need more bucking.

We break the rest of this chapter into two sections. In the first, we explore what just access looks like for students. Not just *access*, but *just access*. In the second, we apply the just access principle to staff.

Just Access for Students

We start by diving deeper into examples of how the just access principle applies to students. We focus first on the curriculum, then move to instruction and assessment.

Equitable Curriculum

The curriculum is perhaps the most obvious domain to which we can apply the just access principle. We could take as our example any discipline at any grade level, but let's begin by focusing on some of the "highest-status" curricula: AP classes. Students enrolled in AP classes tend to be disproportionately white and economically advantaged as compared with the student bodies at their schools (Crabtree et al., 2019). Harkening back to the fix injustice, not kids principle, if we employ a deficit lens, we might interpret these gaps as evidence that Black and Brown students and students experiencing poverty do not value, or simply are not capable of succeeding in, those courses. With a structural ideology, however, we understand that there is something institutional or *structural* preventing some students from enrolling while encouraging others to enroll. The trouble is the inequity, not the people experiencing the inequity.

In a practical sense, this understanding means we need to address inequity with a varied, holistic approach. Our first impulse might be to ask, *How might we be tracking students regardless of their abilities or interests?* That's an important question. It's critical that we examine our tracking processes to determine how bias might be operating, because it almost certainly is.

Many schools have attempted to address this sort of question and reduce barriers to AP classes. For example, some have removed prerequisites. Others no longer require teacher recommendations. We come across more and more schools that provide financial aid for AP exams. If our only goal is to provide opportunities that help facilitate college admission and completion, simply trying to expand who has access to and successfully completes AP classes might make at least partial sense.

However, if we're trying to provide equitable, fair, and *just* access, we should dig deeper. How do students experience "high-status" courses, or any courses, in ways that discourage, dehumanize, and misinform them? How might curriculum be at odds with efforts to work toward equity by normalizing, obscuring, or justifying oppression? The more committed we are to equity, the deeper we want to dig into what is *actually* happening in classrooms to determine whether less disproportionality should be our sole goal or whether we need to rethink the very heart of what we're doing.

There are other, perhaps subtler, mechanisms to consider. We might ask ourselves, *What messages are being communicated, implicitly and explicitly, to students about who belongs in which classes?* We might go out of our way to strengthen representation of gender, gender identity, and gender expression in math or science curricula but fail to address predictable gender bias related to who we encourage to take which math or science courses or who we assign to what track as early as elementary school.

Remember, part of our equity responsibility is to be responsive to the bias and inequity that exist outside our spheres of influence. So even if we don't find evidence of consistent bias in messaging about who belongs in which course within our spheres of influence, we still might be missing the mark if we don't find ways to actively counteract that messaging in the larger society. Perhaps we need to be intentional about who we're hiring to teach those courses. We can develop curricula that purposefully challenge raced or gendered presumptions.

This sort of thinking and action is the difference between just *access* and *just access*.

Then there is this: when students of color and students experiencing poverty do enroll in AP classes, they are less likely to pass AP exams than their more economically or racially privileged peers (Solorzano & Ornelas, 2004). If that's true in our spheres of influence, do we think, *We've done our best to make it accessible; if they don't succeed, then that's on them*? Or, assuming it's a simple sign of ability, perhaps we offer academic supports but ignore any other potential cause of the disparity.

Once we dig a little deeper with an equity lens, we would not necessarily rule out offering academic support to students; we want to offer whatever academic supports students need, especially those who previously have been cheated out of equitable access. But we also would be attentive to other potential contributing factors. We would wonder how students experience the curriculum and instruction, especially those who are the only student of a particular identity in their class, or one of few, and whether they might feel isolated or alienated. We would examine what teachers are doing to mitigate or reinforce that marginalization. And, of course, we would consider the class's content and how it might exacerbate bias and exclusion.

As a more specific example, consider AP U.S. history. Scholars, think tanks, parent groups, and others have engaged in generations-long debates about what ought to be the prevailing narrative in the U.S. history canon (Evans, 2006). Traditionally the narrative has focused on military conflicts and the federal government, inevitably centering the perspectives of white, Christian, economically privileged, presumably cisgender and heterosexual men. Often, authors of textbooks and other resources have depicted this narrow but popular and marketable narrative because it helps to sell more books (Loewen, 2008). James Banks (1993) called this "popular" and "mainstream academic knowledge"; others have referred to it as a "master" or "dominant" narrative (e.g., Salinas & Blevins, 2014).

Of course, at best this approach to history is narrow and inaccurate. But it's also dangerous because it normalizes dominance and oppression. Expanding access to this sort of curriculum to students who have been denied access, especially if they're invisible in it, is no equity triumph. Nor is helping students test better on inaccurate or privilege-sustaining content. This is true for students who are marginalized by that content and for dominant-identity students who also are miseducated by it.

"Transformational academic knowledge" and "counternarratives," on the other hand, expand this narrow focus, highlight social movements, and spotlight the contributions of people who historically have been tokenized in or omitted from curricula. The stories of diverse Black and Brown people, Indigenous and Native people, people experiencing poverty, disabled people, LGBTQIA+ people, and the stories of people with all the intersecting combinations of these and other identities are purposefully, deeply, accurately, and substantially visible and central rather than obscured, relegated to special months, or squeezed into the margins and shaded boxes of learning materials. White supremacy, patriarchy, colonialism, and other systems by which people have maintained the power to oppress are open for examination and critique. With an equity lens, we reject the idea that telling the truth is indoctrination, no matter whether we're talking about an AP class or a general education class. Students need the truth. They need to wrestle with important questions to understand, and act ethically in, the world.

Unless *that* is the kind of curriculum we help students access, we fall short of our equity commitment even if we revise the ways we sort those students. We might be providing *equitable access* to something, but it's not an *equitable something*.

To be clear, we're not encouraging you to eliminate efforts at diversifying the students who have access to those classes. We want to think about and address how the sorting begins far before anybody has access to AP or honors courses. But again, that's just *access*. We also want something deeper, something more transformative, so that we don't think our job is done once we've reimagined the sorting. We want *just access*.

You might be thinking, *Sure, it's easy to imagine this principle in relation to high school history, but what about other subjects or grade levels? Every* subject and *every* level of schooling can be reimagined using the just access principle. Even elementary math. For example, Anita Bright (2016) shares this story problem:

> An orange grower in California hires migrant workers to pick oranges during the season. He has 12 employees, and each can pick 400 oranges per hour. He has discovered that if he adds more workers, the production per worker decreases due to lack of supervision.

The problem, Bright notes, goes on to ask students to determine how to maximize a grower's profit "rather than exploring the dehumanizing conditions of migrant workers. It also reinforces stereotypes, describing migrant workers as needing close supervision to work effectively" (para. 24). As another example, LaGarrett King and Ashley Woodson (2017) describe an elementary math story problem requiring students to calculate how many beatings per week Frederick Douglass received if he was beaten twice a day. That was a real math problem in a real elementary school.

Applying the abilities of equity literacy described in Chapter 2, we assume everybody reading these examples *recognizes* that these story problems are all kinds of harmful. We might *respond* by no longer adopting learning materials in which this sort of story appears, or, if the story problem was created by one of our teachers, by working with that teacher to remove it from the curriculum. *Redressing* the situation would require deeper work, exploring and addressing how we ever adopted learning materials with this sort of story or what kinds of misunderstandings undermined the teacher's ability to avoid these awful problems. Maybe we need to provide broader professional development so staff can practice identifying and modifying potentially traumatizing curricula. This would be one important step toward just access.

Another step would be reworking these examples to explicitly embrace equity. One longtime colleague of ours, a recently retired elementary school teacher, often created math story problems that encouraged students to examine human rights issues in their communities. In one example, students learned about "time poverty" and food deserts by comparing how long it took people in a nearby middle class neighborhood to get to and from a grocery store with how long it took people in their high-poverty community, where there were no supermarkets and many people relied on public transportation. They were still learning and applying the math skills, but in ways that were relevant and meaningful to them.

So let's say we make some progress. Beyond adjusting curriculum, we eliminate tracking altogether, providing all students with access to what might previously have been deemed advanced or honors curricula, which many equity advocates have argued is our most equitable course of action. We might rightly see that move as progress, as identifying and eliminating a source of inequity, or even as actively cultivating equity. But we also must be, and prepare the educators around us to be, attentive to content and its impact. Otherwise, we're still in equity infancy, practicing what Stephanie Jones (2019) calls "curricular violence."

The just access principle challenges us to interrogate the *what* and the *how* of teaching. It challenges us to recognize and eliminate curriculum that reinforces oppression while also addressing institutional conditions such as tracking.

What is something you're doing in your school or district to provide more equitable access to a class or program or any other learning experience? Dig deeper. How equitable is the class, program, or other learning experience to which you are increasing access? Whose communities, values, and knowledges are centered, presumed, or affirmed? Whose are tokenized, omitted, or whitewashed? How can you ensure that the thing to which you're providing access is equitable?

Equitable Instruction and Assessment

Several years ago, Kimberly, a math teacher in Minnesota, shared with us a math exam used in her school. The test included a section of story problems about "hiking and camping in the Northwoods," a region several hours north of the state's Minneapolis–St. Paul urban hub. Kimberly taught at an inner-city, high-poverty middle school. Most of her students had never traveled outside the Minneapolis metro area. Their parents didn't own vacation homes on lakes or in nature preserves. Virtually none of Kimberly's students were familiar with the technical hiking and camping terminology sprinkled throughout the problems—words such as *portage*, which refers to carrying a watercraft over land between bodies of water. There wasn't a lot of portage happening in their neighborhoods.

The school had begun to receive attention and accolades, especially from equity advocates, for its detracking efforts. "This is the sort of thing the people celebrating us don't see," Kimberly said. "We're detracking, which is good, but we're still falling short on equity when it comes to much of what's happening in our detracked classrooms." She described an institutional culture still rife with deficit ideology, the predominance of skills-and-drills teaching, crowded classrooms, and a lack of professional learning opportunities preparing teachers who wanted to do better, which, she insisted, was "a vast majority" of her colleagues. The math exam wasn't part of a purposeful plot, but a symptom of these equity shortcomings. Fortunately, her colleague who created the exam was open to Kimberly's feedback.

When it comes to inadequacies in applying the just access principle, curricular examples are easy to come by. But curriculum is only one relevant site for just access. We also want to consider instructional and assessment frameworks and other conditions that belie surface-level attempts at equity. An attempt at equitable curriculum without sufficient attention to equitable pedagogies and assessment still leaves us at inequity.

Many powerful resources are available to help us inject transformative equity not only into *what* we teach but also into *how* we teach and how we define and assess success. For example, we've drawn inspiration from *culturally relevant pedagogy* (Ladson-Billings, 1995) and its more recent offshoots, including *culturally sustaining pedagogy* (Paris & Alim, 2017), which focuses on how to "explore, honor, extend, and, at times, problematize [students'] heritage and community languages" (Paris & Alim, 2014, p. 86). *Culturally revitalizing pedagogy*, another framework that has informed our approach, highlights the recognition and reclamation of Indigenous sovereignty and traditions (McCarty & Lee, 2014). Like equity literacy, these frameworks require something more than celebrating students' surface-level cultures. They insist upon deep learning that takes students' contexts, cultures, voices, and experiences into account.

Let's say your school has embraced culturally sustaining and revitalizing pedagogies. That is an important step. But many staff will need significant support transitioning from old habits and presumptions into these transformative approaches. Some may need support to avoid presuming "it's not working" when students don't immediately embrace a new instructional approach. Even very young children have learned to play the game of school, so teachers sometimes have to *explicitly* transition them into more humanizing and liberatory practices (Wheeler-Bell & Swalwell, 2021). It can take time. It also requires a transformative mindset, so that we're not just implementing the lowest-hanging fruit on the equity tree.

Take a moment to consider: What instructional and assessment traditions and models are most entrenched in your school and district, and why? What mindsets, policies, and practices fuel them? What are you doing to facilitate and support the shift in mindset that must undergird shifts in practice toward just access?

Some students may feel empowered by new instructional and assessment methods, invigorated by new expectations and opportunities for engagement, whereas others could experience growing pains as they learn how to navigate spaces that no longer advantage them. Students accustomed to getting the short end of the equity stick may need time to trust that the change we're making is substantial and not tokenistic, whereas students accustomed to privilege might need help adjusting to not being constantly centered (Swalwell, 2015). Students who measure their own worth or success by gold stars may mourn the loss of a system they had mastered.

San Pedro's (2018) notion of *culturally disruptive pedagogy* can be helpful in this regard. He explains:

> Teaching youth to better understand themselves in relation to larger systems means that we encourage discussion, thoughts, and ideas that are in process and in transition. It means that we offer encouragement, love, and support to continue to remain in schooling spaces that may eventually challenge and change one's ideas.

It means that we create sacred truth spaces where multiple truths can be voiced, shared, and understood, which may lead to moments where students begin to consider new perspectives offered by their peers. It means that we listen closely and carefully to students' emergent identities—particularly as Whiteness becomes more and more visible—and forward their questions, comments, and moments of tension as legitimate sources of knowledge. (p. 1221)

Challenging that "plug and chug" pedagogical approach, San Pedro continues:

Rather than forcing them to memorize and regurgitate unchallenged "correct" answers on tests, we ought to be providing opportunities for them to voice their new identities and thoughts as they make sense of new paradigms that include others' realities. It also means that we create meaningful "pauses" where students have moments to consider the many positions they've been exposed to in order to consider a deeper question: What truths do I want to hold as my own and what pieces of my prior cultural understandings must I disrupt and let go to make room for this new reality? (pp. 1221–1222)

These commitments, these transformations, are bigger than improving test scores, bigger than making curriculum a little more inclusive. It requires that we fundamentally transform our interactions with students. Even if the curricula, instruction, and assessment seem equitable and inclusive, we're not providing just access until we engage students in critical and creative thinking about issues that matter, until we are willing and able to effectively enact culturally sustaining, revitalizing, and disruptive pedagogies. As leaders, we must equip the people around us with the knowledge and skills necessary to pull this off. We all could use time and opportunities to seek critical feedback and identify resources to add to our pedagogical toolboxes.

To what extent are staff at your school or district prepared to enact a truly transformative approach to equity? To what extent are they prepared ideologically and practically? How can you support their growth and risk taking?

Part of the accounting we need to do as leaders is examining the ways schools and districts, as well as states and policymakers, incentivize *against* this kind of instruction and assessment, so that even if our curricula are equitable, our instructional strategies and assessments remain troublingly inequitable. It's a bit of a setup for teachers if we tell them that this is what they ought to be doing while we simultaneously enforce policies, practices, and assessment systems that undermine it. One of the most frequent requests we hear from teachers, school services personnel, and other people who work in schools is to convey to their leadership teams that they are, in fact, willing to make equity changes, take equity risks, and push themselves to grow. But they want to trust that leaders are doing everything they can to incentivize and celebrate their equity commitments and efforts.

Of course, this undertaking can feel like a monumental task these days, with efforts popping up all over the United States to restrict, or even criminalize, this kind of teaching. But we should read that context as an indication that we need additional layers of equity urgency. We should read it as a call to be unequivocal in our support and protection of staff who commit to applying the just access principle in their roles.

Just Access for Staff

"I am a lesbian and there is *no way* I'm coming out at this school," Patricia, a middle school language arts teacher, told us.

We had just finished meeting with Patricia and the other members of her school's equity committee. Timothy, the principal, had taken substantial time during the meeting to emphasize how welcoming his school was for LBGTQIA+ youth and staff. "It's one of our equity strengths," he said.

We asked whether any LGBTQIA+ students at the school were open about their sexual orientations or gender identities. "A few," Timothy said. We asked whether any LGBTQIA+ staff were out. He answered, "To my knowledge, we currently don't have any LGBTQIA+ staff. If we did, I'm sure they'd feel comfortable being open about it." We reminded him that often when nobody identifies openly at a school as, say, gay or gender-nonbinary, it can be a better indication of heterosexism or cisgenderism than an indication of the absence of LGBTQIA+ people.

It can be easy for people with privileged identities, including heterosexual and cisgender equity leaders, to presume things are better, more equitable, than they are. Timothy was riding his self-perception into dangerous, presumptuous equity waters. We explained as much, but Timothy remained insistent. "Maybe we struggle with some other equity concerns," he argued, "but this is a personal passion of mine."

After the meeting, as committee members filed out of the room, Patricia stayed to chat. As soon as she was alone with us, she opened up to us.

"This school is not safe, and Timothy is not safe." Patricia explained how, although Timothy did hire trainers to lead workshops about heterosexism and cisgenderism, staff largely felt that applying what they learned was optional. "Sure, the library has some books with queer characters, and we have an annual PD, but there's no accountability for staff who continue doing damage," she explained. She then clarified, "Sometimes that damage is to students or families, and sometimes it's to fellow staff members."

As Patricia reminds us, students aren't the only members of school communities experiencing bias and inequity. The just access principle applies to staff too. We've heard or observed instance after instance of awfully oppressive experiences among people in all sorts of professional education roles: a Black teacher whose colleagues keep asking about or even touching her hair, a teacher who speaks English with a Salvadoran accent routinely receiving lower student evaluations that students attribute explicitly to how he speaks, a Muslim teacher enduring bigotry posing as jokes about her religion in the teacher lounge. Regardless of what accolades or promotions those educators receive, these experiences do not signify just access.

We think about schools and districts where leaders invest a significant portion of equity energy recruiting a diverse teaching force. *We need to get our numbers up,* the thinking goes.

Yes, we do. Diversifying staff is an important equity move. But if we're focused only on the input or output, such as increasing the number of teachers of color, we are doomed to trap ourselves in perpetual hand-wringing over why our recruitment and retainment efforts so often fail. If we focus on just access, however, on ensuring that interactions, policies, and spaces are equitable, then those recruitment and retention numbers likely will take care of themselves.

So let's ask, *What, exactly, are we giving people access to in our recruitment efforts? Are we inviting more teachers of color, for example, into an institution where we're expecting them to* be the antiracism *rather than investing in institutional antiracism efforts?* Racially "diversifying" an organization is a worthy goal but does not in itself make that organization antiracist. If we make an organization antiracist, however, we may drastically increase the possibility of diversifying it and sustaining the diversification.

This is the just access principle in action: considering what we're doing to better reach or rethink our equity goals. We could offer increased salary and loan forgiveness and all sorts of other incentives to recruit people to work at our schools, but if they're walking into a toxic system, all the small equity moves in the world won't make their experience equitable.

A story from one of our recent school partnerships illustrates how a failure to apply the just access principle may combine with a lack of commitment to the principles we've described in previous chapters. Over several years, a small but committed group of students and faculty had been pushing the leadership team at Streamside High School to acknowledge and to take more serious action on racial inequities. Under pressure from this long-standing effort, coupled with the intensified focus on anti-Black racism in the wake of George Floyd's murder, the administrators announced that they did, in fact, desire change. Finally, it seemed like they were ready to *directly confront* inequity. They were embracing a willingness to examine inequitable systems within the school rather than leaning on *deficit ideology*. They would *fix injustice, not kids*.

Streamside's administrative team recognized a few staff, most of whom were staff of color, as having the skills and knowledge to help lead these efforts, so they tapped them ostensibly to reorient policy and practice toward equity. Initially, many staff members grew excited as momentum around the initiative built. They felt that maybe, just maybe, current equity efforts would be different from the false starts to which they had grown accustomed.

But this small group repeatedly faced administrators' concerns that they were pushing too hard, too fast: a classic example of the need for *prioritization*. When the group requested the opportunity to provide ongoing professional development for the entire Streamside staff, leadership resisted: "I don't know if we have time. Maybe you can call a voluntary meeting?"

One member of the leadership team cautioned the group, "It seems like you have an agenda that might alienate some people."

"You have to remember that not everyone is as comfortable or confident with this material as you are," the group was told.

Leadership supported performative steps such as launching town hall listening sessions but suggested that a task force should collect more data and propose changes that could be reviewed by another committee. "Don't forget," their principal said, "that pandemic-related budget cuts mean that ideas that cost money are off the table."

Meanwhile, as they buried every attempt at institutional change, Streamside leaders went out of their way to ensure that the district's communication department highlighted the work of student activists. This was leadership's way to demonstrate how antiracist the school was while refusing to embrace any real semblance of antiracism. In the wake of the biggest uprising against anti-Black racism and violence in a generation, the school fast-tracked the *optics* of antiracism and slow-tracked institutional change. And to do it, they drained the emotional and physical labor of a few passionate educators, mostly teachers and counselors of color.

Over time, staff at Streamside who once felt desperate to create change grew cynical. Some simply shut their classroom doors, resigned to focusing their energies on what they felt they had control over. "I learned once again I couldn't trust this school's equity intentions," one teacher shared. "It's always a bait and switch." Those who challenged leadership to push harder, to move more quickly, risked being reprimanded as difficult. The situation turned into an equity brain drain as some became so frustrated that they sought jobs elsewhere. Staff of color started leaving in droves.

Streamside administrators struggled to associate these turns of events with their own actions or inactions. When asked, they listed a litany of reasons staff of color left at a much higher rate than white staff: *They wanted to be closer to family. It just wasn't a good fit. They had a great opportunity at a different school. They wanted to be in a more diverse city.* They opted for gaslighting while ignoring the racial inequities that many educators suffered (Magwood, 2021).

To a person, the people leaving Streamside pointed to the administration's lack of resolve. "Racism is everywhere," one particularly frustrated teacher told us. "I knew what the larger community was like when I moved here. And I would have stayed, but the school was just as bad as the town. Maybe even worse."

School leaders could point to Streamside's diversity-oriented mission statement as evidence that they supported equity. They made a point to celebrate the diversity of the incoming staff, then shrugged off responsibility for the rotating door as they continued to undervalue and undermine an amazing cadre of equity-committed educators. Rather than *just access*, these leaders embraced optics and illusions of equity. They promoted and protected the *veneer* of equity, attempting to hide the reality of inequity underneath.

As we do with students, we must consider ways we might be falling short on *just access* for staff, making it harder to reach the equity goals we value. It happens when we pay lip service to equity but continually promote and hire people who lack basic knowledge or skills related to equity. It happens when we make empty statements in response to specific incidents and lean on bureaucratic regulation rather than the moral imperatives to disavow unjust conditions or behaviors. It happens when we run the same "Diversity 101" professional development programming over and over. Like a hamster running on a wheel, there *appears* to be forward motion without any real motion. It happens when we encourage a commitment to equity, then leave hanging the people leading the charge as soon as a powerful board member or parent complains.

In these ways and so many more, we convey what we value to staff. We must ensure that what we're communicating is that we value, that we *insist upon*, an institutional culture rooted in transformative equity. We insist upon cultivating learning and working spaces where the people most passionate about and capable of enacting transformative equity feel valued, supported, and indispensable rather than perpetuating spaces filled with equity trapdoors and landmines.

So yes, let's diversify our staffs. Let's do that now. Let's critically analyze all the code language such as "good fit" that undermines diversification efforts and build staffs that reflect the communities around them. That's an important step. But let's also ensure we are bringing staff into an actively anti-oppressive learning and working environment rather than inviting people into the oppression. That's how we sustain the diversification.

Conclusion

A school or district can have the world's best equity-oriented mission statement with the shiniest new buzzwords, and even equitable outcome data, and *still* be a place where students, families, and staff contend with xenophobia, cisgenderism, racism, ableism, and other forms of oppression. That's not equity. The just access principle demands we dig deeper.

Applying the just access principle is no small task. In many places, convincing power brokers to acknowledge and address even the most basic of inequitable outcomes is a hard- and long-fought battle. But committing to equitable outcomes without questioning what it is we're trying to accomplish in the first place won't get us very far.

The just access principle forces us to ask: *To what, exactly, are we giving people access with our equity efforts?* It forces us to reckon with whether what passes for equity in our spheres of influence is illusory, providing students with more access to curricula or courses or cultures that are still inequitable, or whether we're embracing a truly transformative equity approach. We applaud families, students, teachers, administrators, school board members, policymakers, and other stakeholders who are willing to reconsider *everything* to reveal the ways inequity is operating and root it out of schools and districts.

Figure 6.1 highlights some of the key points presented in this chapter. It summarizes the just access principle by illustrating, from a leader's point of view, the difference between mitigative equity and transformative equity in terms of actions and attitudes.

FIGURE 6.1

The Just Access Principle: Comparing Leaders' Mindsets Related to Mitigative Versus Transformative Equity

Mitigative Equity	Transformative Equity
I am reluctant to let go of traditions and rethink requirements. What we're doing is good; we just have to bring everyone up to speed.	I am willing to let go of traditions and rethink requirements. We may need fundamental shifts to build a school that is truly equitable, inclusive, and just.
I trust that if people have concerns, they will file them through the appropriate channels.	I follow up on whisper networks, presuming that there may not be enough faith in reporting systems for people to use them.
One of my equity goals is to help more students who have been underrepresented in AP and honors tracks be admitted into those tracks.	In addition to diversifying AP and honors tracks, we must ensure that what is happening in those tracks and in all classrooms is equitable. Equity might even mean rethinking tracking altogether.
I am determined to diversify the staff at my school or district so that it better reflects the student body and community.	I am determined to transform conditions in my school or district so that it is an equitable working environment for staff of color, LGBTQIA+ staff, and staff whose identities are underrepresented or who have had to hide parts of who they are to survive working there.

7

Interpreting Data with an Equity Lens: The Evidence-Based Equity Principle

As we sat in his office, Carter, a seasoned principal, waved a report in the air, then handed it to us. "Look at these numbers," he pleaded.

Carter had asked the district's data specialist to analyze data his school had started collecting to track participation in sports, student clubs, and other extracurricular activities. We were eager to explore the results. We appreciated that the school had disaggregated the data to a greater degree than we were accustomed to seeing. Instead of combining all Asian American and Pacific Islander (AAPI) students, for example, the data specialist had teased out for different ethnic groups.

Even though AAPI students had high rates of participation overall, students from Hmong families were the *least* likely group to participate in extracurriculars. Few of them participated in the school's sports or student clubs.

Carter was right to be concerned about this disparity. His concern was a good start. Studies have shown how participation in extracurriculars can foster a sense of belonging at school, predict higher student achievement, and increase postsecondary opportunities (Lang, 2021). But although the data indicated the *what* of the disparity—it showed what the disparity was—those data did not indicate the *why*. When it comes to equity, and especially to redressing inequity, we need to know the *why*.

Carter projected the *why* onto the *what*, misattributing the source of the problem. "This is what I've been trying to tell you," he said. "Don't these numbers prove that Hmong students just don't value school as much as other students?"

No, they didn't prove that. The results didn't prove anything at all about the *why*. They only showed that these students were less likely on average to participate in extracurriculars. In his desperation for answers, Carter had leaned on deficit-based presumptions and stereotypes rather than equity-based understandings. He jumped to pressing us for solutions that would fix the kids: "How can we convince Hmong families to value extracurriculars more, to value all the school has to offer?"

Carter had the data. But he didn't know how to interpret the data with an equity lens. In a way, that made his access to the data dangerous when it should've been helpful to the school's equity efforts.

Drawing from everything we've discussed in this book so far, can you think of examples of how data in your school or district have been, or are being, misinterpreted in ways that could exacerbate inequity? How would you interpret those data differently?

We arranged to speak with a group of Hmong American students so that we could understand their experiences more clearly. These conversations clarified the *why*.

"I don't want to spend one more minute at this school than I have to," Dieu-Anh said, eliciting snaps from her peers. They needed a break from the relentless stream of microaggressions they withstood at school from peers. Their interactions with teachers, coaches, and other staff had taught them not to rely on anyone to intervene. In fact, sometimes those adults were the sources of their harm.

One student pointed out that some of the activities required teacher referrals. "I don't feel like I have anyone to ask for a referral," he lamented.

"Honestly, I just don't care about football or hockey," Kevin told us toward the end of the focus group, initiating a conversation about the kinds of clubs or sports the students wished the school offered. "Nobody has asked what I'm interested in."

Whereas Carter embraced a deficit explanation for the low participation rates, the students pointed to an array of institutional explanations that made opting out the most reasonable option for them. Without those data, without those rich and nuanced explanations from the students whom Carter identified as needing intervention, he would have continued to misdiagnose the problem and, as a result, to intensify the inequity.

Those conversations helped refocus Carter's attention on solutions that would eliminate barriers for the Hmong American students: hosting meaningful professional development, holding staff accountable for culturally relevant and sustaining interactions with students, educating white students about how their interactions with peers did harm, seeking ideas from students about what sorts of activities they wanted to participate in, offering transportation options to make existing clubs and sports more accessible, finding antiracism training for the principal whose deficit views rendered him incapable of understanding fairly straightforward data. These solutions never occurred to Carter. As we discussed in Chapter 4, that's the danger of deficit ideology.

This is where the *evidence-based equity principle* can help us refocus our equity lenses on what data we ought to gather, how we ought to make sense of those data, and what we should do based on what we've learned from the information. Relying solely on quantitative data, interpreting data through a deficit lens, misapplying data collection tools: these are some of the ways we get stuck in mitigative dead ends or even create new layers of marginalization for students, staff, and families to navigate. If we hope to develop action plans that lead us toward transformative equity, we must expand our understanding of what counts as valuable data, interpret it through an equity lens, and exercise caution about the data collection tools and methods we embrace.

Remember the story we shared earlier about the woman who marches upstream to learn why babies are floating down the river? She's on a fact-finding mission, seeking the information necessary to create a plan of action that will address the root causes of the problem rather than the symptoms. Our efforts need to be similarly evidence-based. If we have any real shot at being transformative equity leaders—of preparing ourselves to recognize inequity, respond to it, and redress it in meaningful ways—then we need data that will help us understand what is really happening and *why*. We need approaches for data analysis that are rooted in systems thinking. And we need to devise evidence-based solutions that target the root causes of our equity problems.

Mining Data to Answer Equity Questions

Every school and district with which we've worked collects loads of data. However, even if those schools and districts do the most meticulous jobs with data collection, there's no guarantee that they will interpret or use those data in ways that support transformative equity. When we present the results of equity audits, we find that some people are bent on twisting them into validations of their existing biases or stereotypes. *Black boys are in the office at disproportionate rates compared with their peers? Well, that makes sense because they misbehave more often than other students.* As we've addressed in previous chapters, that is a bad, deficit-laced interpretation that will lead to bad, deficit-laden solutions. But it's also a common, and profoundly racially presumptuous, interpretation.

We may not even have the right data to help us understand as deeply as necessary how inequity is operating around us. For example, we know that, in many schools, we can predict which students will be referred disproportionately for behavior and which students will be suspended or expelled disproportionately. Often, as we've mentioned previously, these disproportionate referrals and consequences can be tracked primarily to a handful of teachers or policies. But if no one is paying attention to those patterns—if we only collect data about who is being referred for behavior, who is being suspended or expelled, without *also* tracking who is doing the referring and what their referral patterns might reflect—then any intervention intending to strengthen equity is unlikely to address the root causes of the disparity. So this is one very practical step: we should make sure that when we're collecting discipline data and other sorts of predictable disproportionality data, we're tracking not just the disproportionality's symptoms (such as which students are being referred and harshly disciplined) but also its causes (such as who is doing the referring, who is doling out the punishments, and for what sorts of infractions).

As a quick equity literacy exercise, can you think of data your school or district collects and analyzes that might paint a picture of inequity's symptoms but that don't reveal its causes? In other words, are there examples of ways you collect *what* data without *why* or *how* data? Try to identify two examples. What other data could you collect and analyze to provide a clearer, deeper picture of how inequity might be operating?

Another challenge we've encountered is that, although regulations require that we collect certain data, those data may not be used in ways that could support transformative equity. We worked with one principal, Abby, who was stunned to learn that she sent students of color to the alternative high school six times more often than white students. "I don't see my students' race," she explained, "so race can't have anything to do with it."

Despite having the data, nobody on her team had ever examined them for those sorts of patterns. They weren't nefariously evading this deeper data collection or analysis process. It wasn't an active refusal to look at the patterns. Instead, the barrier was a lack of equity understanding, of equity curiosity. It was a missed opportunity for the principal to better understand the nature of racism and racial equity and to examine the ways she might be perpetuating it despite, or *because of,* her claim of "color blindness."

In fact, our sense is that, in most cases, these inadequate systems of data collection and interpretation aren't caused by leaders who make decisions with the specific goal of evading or burying important information (although we have seen that happen, too). In most cases we don't see it as intentional neglect. As with Abby, we usually see it as a missed opportunity. These data can inform professional development for staff members who contribute to disproportionate referrals; they can inform policies and practices; they can bolster our equity efforts. But they can help us do these things only if we use and interpret them with an equity lens.

In fact, as equity leaders, we should be curious enough to make sure somebody is tracking *our* patterns, somebody who will be honest with us about the damage we might be doing. We can't rightly expect staff to buy into this sort of accountability system if we are unwilling to model self-accountability.

What sorts of data might somebody collect to ensure you are leading in equitable ways? Who in your school or district can you trust to be frank with you about what those data reveal?

The Equity Limitations of Data Collection Instruments

Sometimes, data collection tools themselves have troubling limitations. A few years ago, while visiting Cadence Creek, a small high school nestled in the hills of the Pacific Northwest region of the United States, we met a student we'll call Simone. We had just spent the day with her school's leadership team, helping them organize an equity audit. Simone hurried toward us as we were leaving the building.

"I have a story I need to tell you," she said as she pulled us aside.

A major challenge at Cadence Creek, as in many schools, was the leadership team's habit of embracing trendy programs while avoiding meaningful interrogations of troubling institutional issues, especially those involving equity. During their most recent foray into fashionable programs, they embraced trauma-sensitive care. The school invested in trauma-sensitive training for teachers. They prepared school counselors to help identify students who carried the impacts of trauma to school with them. The emphasis was building-wide.

Earlier that day, Patricia, Cadence Creek's principal, was beside herself with enthusiasm when we discussed this initiative. "I tried something like this at my previous school," she shared, "but it didn't take." She explained that staff were more open to the idea now that she presided over a more racially and economically diverse school.

Simone wasn't as enthusiastic about this new effort as her principal. "I'm a Black woman, transgender," she told us. As far as she knew, she was the only openly transgender student at Cadence Creek. She explained how, several weeks earlier, her counselor had summoned her to his office. When she arrived, he invited her to sit, then began administering a questionnaire to her. "He asked a lot of personal questions about my life, what I've experienced at home," she told us. "It was intrusive."

When Simone inquired about the questions and why her counselor was asking them, he explained that she exhibited signs of trauma. Her grades were slipping, and according to some teachers, she seemed to be withdrawing socially. He told her the questionnaire would help him learn more about the challenges she faced so that he could support her more effectively.

"He called it 'ACEs,'" she shared, "for 'adverse childhood experiences.'" Simone grew animated describing how awkward and offput she felt. After all, she explained, she had no reason to trust her counselor enough to answer such personal questions.

"Here's what I want you to know," she told us. "The most adverse experiences in my life have happened *here*. My biggest source of trauma is how I'm treated at this school. That's what I told my counselor."

"How did he respond?" we asked.

"He said there was nothing on the ACEs questionnaire about that."

Simone looked around, worried somebody might overhear her. Then she described unrelenting transphobic and racist bullying at Cadence Creek and how inadequately adults in the school addressed it. She explained what a struggle it had been trying to convince teachers to use her correct pronouns and name, how humiliated she felt by her absolute invisibility in health and other curricula, and how traumatized she was by a whole host of other conditions that made school the bane of her well-being.

"Nobody has asked me about any of this," she said. "Not my counselor or anybody else. And when I mention it, they act like there's nothing they can do."

Here's what we appreciate about what was happening at Cadence Creek. School leaders had sufficient insight to know they needed to take a closer look at how equity was or wasn't operating. That takes some measure of humility. They were willing to collect data to identify problems, look for solutions, and invest resources in those solutions. Many of the staff with whom we met were deeply concerned about students, including Simone. At least that's how they saw it.

The trouble was, they tapped the wrong knowledges, the wrong voices, in their data collection. They weren't considering the right kinds of evidence. It is all kinds of disconcerting that they would go through the trouble of implementing trauma-informed care, embracing the ACEs tool, and investing in several days of training, but never get around to asking Simone what her most significant barriers were, what she needed, or what, if any, harms had befallen her *at school*. So that measure of humility may have been overmatched, either by a measure of overconfidence or by significant misunderstanding.

It hadn't occurred to Simone's counselor or Cadence Creek leadership that any authentic approach to trauma-informed care begins with an honest reckoning of the ways students, families, and even staff experience trauma *at school*, that when we skip that sort of accounting the entire trauma-sensitive project becomes an unmitigated hypocrisy (Gorski, 2021; Venet, 2021). Notably, the original ACEs questionnaire and many of its most popular revisions are also silent on the adverse childhood experiences of systemic racism, institutionalized cisgenderism, and most other forms of oppression. Because nobody knew to, or because everybody chose not to, ask the right questions, and because they relied on programs and initiatives that created the optics of equity progress while obscuring the lived experiences of people experiencing inequity, they interpreted the problem as "Simone has experienced trauma." And they assumed this happened outside school. That's what the ACEs instrument revealed. But that wasn't the problem. The problem was that *they were traumatizing Simone*.

The solution to the former: offer Simone emotional and academic supports. The only possible solution to the latter: eliminate the racism and transphobia. That's what the school wasn't doing. So even in the context of trauma-sensitive education, the school was deteriorating Simone's trust and enabling her biggest source of trauma. That wasn't the intention, of course. But it was Simone's experience; it was the impact the school's approach was having on Simone. And that, after all, is a much clearer measure of equity progress than intentions.

This example illustrates how the evidence-based equity principle interacts with the prioritization principle: the people experiencing the harm are the most important experts on the harm's nature and impact. As we collect data, we must prioritize their perspectives, needs, wants, and joys before we (preferably jointly) develop solutions to the harm. Simone had pleaded with one of her assistant principals to hold teachers who refused to respect her name and pronouns accountable. Instead, her counselor gave her the ACEs questionnaire. The school answered harm with harm.

Data on Experience, Not Just Achievement

Here are the two big lessons from the evidence-informed equity principle: (1) we must exercise caution about how we collect and interpret more conventional quantitative data that are focused on inputs and outputs such as discipline referrals and graduation rates, and (2) we should consider other kinds of data that can help us learn more about how students experience schools. Before we dive into ideas for considering what constitutes a broader range of meaningful evidence, we want to recommend the book *Street Data: A Next-Generation Model for Equity, Pedagogy, and School Transformation*, by Shane Safir and Jamila Dugan (2021). It's an enlightening nuts-and-bolts resource that has expanded our understandings of what data to solicit and what existing data to reinterpret.

Soliciting Equity Feedback

Qualitative data such as stories we collect using focus groups, observations from equity walk-throughs, and survey items that elicit short, open-ended answers can help paint more detailed pictures than quantitative metrics alone of how deeply inequity runs in a school. They can help us dig beneath the *what* to excavate the *why*. We would like to offer a few words of caution, however, about gathering this type of data.

For example, inviting people to revisit their trauma for public consumption during focus groups or listening sessions with unfulfilled promises of follow-up action can do more harm than good. Remember, focus groups, listening sessions, and town halls do not constitute the equity action. The question is, what do we do with what we learn during these activities? If we don't intend to respond directly to people's concerns by changing what we do in schools, it's unethical and inequitable to request that they share their experiences.

When we conduct focus groups with students, they often voice this concern. For example, Maria, who identified as a "proud Chicana student," shared, "To be honest, I didn't want to do this focus group. . . . We talk to people all the time, and nothing happens." Based on previous experiences at her school, she was worried that meeting with us would be at best a waste of her time and at worst another way she would be exploited without any real hope of her school experience changing. She had tried to communicate her frustrations to adults in her school. Her attempts to use formal channels were ignored, and her informal attempts were deemed "disrespectful" by several adults. Why should she want to continue making herself vulnerable?

How can you ensure that the gift of honest feedback you ask students and their families to share will lead to the change they demand? How can you ensure it will not lead to more inaction, empty promises, or, worse, retribution?

We also need to be careful about documenting our *attempts* at equity as evidence of *actual* equity. For example, during a conversation with LGBTQIA+ students, we asked about the large number of "Safe Space" stickers we saw throughout their school. If we judged by the number of those stickers alone, we might presume the school was overwhelmingly safe, welcoming, and equitable for LGBTQIA+ people.

"Those 'Safe Space' stickers are cosmetic trash," one student shared. The students with whom we talked didn't trust several teachers who displayed the stickers. "If our Gay-Straight Alliance could post those stickers where we actually felt safe, there would be *far* fewer," one student insisted. The equity evidence is not the presence of the sticker, but whether the lived experiences of the students are changing. The only way to gather that evidence is by talking with the people experiencing the oppression.

We are reminded of a story we heard from a friend, a powerful equity leader who identified passionately with her Puerto Rican heritage. She sounded frustrated as she described how a white colleague had confided in her over lunch one day. "Don't worry about working here; I'm your ally," the colleague told her.

"*I* get to decide who my allies are," our friend noted. "*I* get to decide when I can trust you."

We are accountable to the people whom we profess to champion in our equity efforts. *Their* assessment of our equity health is our gauge for the direction we're headed. Sometimes this means we need to formally collect and analyze data. But there are other forms of evidence, as well, as we discuss below.

No Evidence of Inequity ≠ Equity

"Nobody has complained to me about sexism," Frederick, a principal, told us. In his view, that meant that sexism wasn't a problem at his school. Of course, we know that in almost every school, students, staff, and others *absolutely* experience sexism. We also know based on hundreds of focus groups with girls and young women and with gender-nonbinary students that the more likely scenario is that they do not trust school leaders enough to report the sexism or cisgenderism they may be experiencing. In several focus groups conducted at Frederick's school, students confirmed our suspicions, sharing one troubling example after another of sexism in the school.

The reality is that sexism is rampant in most schools. The other reality is that most students worry there's a bigger price to pay by reporting it than by keeping it to themselves. They have lost faith in school leaders who often don't believe them or minimize their concerns. Some express fear of retribution.

As we use data to determine the genuine equity health of a school, we mustn't mistake the absence of official *reports* of inequity for the actual absence of inequity. In fact, we might better interpret the absence as evidence that students, staff, or others don't feel safe reporting inequity. Perhaps we need to build stronger systems of accountability. Perhaps we need to establish more trusting relationships with students by demonstrating consistently that we're taking their concerns seriously.

Reams of narrative data swirl around us constantly. Be sure not to ignore or dismiss them. They are as important as any other data. For example, whisper networks among students often point directly to an inequity and its source: a problematic policy or an inequitable application of policy, a demeaning school tradition, a deficit-minded staff member. When we catch wind of these conversations, we need to follow up rather than dismiss them as gossip or outlier experiences. Simone's experiences at Cadence Creek, the stories she shared with us, were critical data. It was notable, and disturbingly so, that she was more comfortable sharing them with us than with her school's leaders.

What dynamics exist in your school or district that might dissuade students who are experiencing inequity from reporting it? What can you do to address those dynamics?

As another example, students who are marginalized at school often congregate in spaces where they feel safe and, to the extent possible, avoid spaces where they don't. We can learn a lot from teachers, counselors, and other educators to whose offices or classrooms these students are drawn. What sorts of relationships are they constructing with these students? How are they establishing and sustaining trust?

We've even helped schools map these spaces. We provide the maps to students of color, LGBTQIA+ students, and other groups of students who disproportionately face inequity and ask them to mark the places where they feel relatively safe and welcome as well as spaces where they feel especially marginalized. When we accumulate their responses onto a single map, it often becomes very clear not only which spaces they avoid but also who they consider a particular threat and who they consider a trusted ally.

One practical thing we can do as equity leaders is to make sure we are providing multiple ways for students to share their stories with people they trust. We want official, formal reporting structures, of course. But we don't want to rely on those alone to gauge the volume of inequity in our schools and districts.

In what ways do students, staff, and families communicate their equity concerns in your school or district? What formal channels exist? What informal channels exist? Are they used more or less often than formal channels?

Your answers to those questions may reveal important next steps for building better data systems that will help you recognize, respond to, and redress inequity, as well as cultivate and sustain equity.

Embracing Negative Feedback

Another important question to ask ourselves is whether we pay more attention to *how* students, staff, and families communicate their concerns than to the concerns themselves. When we find ourselves growing defensive or wanting to explain away an inequity that someone has bravely, generously chosen to share with us, remember this tweet advice from our friend and colleague Marceline DuBose (2022): "Anyone who takes the time to . . . share with you that a choice you made had a ripple effect is giving you a gift. Of information. Of relationship. Of connection and caring. They haven't written you off yet."

That word, *yet*, is important. How we respond to repeated efforts to communicate with us may determine whether we are written off. As we've mentioned several times, *feedback is a gift* even if it comes wrapped in packaging we don't like. It's crucial data. If we continuously refuse to receive it, if we toss it aside, eventually the giver will stop giving. That is the worst possible scenario. Learning how to embrace this gift is crucial to enacting the evidence-based equity principle.

Next we describe three sources of this sort of data or evidence that we, as equity leaders, might not immediately recognize as data or evidence: troublemakers, wallflowers, and whistleblowers. If we can adjust our lenses to see the evidence they're gifting us, we might uncover a wealth of guidance for achieving transformative equity.

Troublemakers. Sometimes the most important feedback comes in forms we might initially interpret as troublemaking or disruption. Christopher Emdin's (2021) description of "ratchet academics" deviating from whiteness in schools and Carla Shalaby's (2017) portraits of young children in the book *Troublemakers* call us to question whether the students who openly, defiantly resist schooling aren't right and brave to do so. They are the proverbial canaries in the coal mine, alerting us to ways our community needs to be more humane, loving, and equitable.

We might consider questions like these: Who are the "troublemakers" in your school or district? What are they communicating? What can you learn from them about how to lead more equitably?

We can start by learning to interpret these behaviors in ways that help us receive the messages students are sending us about the ways we may be failing or harming them. In many districts we hear about incidents in which racially and otherwise marginalized students are involved in some sort of disruption. Leaders often reactively apply punitive measures in these situations, missing another opportunity to practice transformative equity leadership.

We're reminded of Gold Elm, a high school we visited several years ago. We happened to be visiting during homecoming week, so that Friday we decided to observe the pep rally for the football team, which would play its homecoming game that evening. As we entered the gym, we noticed, as we often do, a dozen or so students sitting in the top corner of the bleachers, as far away from the action as they could possibly be. They were making faces and gestures that appeared to be mocking the pep rally. They seemed annoyed at having to sit through the cheers and the cajoled expressions of school spirit, and they seemed to want people to recognize their annoyance.

Eventually an assistant principal was dispatched to insist they stop disrupting the pep rally. Later we learned that a couple of the students asked at that time if they could go to the library during the rest of the pep rally. "Why do we have to sit through this?" one of the students asked. As that conversation grew louder, more and more students turned to see what was happening up in that corner of the bleachers. The assistant principal who had just refused to allow those students to go to the library then took them to the office.

Later that day we asked the leadership team how they intended to handle the situation. We had been working with them on how to find important data in these sorts of incidents rather than responding reactively, punitively. The assistant principal who had escorted the students to the office shared that several of them were "known troublemakers" at the school, "among our most disengaged students." His impulse was to respond to our question by exploring disciplinary options. Then Pamela, the principal, modeled exactly what we had been working on with her team. She asked, "What can we learn from the students you're calling 'known troublemakers'?"

"Let me tell you," she continued. "I likely would've been one of those students in high school. When I look at this another way, I might argue that those quote-unquote *disruptive students* were the only people in that gym who saw through our shaky expectation that everybody ought to have school spirit."

That's when the other assistant principal shared, "I'm wondering why students who don't feel like they belong here would have school spirit. I'm wondering how many students feign school spirit just to try to survive here socially. I mean, if I was a gay student being pounded every day with homophobic jokes, would I *really* feel excited to be here just because of the accident that my family lives near the school?"

That was a powerful bit of data analysis, of data interpretation.

Notice the shift in the conversation. Perhaps by some rigid definition, the students were being disruptive. But they also were being honest. Their behavior was data, not just about who they are but also about what the school is. Imagine how much of a missed opportunity this could have been if it had been interpreted solely as a disciplinary issue.

Taking this road can be difficult. Sometimes as leaders we are under tremendous pressure to punish troublemakers regardless of cause. For example, a district we recently worked with exploded with controversy after a principal refused to escalate punishment for a student who pushed her. Instead of expelling him, she opted to engage with him to learn what he was experiencing and why he would resort to an action that could risk his educational future.

His actions weren't without consequence. We certainly aren't condoning physical violence. But rather than reactively applying the harshest discipline, what we call *reactive rule-flinging,* the principal leaned into relationship building with him and his family, trying to model the commitment to equity she was cultivating in the school. She knew that the school-to-prison pipeline was very real, especially for a young man of color, and that her actions, and her interpretation of *his* actions, could affect his life trajectory for years to come.

Upon receiving several complaints from families and staff that her "inaction" made them feel unsafe, the school board terminated the principal's contract. This, too, is data. It turns out, this student had *never* felt safe in the district. After more than a decade of alienation, he had given up trying to play the game of school. Giving up felt easier than buying into school and repeatedly being disappointed. The anxiety and hurt spiked until he did something he regretted. Understanding this context, attempting to see the data in the incident and what it evidenced about his school experiences, the principal was trying to help him through the situation and to learn from it.

Situations like this remind us to ask: *Whose safety do we prioritize? To whose concerns do we respond, and how?* In your school or district, to what degree are you focused only on moment-to-moment safety, responding only when big disruptive events occur, and to what extent are you responsive to the impacts of longtime, ongoing, grinding institutional and structural harm? How do you collect and interpret data about that harm?

If we're embracing transformative equity, we should have a plan for how we respond when students are "disruptive" or when they "misbehave" or "act up" because they have reached a breaking point with racism, heterosexism, or any institutional cause of marginalization. We need to consider what we'll do when students decide to take an issue into their own hands after we, the adults, inadequately address the heterosexism, economic injustice, or sexism they're experiencing at school. And again, we need to learn how to see the data in incidents that can tell us something about equity, about ourselves. How are "troublemaking" students in your school seen by their peers and staff? What does that interpretation say about the school and its degree of belongingness?

Wallflowers. Sometimes resistance to inequity doesn't take the form of disruption. Instead, it's expressed through withdrawal. Some students might silence themselves as a survival technique, avoid certain spaces or people, or find other ways to fade into the background with the hopes of protecting themselves from harm (Rodriguez, 2020; San Pedro, 2015). We often come across educators who do the same within their schools, especially educators who are routinely shushed or shamed for speaking up about inequity. When it comes to students and the need to better identify and understand potential inequity, we must examine *why* they might choose withdrawal rather than rely solely on output data suggesting they're not engaged.

We've heard countless stories from Black and Brown students who, like the Hmong American students we discussed earlier, face such overwhelming micro- and macroaggressions that they no longer have energy to, or simply choose not to, engage in certain classes or experiences. Of course, sometimes students are just reserved or introverted. But something more institutional could be at play, especially if the input and output data demonstrate predictable demographic patterns.

If we are trying to document and analyze inequity, then we must be willing to ask what it is about a policy or practice that could make shutting down, blending in, or fading away the most rational, safest choice for some students to make. And when students do shut down, what does it tell us about ourselves?

Whistleblowers. Another form of feedback or data that we might initially interpret simply as resistance happens when people forego official channels and speak out publicly about injustice in a school or district. We've been particularly inspired by the #BlackAt campaigns in which schools' alumni and students take the institution to task by publicly naming and demanding action on institutional racism. We've also witnessed walkouts and marches meant to draw attention to racist or sexist dress codes, the firing of an LGBTQIA+ teacher, book banning, and more.

The question for us as equity leaders is, are we inspired to learn, grow, and act in the face of this criticism? Can we accept it as a gift, as important data, as feedback about what we need to do better? Or is our instinct to resort to reputation management, to downplay or dismiss publicly expressed concerns? If it's the latter, we once again might be missing an important opportunity to learn from data that are falling right into our laps.

In 2015 in Pearland, Texas, just south of Houston, high school freshman Coby Burren texted his mother a picture from his McGraw-Hill world geography textbook (Fernandez & Hauser, 2015). The image included a map titled "Largest Ancestry Reported by Country," with color-coded regions of the United States indicating a range of ethnic demographics. One of the captions linked to the Southeast, where the largest ancestry group was recorded as "African American," read, "The Atlantic Slave Trade between the 1500s and 1800s brought millions of workers from Africa to the southern United States to work on agricultural plantations."

Roni Dean-Burren, Coby's mother, posted to social media the photo and a video of her flipping through the book. After her posts went viral, McGraw-Hill promised to change the caption so that it described the enslavement of Africans as "forced migration." The Pearland School District promised not to use the textbook to teach that specific content.

Recently we shared this case with a district leadership team as part of a professional learning exercise. When we asked for participants' responses, without missing a beat the superintendent exclaimed, "That is *outrageous*."

We agreed, and then quickly realized we had very different motivations for being outraged. "The mother should have come to the school with her concerns!" he argued, marking her, rather than the racism, as the problem. As the conversation unfolded, several members of his cabinet shared their frustration with similar events in their district—times when students or families had taken to social media to express their inequity concerns. "They should have gone through the proper channels," one department head insisted. Instead of interpreting this case as a multilevel failure of district equity leadership—the selection of the textbook, for example—the leadership team chastised the student and his mother, sympathizing with the district administrators for being dragged unfairly.

In response, we asked *why* a Black student or parent might not trust the school and might be hesitant to bring their concerns to school or district leadership. What rationales might this student and his mother have for avoiding "proper channels"? We challenged the team to distinguish between people using social media to point out valid concerns about structural racism and people using it to protect racist structures through disinformation campaigns. Drawing upon the prioritization principle, we asked whose interests the team was prioritizing when they focused on policing a response to racism rather than focusing on the undeniably racist framing in the textbook and the harm it could do to students.

Notably, the leaders' response illustrated why Coby and his mother might have avoided formal channels. When we pointed this out, the superintendent replied, "When you put it that way, I see what you mean."

As we talked, we encouraged the team to shift their interpretation of this case. It was a great example of the evidence-based equity principle in action. Coby pointed to the kinds of experiences that made his schooling inequitable. That was a gift. It was data. The family's use of social media to pressure the publishing company and the district encouraged a more equitable and just curriculum; their action also was a sort of data, perhaps evidencing that the district had a lot of work to do to earn the trust of Black families. And although the publisher and school district taking note of this flawed textbook page was an important first step, their responses left *much* to be desired when viewed through an equity lens. Those responses constitute a kind of data too.

Responding to Equity Feedback

The best-case equity scenario has several elements. First, the data we use to make decisions about the inequities we need to eliminate and how best to eliminate them include appropriately disaggregated quantitative measures *and* qualitative accounts. Second, they include information we have collected intentionally as well as unsolicited feedback communicated to us in a variety of ways. And third, we're analyzing these data through a structural lens that avoids deficit interpretations or explanations.

Another important piece of the evidence-based equity principle is to consider what we as equity leaders do with that data. A few key commitments can help.

Commitment One: Listen, Believe, Validate

We should never, under any circumstance, invalidate or attempt to soften people's experience of bias or inequity when they share it with us, whether it's part of formal data collection or an informal conversation. Far too often, the Simones of the world are told that they're misinterpreting things and admonished to be less sensitive. *That couldn't happen here. I'm sure it's just a misunderstanding. That doesn't sound like something they would do.*

Instead, we should listen, believe, and validate. *That's terrible. I can't imagine how difficult that must be. I'm so sorry you're experiencing this. Thank you for sharing this with me.* And we need to make sure *everybody* in our sphere of influence is committed to these three actions: listen, believe, validate.

Remember our gaslighting discussion in Chapter 3? One of the best ways to deteriorate trust and to layer on additional harm is to invalidate or even suggest that we don't believe that what someone is telling us could be true. This doesn't mean we don't follow up with questions or seek additional evidence as we determine a course of action. However, when we dismiss out of hand someone's story about experiencing ableism, racism, cisgenderism, or some other form of oppression as impossible or incomprehensible, we create another obstacle for the person to overcome and additional evidence that we are untrustworthy. We also cheat ourselves out of the possibility that people experiencing harm will continue sharing their experiences with us.

Commitment Two: Listen, Believe, Validate, and Then *Act*

Remember that listening to and validating people's stories is not itself the equity change. The equity change is what we do in response to that information. If we are unwilling to hold ourselves and one another accountable for harm, then we are not committed to real equity change. If we are unwilling to fundamentally change a policy, a practice, a curriculum, or an entire institutional culture, wringing out the xenophobia, ableism, or Islamophobia, then our commitments are shaky at best. If we're unwilling to *act*, then it's exploitive to ask people to make themselves vulnerable by sharing their experiences or rehashing their trauma. In those cases, our listening sessions, focus groups, or town halls become spectacles that may be more unjust than doing nothing at all.

We see this happen far too often: a school arranges a listening session with, say, families experiencing poverty, asking them to make themselves vulnerable and talk about experiences that are painful, even embarrassing. Maybe staff members nod and applaud and voice appreciation, but then *nothing changes*. Or maybe leaders make changes that have little to do with the parents' suggestions; everything proceeds as though school leadership knows better than those parents what the school ought to be doing to achieve equity. Or, worst-case scenario, the criticism of the school comes back to bite the parents through some kind of retribution against them or their children by leaders who feel threatened in some way.

The ultimate question is not what we learn when we collect data but how we use what we learn. When it comes to equity, sympathy, pity, or guilt without any subsequent effort to address the root causes of the problems people share with us is at best meaningless and at worst additionally harmful. Determination to foment change and do better, and then actually fomenting the change and doing better: this is what equity leaders do.

Commitment Three: Own It

As we argued in Chapter 5, somebody who has been harmed by heterosexism, racism, or economic injustice in school should never be cajoled into a restorative encounter with the aggressor or into any other arrangement that risks further trauma or oppression. It's *our responsibility*, as leaders, to hold people in our spheres of influence accountable when they do harm. We should never pass that responsibility onto the people who have been, or continue to be, harmed.

Returning to Simone's story, we were most struck by her comment that she was less exhausted from the abuse she endured than from the effort she exerted trying to convince adults in her school to use her correct pronouns and name. Her experience was a failure of equity leadership. It wasn't Simone's responsibility to convince adults who had power over her to treat her equitably. Nobody who is being oppressed should have to convince anybody doing the oppressing of anything. That is *our* labor as leaders.

Conclusion

If we hope to maximize the power of the evidence-based equity principle, we must apply it in concert with the other equity leadership principles. In terms of the direct confrontation principle, this means consistently, routinely, and explicitly collecting data that illuminate the equity health of our schools and districts with regard to ableism, cisgenderism, economic injustice, racism, heterosexism, and other forms of oppression. In relation to the fix injustice, not kids principle, we collect and interpret data using a structural rather than a deficit lens. Adhering to the prioritization principle, we consider what is best for the people who the system has harmed, alienated, or excluded *according to the people who have been harmed, alienated, or excluded.* If we apply the just access principle, it means considering what data we are collecting about student *experiences*, not just outcomes or inputs.

Ultimately, the evidence-based equity principle is about recognizing and collecting meaningful data that help us as leaders understand when, where, and how harm has been done, how inequity is operating, and why disparities exist. But if our goal is to redress, repair, and heal, we also need to accurately interpret data and act transformatively in response to what we learn.

Figure 7.1 highlights some of the key points presented in this chapter. It summarizes the evidence-based equity principle by illustrating, from a leader's point of view, the difference between mitigative equity and transformative equity in terms of actions and attitudes.

FIGURE 7.1

The Evidence-Based Equity Principle: Comparing Leaders' Mindsets Related to Mitigative Versus Transformative Equity

Mitigative Equity	Transformative Equity
If we can ensure equitable access and outcomes using traditional metrics, we've been successful.	I am aware of the inequities baked into common metrics and assessments and seek out a variety of other data to document (in)equity within the school.
I regularly review disaggregated data to set goals for future metrics.	I regularly review disaggregated data, looking for any disconcerting patterns or trends, and then follow up with more qualitative data collection to understand why those patterns or trends exist.
When students resist, we need to find better ways to support them.	I consider how various forms of resistance are a type of feedback about the health of our community.
People need to learn the most effective way to express concerns about equity before I can hear them.	I welcome feedback about inequity as a gift, even if it comes in ways I would not prefer.

8

Strengthening Community Through Equity: The Care, Joy, and Sustainability Principle

When we started writing this book, we had no idea what was in store for our lives and our world. Our best-laid plans fluttered away. It has been a time full of tragedy, injustice, and hardship. At a time when a global pandemic exacerbated long-standing disparities, other challenges loomed: devastating natural disasters linked to climate change raged, grief and anger intensified over the flagrant disregard for Black life, anti-Asian attacks and other forms of racism and xenophobia flared. In some districts, groups of parents and teachers fought fiercely over mask mandates and in-person schooling. Parent organizations, sometimes backed by national political interests, waged war against more or less everything related to equity in schools. Multiple school shootings took the lives of students and teachers. We could go on.

Despite the ugliness and pain of these struggles, many people found seeds of hope. Whenever we come together to work against injustice, we create the possibility for something new, something more just. There is beauty, hope, and joy in that possibility, fighting for space and voice alongside the cynicism, outrage, and hurt.

It's not always easy to hold onto that hope, especially when enthusiasm for a more equitable world is fleeting or gains are so easily erased. For example, when Darnella Frazier's video of police murdering George Floyd went viral, we witnessed an unparalleled and global wave of support for Black Lives Matter, shifting public opinion in the United States and around the world. Suddenly, greater numbers of people, especially white people, were more likely to support structural changes in policing and other institutions. Superintendents, principals, heads of school, school boards, and boards of trustees penned a flood of public statements claiming solidarity with Black communities and asserting their commitments to equity. The wordsmiths at Merriam-Webster even changed their definition of *racism* to incorporate its systemic nature (Cineas, 2020).

Then came the blowback.

Media and organizations hostile to equity efforts intensified anti-equity rhetoric, drumming up fear around critical race theory in schools. Legislators passed, and continue to pass, "divisive concept" bills that in essence ban teachers from teaching the truth about racism, heterosexism, cisgenderism, and other forms of oppression. Well-organized parent groups descended on school board meetings to excoriate leaders who invested in even the faintest equity efforts, sometimes demanding their firing. Some fought to criminalize curriculum and ban books. Political candidates began running on anti-equity platforms. The backlash was just as passionate as the movement to which it was responding.

Cowed by the backlash, the initial apparent spike in antiracist interest proved shaky. Many of the antiracist book clubs white people had joined in droves led to little action. Public opinion polls showed sliding support for Black Lives Matter. Districts canceled equity-related professional development, sometimes under the orders of school boards. Some of the leaders who had penned those passionate letters of solidarity with Black communities suddenly requested that we talk about equity without using the word *equity* during our professional development workshops, or that we avoid using terms such as *racism*, *privilege*, and *whiteness* to describe racism, privilege, and whiteness.

If any of this surprised us, we weren't paying very close attention. Bias, inequity, and systemic oppression do not slip quietly into the night. The racism wasn't new even if it was intensified in response to what might have seemed like bits of progress toward racial justice. The antiracism wasn't new. The well-organized resistance to the antiracism wasn't new. It was the same old story. And where has it left us? With racism, with inequity.

Nurturing transformative equity has *always* been challenging. Even in the best of times, consistently recognizing, responding to, and redressing deep structural inequities is emotionally and intellectually taxing. Cultivating and sustaining equity is too. And these are not the best of times.

Even the most benign forms of diversity, equity, and inclusion efforts in schools are under attack by people angling to protect their privilege. Equity and critical race theory are their bogeymen.

However, as we've stated before, these struggles are not our reason to back off. They're our reason to dig in.

So with all the pushback and resistance, with the threats of lawsuits against our schools and districts and perhaps even threats to our own jobs, how do we garner support for transformative equity, avoid despair and discouragement, and plug into the joy and connection we unlock by building more equitable school communities? How do we sustain ourselves for the long haul? That is what the *care, joy, and sustainability principle* is about; it grounds everything else in this book. It's a reminder that there is no transformative equity without caring for ourselves and for one another. As Audre Lorde (2017) and many others have pointed out, there's room for joy in justice work.

As difficult and precarious as transformative equity leadership can be, especially for leaders experiencing the inequities they're also bent on upending (Irby et al., 2022), it also can fill our metaphorical cups. Care and joy can help sustain us in the face of exhaustion, so it's worth spending time outlining ways to nurture them. In this chapter, we explore what this looks and feels like, and how we can sustain ourselves and our equity efforts by embracing an approach that has room for care and joy along with anger, outrage, and disappointment. These feelings are not mutually exclusive.

To be clear, we're not talking about the care and joy of false positivity, the kindness or niceness that people weaponize to avoid the realities of injustice. We're talking about care and joy as ingredients for equity leadership, something we can mix with our urgency and outrage. That is what the care, joy, and sustainability principle is about.

Before we explore this principle, we want to mention that we fretted over whether to include this chapter at all. We worried how it might come across, two white authors writing what might be read as a fluffy, feel-good principle after spending all these chapters establishing a direct, institutional, transformative vision for equity leadership. We decided to include it in large part because we've witnessed so many of our equity-committed colleagues burning out. Many express how hard it can be, believing they are completely alone in their commitments, individuals feeling as though they are struggling against entire systems. So, we thought, why not acknowledge that reality and discuss what we might do about the exhaustion and despair the effort could engender for some of us?

We also want to clarify that, in our view, this principle is not fluffy at all. Here's what we know from the research on burnout among people doing equity- and justice-oriented work (Gorski, 2019): burnout and turnover among the people most ardently committed to equity and justice is one of the biggest threats to the sustainability of equity efforts. Yes, burnout is an individual issue; we must do a better job taking care of ourselves. But it's also a *community* issue.

For example, although as far as we know there are no data on turnover rates among school- and district-level equity specialists, our experience suggests the rates are *very* high. It's not uncommon for people in those roles to move between schools or districts every couple of years, hoping to find some place, *any* place, where they feel supported to do what they ostensibly were hired to do. That turnover is disruptive and oppressive to the people in those roles, which is reason enough to be concerned. But it's also disruptive to the work they are doing. It's disruptive to equity progress in schools and districts. These are serious, not fluffy, concerns.

Maybe you aren't on the verge of burnout. Maybe you already have found ways to channel the outrage and disappointment that are inescapable for people deeply invested in equity so that they don't threaten your well-being. Even so, we all can learn how to support one another better.

We begin by exploring what it means to embrace and enact equity in community and to build a community with the intention of cultivating and sustaining equity. Then we discuss what a care ethic looks like, in terms of both caring for our own well-being as equity advocates and caring for one another in the context of this important work.

Community for an Equity Commitment

As we've argued throughout this book, transformative equity requires us to enact big, systems-level change. That's why we've used a lot of systems-oriented framing, with terms such as *institutional, structural,* and *root causes.* That systems view is a foundational aspect of transformative equity action.

Another foundational aspect concerns relationships. It's about community and belonging, but not just in the let's-all-join-hands-and-sing "We Are the World" way. It's about our relationships with one another and how power and oppression operate within them, but it's also about our relationships to and with institutions and systems. It requires that we ask ourselves questions such as *How do we distribute institutional power? Who do we encourage to participate and who do we incorporate into institutional decision making?* These questions push us toward a deeper, more meaningful kind of community with equity at its center.

Community Through Equity, Not Vice Versa

During a recent visit with a school district, we met with a team of teachers charged with revising the language arts curriculum using equity as a core component. "I'm a big believer in *e pluribis unum,*" Philip, a white man, shared after the first session. "I don't like all this pitting people against each other or saying that everything boils down to our identities like we can't ever get past anything." His concern wasn't unique. "Why can't we just focus on what we have in common?" we're often asked.

He exhibited a fundamental confusion about the nature of equity. Philip preferred to start the conversation at *unity* without accounting for the *disunity* of racism, sexism, and other forms of inequity. This is a privileged view: wanting to hold onto accrued advantage but also to be in unity with the people whose marginalization is tied to that advantage; wanting the accumulative fruits of advantage without the responsibility to acknowledge it or to do something about it. These are the conditions we create when we expect, for example, newcomer Salvadoran students to celebrate diversity in a school where they are racially, culturally, and linguistically marginalized while we do little to address their marginalization. It's a sort of unity for white people, for people with other privileged identities.

We're certain that, in the moment, Philip was not looking at it that way. We might even extend a considerable benefit of the doubt and, misunderstandings aside, assume he sincerely yearned for community or for what antiracist educator Ayo Magwood (2021) calls a united "we."

"Equity is related to the *'unum,'*" we explained, "but it's what that unity looks like and what we build it upon that matters most." Have we built trust through transparency and honesty, or do we dance around equity problems to maintain a façade of togetherness? Do we provide space to recognize and redress systemic inequity, or do we skip that step because it's too uncomfortable for people like Philip, whose actions or advantages are being scrutinized?

What kind of unity have we achieved if it's not rooted in equity and justice? Unity for whom, exactly?

Reimagining Community for Equity

Throughout time and across cultures, this notion of community has had various names: *ubuntu*, "all my relations," *eres mi otro yo*, "beloved community" (Rodríguez & Swalwell, 2022). We can't escape the ways we are linked to one another and to everything on this planet. Our actions and inactions have consequences. We are connected, not just in the present, but through what's happened in the past and the possibilities we're carving out for the future.

That sounds like a big reality, we know. But it's also a sort of grounding.

As we ground our equity efforts in this sense of community, the recent accusations of equity being "divisive" feel especially galling. *Inequity* is divisive. *Racism* is divisive. *Cisgenderism* is divisive. Equity is the annihilation of divisiveness. Still, we both, along with many other equity leaders, have been accused by policymakers or anti-equity parent groups of making children feel bad about themselves, promoting hatred, fanning the flames of victimhood, and perpetuating inequity simply by naming and trying to eliminate it.

People raising these concerns manufacture some of their criticism to undermine the credibility of equity efforts—efforts that threaten to rearrange existing distributions of advantage and disadvantage. Some of these concerns, however, may arise from a genuine but misguided belief that focusing on inequity makes it harder to build and sustain community. *Why do we need to focus on the negative? If we just stop talking about all this equity stuff, won't the racism and cisgenderism disappear?*

The clearest analysis we've ever heard on this point came from a student in 8th grade. We'll call her Pam.

We happened to be visiting her school the day before an annual event called Diverse Friends Day. For one lunch period, the school encouraged students to sit with classmates with whom they normally wouldn't sit. Although we never heard any adult explicitly associate Diverse Friends Day with race, everybody seemed to know it was the school's attempt to force-integrate the cafeteria and encourage cross-race interaction for a day.

We ended the day by visiting a language arts class. As we chatted with Pam and Tariq, the only other Black student in her class, we decided to ask how they felt about the following day's Diverse Friends Day.

"That program is racist," Pam said.

"I don't know about 'racist,'" Tariq responded, "but I don't want to do it."

When we asked Pam what made Diverse Friends Day racist, she explained that there was a lot of unresolved racism in the school. Then she paused for a moment and said, "Really, I think Diverse Friends Day is for white people."

She's right, isn't she? In a predominately white school, does Pam need to spend a lunch period with white students to understand "diversity"? Or is it, like a lot of diversity programs, really designed to be a soft landing for white students, a gentle bit of diversity learning without the antiracism? These are the sorts of questions we should be asking about all our diversity and community efforts. What does it mean to build and sustain community while some students continue bearing the brunt of unaddressed racism, heterosexism, or ableism, the biggest barriers to authentic community?

Sure, it can be fun, even powerful, when we connect across difference by learning what we have in common. Maybe we learn that we enjoy the same music as someone else, or that we have experienced similar childhood traumas, that we crave the same junk foods or have similar hobbies. Connecting on this level might help us work together more effectively. As we work toward transformative equity, creating space for people to connect over similarities is helpful but insufficient. These opportunities become most meaningful when we are confronting racism, confronting ableism.

We also must understand how we are linked across, sometimes even *because of,* our differences, not just in terms of personal tastes, but also in terms of levels of access, opportunity, privilege, and power. What we want to highlight here is *connection as interdependence.* Being in the same institution, the same proximal community, weaves us together in a way, but we also should account for the reality that people woven together in this way can occupy very different positions when it comes to how they experience a classroom or school. Two students or staff members can experience the same institution in vastly different ways. We would guess that although they too might not be thrilled at having to participate in Diverse Friends Day, most white students at Pam's school aren't experiencing it as something that caters to them while exploiting their classmates of color. Other students, including LGBTQIA+ students and students who are masters of languages other than English, might also have good reason not to feel enthusiastic about being thrust into a social situation with classmates they don't know or trust.

Yes, the identifiers we keep discussing, including race, ethnicity, gender, class, and disability, are *social constructs*. In a sense we can say we are all human beings, a significant commonality. But if we focus only on what we have in common, we risk obscuring this sort of inequity. We risk obscuring the fact that advantage and disadvantage are tied together. What kind of community, what kind of unity, have we achieved if we're not accounting for that?

To help educators surface these interconnections and to highlight these points of difference that bind us together, we've used a reflection activity adapted from the book *Social Studies for a Better World: An Anti-Oppressive Guide for Elementary Educators* (Rodríguez & Swalwell, 2022). In pairs, we ask leaders to respond to prompts such as these:

- Where have I felt a sense of belonging, and where have I felt like I didn't belong?
- What's the most salient dimension of my identity, and why?
- What's the most pivotal decision I've ever made related to equity?

These questions can help colleagues, some of whom might have worked together for years, get to know one another more deeply. It can be meaningful when we find similarities in our responses. But it may be even more powerful when we realize how our positionalities, the proximity to power our identities afford us, inform how we answer these sorts of questions.

Full transparency: we encourage you to use these prompts only if you're deep into the process of eliminating bias and inequity from your spheres of influence. We don't want this to become yet another exercise in which people experiencing oppression are expected to educate their privileged-identity peers. It only works if we're already deeply invested and engaged.

In that spirit, take a moment to list community-building efforts in your school or district. Which of those efforts focus on an assumption of community-as-sameness, and which highlight our interdependence and acknowledge differences in access and opportunity?

If we're seeking healthy, sustainable community, then we ought to ask ourselves whether we're willing to embrace the level of equity literacy that is required to realize it. All the "No Place for Hate" posters in the world don't make for a stronger school community if we don't identify and eliminate cisgenderism, ableism, and other forms of oppression. Similarly, land acknowledgments at the beginnings of meetings eventually may come across as empty performances without efforts to decolonize our curriculum or address the impacts of settler colonialism in educational systems. All our pep rallies, spirit days, and antibullying assemblies are of little consequence for community if groups of youth or staff continue to be marginalized for their gender identities or expressions. That kind of community is a sham. People experiencing bias and inequity know it.

This brand of unity doesn't lead to equity. It leads to a community that is fragile and illusory, fooling only the people who benefit from the inequity we're ignoring. Our only shot at real community starts with equity.

So let's start our discussion of care with this observation: it's important not to cajole people into community-building exercises or processes that don't account for inequity. Authentic community building is a matter of genuine care, well-being, and love.

Channeling Love and Joy

By love, we don't mean romance or even a sentimental attachment. Neither do we mean touchy-feely affirmations and feel-good compliments. We often hear educators say that they *love* their students as though the word is a shield against claims they might be doing harm. We're talking about something deeper.

The question is, what kind of love allows inequity to fester? Without attending to the ways students are suffering *and* taking action to stop systems from disadvantaging them, any love we claim is somewhat twisted. Lamar L. Johnson, Nathaniel Bryan, and Gloria Boutte (2019) call this "fake love." They explain how it rests in educators' "inability to critically read the world and themselves" (p. 55). Refusing to acknowledge painful realities and focusing only on whatever we might deem positive isn't love—at least not the kind of love we as equity leaders ought to embrace.

An equity-centered love might not be quite as fuzzy as this sort of love, but it's far more powerful. We've hinted at it throughout this book. It's the kind of love that inspires us to share, and to openly receive, critical feedback. It's the kind of love that makes us incredulous about any injustice and desperate to act with informed urgency. It insists we have high equity expectations for ourselves and one another. *We can do better. We must do better. We will do better.*

Let's explore what those high expectations of equity love might look like. In his article "Why Emotionally Intelligent Leaders Avoid the 'Feedback Sandwich'," Jeff Haden (2021) pokes at the popular feedback formula. You're probably familiar with it: give a compliment, sneak in a criticism, then quickly follow the criticism with another compliment. It rarely works. This approach says,

> "I need to give you negative feedback . . . but first I'll say something nice so you won't think I hate you. And then I'll say something nice so you won't be mad at me when you leave." That's the problem with the feedback sandwich. The recipients feel manipulated. And even if at first they don't, give it time: Since our positive qualities tend to stay consistent, the same bread eventually starts to taste stale. (para. 6–8)

Haden instead points to "benevolent honesty" as the most meaningful expression of love and care: "No manipulation. No platitudes. No irrelevant compliments. No false hope. Just clear, direct feedback—delivered inside a message of connection, belonging, and trust" (para. 16–17).

Does the culture in your school or district support this kind of honest feedback? If not, what might you do to model and help cultivate it?

Gloria Ladson-Billings (2009) explored this kind of love as it relates to classroom practice in her classic book *Dreamkeepers: Successful Teachers of African American Children.* The teachers she profiled eschewed pity and refused to lower standards or expectations; they rejected the notion that this approach was how they could love their students. Instead, they developed a layered awareness of students' contexts to support rigorous learning and growth. They didn't settle for "idiosyncratic connections with students" (p. x), opting instead to cultivate deep community through classroom experiences, learning activities, and an emphasis on collective responsibility. Over the years, other inspiring educators have written about this kind of love in schools (Love, 2019; Muhammad, 2020).

Critical educator bell hooks (2000) noted that embracing love means rejecting the fear that drives human action and inaction. "Our fear may not go away," she admitted, "but it will not stand in the way" (p. 101). She continued:

> Cultures of domination rely on the cultivation of fear as a way to ensure obedience. . . . Fear is the primary force upholding structures of domination. It promotes the desire for separation, the desire not to be known. When we are taught that safety lies always with sameness, then difference, of any kind, will appear as a threat. When we choose to love we choose to move against fear—against alienation and separation. (p. 93)

When we act out of love, when we demonstrate care, we don't deny those fears. We examine them. We understand why we're socialized to accept them. But we also don't let them dictate our actions.

To be clear, we're not arguing that people who are marginalized ought to love the people or institutions marginalizing them. Instead, we're arguing that authentic love moves against injustice.

This kind of love also can help nurture compassion and solidarity as we learn more about how systems harm people in our communities. Recounting how she responds to everyone from resistant students in her methods courses to bigoted strangers at the grocery store, Muna Saleh (2021) stresses the lessons she learned from her grandmother about how "love and compassion inherently dwell alongside equity and justice" (p. 11). She explains that

> as an educator who is always simultaneously learning, I must try to be radically loving by holding in tension the need to be unflinchingly truthful about these violent systems and also as patient/compassionate as possible with those encountering difficult knowledges, sometimes for the first time. This is sometimes (often) a struggle for me, especially in the face of outright bigotry and/or vitriol. However, . . . I have learned to make these tensions and commitments explicit to students when we first meet and throughout our time together. (pp. 11–12)

Saleh recounts repeatedly fighting the impulse to write people off or to continually validate her own humanity. Instead, she focuses on how dehumanization operates and invites the people perpetuating it to recognize the mechanics at work (which dehumanize them too) and the harm they are doing. This kind of radical love does not require that we pretend we're all the same or ignore harm. Quite the opposite: it requires us to name and then directly address the harm.

This requirement can be tricky because sometimes the fears are informed by our understandings of actual conditions. We've mentioned several times how, for example, leaders of color often face harsher reprisals than their white colleagues for taking strong antiracist stands. We can't pretend this dynamic, this racism, doesn't exist. Recall the idea of *informed urgency*, part of the prioritization principle. We need to move our institutional efforts at the pace of the people who are ready to move, who are desperate for us to do better right now. We also must build bridges for people who are open to moving but need support to do so. For those who refuse to move, we may need to bridge them out of our school or district, or out of education altogether.

It can help to remember that we're all tripping over ourselves to some extent when it comes to leading at least some dimensions of equity. Maybe we're deeply knowledgeable about and committed to equity related to class and poverty but still working on developing the same levels of knowledge and commitment with racial equity. Maybe we're primed to sprint forward on racial equity but struggle to recognize everyday examples of cis- or hetero-normativity. An equity-inspired love means not only holding one another accountable for moving forward but also supporting one another on that journey. Self-love means not only holding ourselves accountable but also building our support networks so we're not trying to do it alone. More on that later in this chapter.

An equity-inspired love might also mean that when we're finding ways to grow around privileged dimensions of our identity, we avoid overloading our colleagues who experience inequity along those dimensions with requests for help and support. And, as we discussed in the previous chapter, when they do offer us feedback, we don't try to police their tone.

If we are building loving relationships in schools with colleagues, families, and students, then we must be willing to both give and receive honest feedback, to hold ourselves and one another accountable in those ways. We also must be willing to face down the fear. No fake love, no feedback sandwiches, no hiding behind our discomfort as a reason not to do the equitable and just thing. This is where equity literacy and community well-being feed one another.

Let's not forget another important ingredient for transformative equity: *joy*. If all we do is focus on trauma and oppression, then we are setting ourselves up for failure. And exhaustion.

In *We Want to Do More Than Survive: Abolitionist Teaching and the Pursuit of Educational Freedom*, Bettina Love (2019) places joy front and center. She doesn't endorse "the type of fabricated and forced joy found in a Pepsi commercial," but a deeper satisfaction and delight that come from a "place of resistance, agitation, purpose, justice, love, and mattering" in the face of oppression (p. 15). She embraces a joy intertwined with an equity commitment, a joy "discovered in making a way out of no way, . . . that is uncovered when you know how to love yourself and others, . . . that comes from releasing pain" (p. 15). This is joy as catharsis, as release, as liberation.

As we have stressed throughout this book, there's no step-by-step recipe that guarantees joy, no magic elixir. But we can cultivate it by talking *joyfully* about equity, framing equity efforts *positively. We're investing in something in which most schools and districts never seriously invest. We are making progress, which means we're alleviating harm and crushing its sources. Instead of celebrating diversity, let's celebrate our commitment to doing the right equity and justice thing.*

We should feel excited about reshaping our institutional cultures around equity. We should feel joy about it. We should celebrate it, as long as our efforts are transformative and not merely mitigative, as long as we are seriously moving against racism, ableism, and cisgenderism, and just as seriously moving toward equity and justice. Nothing is more positive.

A Deeper Belonging

All this talk about love and community harkens to the latest education buzzword, *belonging.* We suspect that its growing popularity is at least in part a counter to accusations from anti-equity advocates that words such as *equity,* even *inclusion* and *diversity,* are divisive. It may be easier to secure buy-in if we frame our goal as cultivating a sense of *belonging* than if we frame it as *disrupting white supremacy* or as *redistributing access and opportunity.*

To be clear, we're not against belonging, rhetorically or strategically. We want people to feel welcome, to experience a deep sense of belonging. We also want something more. We want *true* community that grapples with tough questions related to inequity and marginalization, prioritization and redistribution: the kinds of questions that make the anti-equity faction worry we're making progress. We don't want a belonging in which people have to contort themselves to fit into an oppressive institutional culture. Instead, we want to transform institutional culture.

As we hear more about how leaders are leaning into *belonging,* we have noticed that they often embrace an approach that relies on an us/them binary. Do *they* feel welcome here with *us*? This brand of welcoming may look like a sort of kindness, but it still marks distinction and uncovers differential power. We welcome someone into *our own home,* right? It would be odd to welcome someone into a space we didn't somehow control. So at any moment, if a guest offends us or we perceive that person as a threat, we might rescind the welcome. This shallow sense of belonging is fragile because it relies on the goodwill of people with power, the kind of goodwill that guests who routinely are harmed by people with power have reason not to trust.

Take a moment to consider your school or district's messaging around being "welcoming." To what degree is it *us* welcoming *them* as opposed to *us* sharing power with *one another,* or *us* creating community *together*? How is it aligned or at odds with the ways people who disproportionately haven't felt like they belonged experience school? How can you adjust your approach to belonging so that it is rooted in transformative equity, if it isn't already?

Muna Saleh (2021) also speaks to these concerns, writing about her personal and professional experiences as a hijabi Muslim woman and daughter of Palestinian refugees. When she recounts attending a recent social studies education conference, for example, she explains how condescending it felt to sit through conversations about the need to humanize "the Other": Muslim people, Black people, transgender people, immigrants, disabled people. She writes,

> My whole body would tense every time I heard this "common sense" assertion, until . . . I finally decided to speak up. I said, "I don't know that we need to 'humanize' those who are *already* human; I think we probably need to focus on why some are *trying to de*humanize other human beings." (p. 5)

She urges us to replace "the need to humanize Others with our relational commitments and responsibilities to and with each other" (p. 5).

If we want to cultivate a sense of belonging that requires more than a vague sense of welcoming, something more like a mutual obligation, then we should yank up our proverbial rugs and take a good long look at the dust and dirt underneath. Set the vacuum to its most powerful level. Tear off that drywall to expose the structural wounds hiding behind it. This is what all the other principles we've discussed help us do.

In his "Letter from Birmingham Jail," Martin Luther King Jr. wrote,

> [W]e who engage in nonviolent direct action are not the creators of tension. We merely bring to the surface the hidden tension that is already alive. We bring it out in the open, where it can be seen and dealt with. Like a boil that can never be cured so long as it is covered up but must be opened with all its ugliness to the natural medicines of air and light, injustice must be exposed, with all the tension its exposure creates, to the light of human conscience and the air of national opinion before it can be cured.

Are our efforts to address the roots of institutional problems going to be dirtier, more painful, or more expensive than we'd like? Probably. Might we find out the damage is even more extensive than we imagined? Almost certainly. But this is our only way to achieve a solid structure. And it's worth it because there's no real community, no real belonging, without it.

In some ways, serious equity efforts are about reallocating the discomfort and mess, removing them from the backs of people who have borne the brunt of injustice and loading them onto the shoulders of the people who have reaped advantage from that injustice. So that grime, that reallocated discomfort, that disarray are evidence that we're digging out the roots of, or *redressing*, the problems that destroy any real possibility for authentic *belonging*. That is equity progress.

Pushback as Evidence of Equity Progress

The most common fear educators express to us revolves around coping with pushback against their equity efforts. School leaders often ask us how they can move forward with equity without angering newly elected school board members or attracting the attention of well-organized parent organizations bent on disrupting equity efforts. They don't want to attract controversy or wake the proverbial beast. Over and over, we hear variations on the question "How can we do equity work without making anyone angry?" That fear seems to be growing and intensifying as more leaders worry about the implications of anti-equity legislation, the threat of lawsuits, and even the stability of their employment.

Our first response is to be curious about its motivation. What concerns, fears, anxieties does it reflect? Whether we are positional leaders or passion leaders, we know that our work is complex and that it can be tempting to do whatever we can to avoid controversy. We can't allow this temptation to inhibit or slow our leadership toward transformative equity. But we do want to make sure we have support systems and, as we've discussed previously, we want to proceed strategically.

Take a moment to make a list or word web of the fears and anxieties you have about enacting transformative equity. Which fears can be allayed with tactical planning, and which are rooted in deeper internal work you need to do? Which are related to your employment stability?

Here's the reality: Efforts toward transformative equity are going to make some people uncomfortable. They're going to make some people angry. They might draw shouting protesters at school board meetings or irate parents in administrative offices. In some places they are resulting in legal challenges. This a hard reality, even for those of us whose entire lives are built around our commitments to educational equity. We would be foolish not to proceed strategically, not to consider how this blowback might affect our emotional well-being or job security. We all must make decisions about what stands to take and when to take them. The last thing we want is for every equity-committed leader to be run out of town. That's why it's important to do the sorts of things we've mentioned throughout this book: Build a system of support. Start with the people already committed. Proceed strategically but assuredly.

Here's the other reality. As we mentioned previously, if there's no pushback in response to our equity efforts, if it all feels like smooth sailing, we're probably not leading transformatively enough. There simply is no way to restructure systems of advantage and disadvantage without making some of the people accustomed to advantage panicky. Sure, we can choose to see their response as a threat. And depending on local politics and who's on the school board, perhaps it *is* a threat. But it's also something else.

We don't want to romanticize the pushback. So we're careful about how we discuss that "something else."

The pushback is a sign, perhaps the best sign, that we're making progress. In that way, it can be interpreted as a kind of positive feedback. We don't want to minimize the challenges it presents. But we do find it helpful to reframe it so that we can see, celebrate, and derive positive energy from the progress it suggests. Chances are, if all we're doing in the name of equity and belonging is Diverse Friends Day or the Multicultural Arts and Crafts Fair, we're not eliciting much shouting. But as soon as we start to transform policies, reconstruct practices, redistribute access and opportunity, talk about racism or heterosexism, we invite the blowback. The blowback feels negative, but it's a response to something positive. Find a way to hold onto that positivity.

Another helpful equity move is to identify the *"push for* folks" in our schools or districts (Rodríguez & Swalwell, 2022). Who are the people—parents and caregivers, students, staff—most committed to equity? Who are the people pushing *for* change, sometimes at the risk of upsetting their colleagues or classmates? Cultivate relationships with them. They're important sources of feedback. They can be that support system, especially when the blowback comes.

In many schools and districts, the *push for* folks are burned out, exhausted from all the pushing that seems to result in little progress. Sometimes they're the most alienated people in a school or district because their truth-telling upsets the *push against* people. So we should avoid the temptation to reactively assign the *push for* folks to an equity committee or workgroup that is going to spend the next three years revising a school or district equity statement. Listen to them, to their concerns and ideas. Acknowledge them publicly. Align with them. And if they do serve in a formal capacity, compensate them. They can be an important support system.

Again, we understand—believe us, we do—that each of us has localized challenges to face, our own navigating to do. We can't prioritize our fears over what's best for students. But we can proceed strategically. Sometimes prioritizing a group of students means making sure the leaders who advocate for them are not pushed out. Whatever strategizing we're doing, it should be *toward* transformative equity rather than *away from* controversy and blowback.

The Inevitability of Resistance

Even though we highlight pushes *for* equity, we aren't naive about the realities of the push*back*. In fact, we haven't known a district where there hasn't been pushback, or at least significant fear of pushback. We should embrace the fact that, no matter how delicately we present something, which words we avoid, or how much care and concern we exhibit, some people will never be on board with our equity efforts.

That said, recognizing where resistance is coming from can help us formulate a more effective response to it or head off pushback before it gains momentum. For example, sometimes resistance is a symptom of confusion and miscommunication. As we roll out equity efforts, it's important to make the relevant information and motivations accessible, transparent, and clear. *This is who we are as a school. We know that students are being harmed. As long as that's true, we will do whatever it takes to eliminate the bias and inequity harming them.* Some critics are potential allies, their questions and skepticism borne out of good faith that can be helpful as we craft better policies and action plans. Some critics have learned not to trust leadership's claims of a commitment to equity. We must earn their trust by demonstrating our unwavering leadership.

In some cases, resistance definitely is *not* in good faith. It can be fueled by media outlets that whip up hysteria or well-funded organizations with long-standing anti-equity goals. It's important that we learn the common talking points, such as calling everything under the sun related to equity "critical race theory," suggesting that antiracism efforts are themselves racist, or arguing that heterosexism and cisgenderism don't even exist. We risk giving too much power to anti-equity critics if we acknowledge their arguments as legitimate points for conversation, as valid perspectives. In the context of an equity commitment, "heterosexism doesn't exist" is not a valid perspective. It's not a useful topic to discuss. It's a red herring meant to distract us from eliminating injustice.

Consider the cisgenderist legislation emerging all over the United States, such as bans on transgender girls playing sports or using bathrooms aligned with their gender identities. How do we respond to these laws as leaders committed to equity? We've seen social media posts from leaders publicly regretting that they must tell girls that they can no longer be part of a sports team. But that regret is cold comfort; it doesn't disrupt the harm. As equity leaders we cannot just extend our sympathies, our hopes and prayers. We cannot simply comply. We have other options. And if we're committed to equity, to any real sense of community and belonging, we exercise them.

We could recognize a law but find ways to subvert it. In response to a divisive concept bill becoming law in her state, elementary teacher Trechiondria Lathan took this public stance:

> I will not simply comply with racist laws, or be disrespected, dismissed, and traumatized by administrators and political leaders

who proudly inflict harm on BIPOC students, families, and educators across the nation. In the words of Angela Davis, "I am no longer accepting the things I cannot change. I am changing the things I cannot accept." (*Rethinking Schools* Editors, 2021a, para. 15)

For her, laws that are overtly racist, policies that inflict trauma, are a thick red line. She will not comply, come what may.

For what would you be willing to take this kind of stand? What is your thick red line?

We've asked ourselves these questions throughout our careers as we've faced watershed moments. To be honest, we're not always proud of our answers. We look back on some of our decisions with regret that we didn't advocate harder or take greater risks. In other instances, we did take that leap and the consequences were not nearly as dire as we had imagined. And in others, we knowingly made drastic, even job-ending decisions in pursuit of equity. As a community of equity leaders, we should acknowledge and appreciate that not everybody is in a position to make job-ending decisions. In a way, that ability is itself a marker of privilege. So these haven't been easy questions for us to ask ourselves. But they're fundamental to the work of transformative equity leadership.

We know what some of you are thinking. *All this reflection is good, but please just let me know what I ought to be doing.* We wish there was a blueprint or playbook for equity leadership, for dealing with resistance. Sometimes it feels like equity leadership is the water in a stream, navigating the rocks and debris. There is no correct path. Tactical disagreements or differences are inevitable, and different sets of variables will require different approaches. Sometimes we catch more flies with honey. Sometimes we don't. It depends as much on our own personalities and quirks as on the particulars of any given situation.

For example, the two of us have very different styles of engaging educators in difficult conversations and actions related to equity. We don't agree on everything. That's OK. What's important is to not let fear detain us, to take strategic risks rooted in justice, love, awareness of ourselves and our contexts, and commitments to community. This will make us a formidable threat to inequity.

Caring for Ourselves and One Another

"Caring for myself is not self-indulgence," Audre Lorde (2017) famously wrote, "it is self-preservation, and that is an act of political warfare" (p. 130). Unfortunately, Lorde's words have been coopted by the corporate "well-being" machine. But Lorde made this claim in a specific context, not only as a lesbian activist of color but also as somebody who had experienced injustice even within justice-oriented movements such as white-dominated feminist groups. She was referring to self-preservation as somebody committed to justice, the opposite of self-preservation as an excuse for sidestepping that commitment.

As we've mentioned, the education world can be hostile for those of us willing to tear into injustice, to name it publicly and respond to it forthrightly. And according to researchers who study burnout among people doing equity and justice work, this is only one of the challenges with which people who do the naming and tearing contend (Gorski, 2019). (We'll explore the other challenges shortly.) Being mindful of and proactively attending to those challenges can help us weather the storm of blowback and resistance. It can help us sustain ourselves as people who insist on saying what needs to be said and doing what needs to be done.

Too many of us burn out and leave education because the storm deteriorates our well-being. As we've mentioned before, this is especially true for those weathering the storm of resistance while also weathering the storm of injustice as educators of color, LGBTQIA+ educators, and other educators disproportionately facing the inequity we're trying to abolish. Add a pandemic, the threat of gun violence, low pay, increasing bureaucratic regulations. There's no other way to say it: it's a lot. It's too much.

We certainly bear no ill will toward people who decide either to leave education or to find ways to make a difference from outside hostile systems. But we do hope to support equity accomplices who want to continue to work in schools and districts by providing tools that may help them do that. One of those tools can be self-care, caring for ourselves.

However, if we're going to talk about *self*-care, we also need to talk about *community* care: how to care for one another, how to create a context for equity and justice efforts that feeds and sustains the people who push the hardest. And if we as leaders are going to set and hold people accountable to expectations that they will engage in that pushing, we should develop policies and practices to protect and support them. When we fail to provide this kind of care, we increase the potential for resentment, discouragement, and burnout.

Self-Care

The growing body of knowledge about burnout among people doing equity work can help us understand why self-care among equity leaders is important. When we talk about burnout, we're not referring to popular uses of the term, to occasional bouts of exhaustion or general vocational displeasure. Of course, those are real concerns in schools too, and another reason educators leave the profession or find a way to do what they're passionate about doing outside the education system. *Equity burnout* refers to the impact of conditions that may be piled atop the threat of vocational burnout for people who actively resist racism, cisgenderism, and other forms of injustice. It's a form of burnout specific to people who have the courage and commitment to stand against inequity despite the blowback, to those of us who can't live with ourselves if we allow inequity to live.

Interview studies with educators who have experienced this sort of burnout (Gorski & Chen, 2015) have pointed to two primary causes. The first revolves around unique characteristics of people whose natural inclination is to stand up to injustice—characteristics that point to the need for self-care, which we discuss in this section. The other cause, the sort of blowback we discussed earlier, is more related to community care, which we explore in the next section of this chapter.

Transformative equity leaders *have* to be deeply aware not just of the impact of interpersonal bias but also of the scope and impact of institutional and structural injustice. As a result, we tend to put pressure on ourselves to do anything it takes to disrupt whatever is doing harm. That could mean working incessantly, foregoing rest. It could mean putting ourselves in harm's way because we can't help but speak up when we hear a colleague make a deficit-oriented remark about families. Perhaps we imagine that if we take time to rest or attend to our own well-being, nobody will pick up the slack.

We might see this impulse as something positive. *Inequity is intolerable. We can't rest until it's eliminated.* And, of course, people who experience inequity don't have the option to take a break from its impact, so perhaps we imagine that any sort of rest associates us with that self-indulgence to which Audre Lorde alluded. So yes, the impulse to want to do whatever it takes to eliminate inequity is admirable. It's necessary. We relate to that urgency.

But if we're in this for the long haul, we also need to sustain ourselves. We unfortunately know many equity leaders who have invested so much of themselves that they ended up physically sick or psychologically or emotionally unwell, sometimes to a degree that rendered them unable to stay in the fight. Some had to leave education altogether. This is the definition of equity burnout: when the physical, psychological, and emotional tolls of acting on behalf of equity and justice become so overwhelming, they compromise our abilities to be effective in our equity efforts or force us to disengage at least temporarily from the work we're so passionate about doing. As we said earlier, this is harmful to the person experiencing it, but it's also a setback for the sustainability of equity efforts. It has both interpersonal and institutional consequences.

So another way to consider our impact is to wonder whether we might be more effective equity leaders, more effective equity accomplices, if we listen to our bodies and slow down when we need to. Might we be more attentive, more apt to recognize those systems of advantage and disadvantage swirling around us, if we attend with similar vigor to our own well-being? Sure, some of us have the tools and dispositions to navigate the rough waters without succumbing to burnout. But for those of us who struggle to do that, we might be better served, and might be more effective in long-term service to equity, if we learn to be more intentional about refilling ourselves spiritually, culturally, or in whatever ways work for us, even if that means not spending all our waking hours on equity and justice.

That effort can look very different for each of us. We know our ability to manage stress deteriorates if we don't sleep well, nourish ourselves, or have quality time with loved ones, but that set of conditions feels like an obvious baseline, not an intentional commitment to care. We both have short-term ways to recharge: going for walks, crafting, snuggling our children, doing yoga, screaming into pillows. Some of our equity leader friends swear by meditation; others swear by running, biking, or other kinds of exercise. Some are intentional about unhooking from technology, trying to eat healthier foods, or spending more time outside.

We know some equity leaders who recharge by attending local get-togethers of equity-committed educators where they can talk about the threat of burnout and the heaviness of anti-equity blowback or just share space with like-minded people. We know other equity leaders who need time away from colleagues similarly passionate about equity and justice.

You do you. But please do *something* to recharge.

Taking care of ourselves also means that we need to structure into our spheres of influence opportunities for other equity-committed educators to recharge. We'll discuss that in more detail when we talk about community care.

What do you do to attend to your own well-being? What more can you do? Remember, we're not asking what you do to attend to your well-being by *avoiding* the hard work of educational equity. What do you do, or what can you do, to attend to your well-being with the goal of maximizing your impact and sustainability as an equity leader?

The other common cause of burnout among equity-oriented educators cannot be remedied with self-care. We discuss it in the following section.

Community Care

When we proceed with an ethic of community care, we intentionally attend not just to our own well-being but also to the well-being of the community of equity truth-tellers and change-makers. We create institutional conditions that support the most adamant equity voices.

This, again, is about sustaining individual advocates; but it's also about sustaining progress toward institutional equity.

This observation leads us to the other common cause of burnout among justice-oriented educators: blowback from anti-equity people and organizations. We've covered that challenge in various ways in this and earlier chapters; we revisit it here as it relates to the threat of burnout.

We have several colleagues, ranging from counselors and class-room teachers to principals and superintendents, who have lost their jobs for taking a strong equity stand or who have left their jobs due to the blowback they experienced for doing so. But burnout isn't always the result of one enormous impact. Sometimes, maybe even *usually*, it's the accumulative impact of the more day-to-day grinding sorts of things that undermine our well-being over time, such as the lack of support from supervisors, the steady stream of resistance, or the continual *threat* of job insecurity (Magwood, 2021). The question for us as equity leaders is, how do we protect people in our spheres of influence from these detrimental conditions?

Recently, after facilitating a webinar on antiracist teaching, a colleague of ours whom we'll call Lynda received a flurry of hate mail and death threats to her work email, cell phone, and home address. Soon after, she was summoned to the human resources office, where she was told the district had reviewed her webinar and determined she was not in violation of district policies. "Case dismissed," HR concluded.

However, HR's dismissal of the case did not end Lynda's struggles. Her district publicly claimed a commitment to equity, but nobody offered support for the trauma she was experiencing as somebody demanding equity. Nobody from the district made a public statement unequivocally endorsing her leadership and antiracist efforts. Nobody seemed to recognize the cooling impact the district's inaction had on students or on Lynda. Their duck-and-cover response began and ended with an investigation seemingly conducted to demonstrate to Lynda's critics that the district attended in "unbiased" ways to their concerns. It was a failure of district equity leadership.

Lynda was devastated, not just by the vitriol and threats but by her district's lack of courage in the face of blowback. In contrast, the

Indigenous-led nonprofit with which she had partnered for the webinar provided volunteers to watch her house at night. They also sifted through her mail, pulling threatening messages to share with the police so that she wouldn't have to read them.

How do people in your employ know that you have their backs if they embrace and enact transformative equity? Can they trust that, if somebody complains, whether a parent or a policymaker, you'll support them rather than avoiding the controversy or suggesting they roll back their equity efforts?

If we embrace transformational equity, then the schools we lead *must* be communities of care for staff as well as students and families. This effort can't be aspirational; we must be able to show our receipts. What are we doing to care for our colleagues? As educator Monica Cox (2021) tweeted,

> Instead of showing me your diversity statement, show me your hiring data, your discrimination claim stats, your salary tables, your retention numbers, your diversity policies, and your leaders' public actions against racism. End performative allyship.

What can you point to that demonstrates your care for colleagues? What actions have you taken, and what actions can you take, to demonstrate you mean business as an equity leader, creating space for other people to speak and act their commitments more freely? In what tangible, material ways does your school or district show care specifically to staff who may be marginalized? How do you protect staff members who take personal and professional risks for equity?

Notably, one consistent bit of advice for longer-term self-care, especially from BIPOC and LGBTQIA+ scholars and educators, is to *be in community together*. As Jennifer Alzate González (2015) explains, *self*-care is impossible without *us*-care, our "collective strength, wisdom, and beauty" (p. 16).

"We need each other." These words end a powerful letter by educator Harper Keenan (2020, p. 10) welcoming LGBTQIA+ teachers to the profession. In his advice for how to "keep yourself alive," Keenan explains how his current justice work as a transgender teacher is "only possible because of the many years of struggle, organizing, and community-making that came before it." He describes a community of care that includes other LGBTQIA+ educators past and present. As he notes, "I have a responsibility to carry that struggle forward in the ways that my position allows" (p. 9).

Similarly, Rita Kohli and Marcos Pizarro (2016) detail how teachers of color often bring a relational approach to their schools, especially around racial justice. They show how structures of schooling where a "Eurocentric, individualized nature of schools was prioritized" conflict with this community orientation, causing teachers of color to feel "isolated and devalued" (p. 77). Their advice echoes Keenan's, that "community-oriented teachers should find a network of like-minded educators with whom to build, plan, and organize" (p. 83).

If you need to find this sort of community outside your workplace so that you are better able to build it within your workplace, many organizations offer educators opportunities to connect. One powerful example we recommend is the Institute for Teachers of Color Committed to Racial Justice (ITOC), cofounded and codirected by Kohli and Pizarro (www.instituteforteachersofcolor.org). Other gatherings and organizations, in addition to our own Equity Literacy Institute (www.equityliteracy.org), include the following:

- Abolitionist Teaching Network (www.abolitionistteaching network.org)
- All Y'all Social Justice Collective (www.allyalledu.com)
- Association of Raza Educators (www.razaeducators.org)
- Black Educators Caucus Milwaukee (www.facebook.com/BlackEducatorsCaucusMke)
- Black Lives Matter at School (www.blacklivesmatteratschool.com)
- DC Area Educators for Social Justice (www.dcareaeducators4socialjustice.org)
- Due East Educational Equity Collaborative (www.dueeast.org)
- Education for Liberation Network (www.edliberation.org)
- EduColor (www.educolor.org)
- Free Minds Free People (www.fmfp.org)
- New York Collective of Radical Educators (www.nycore.org)
- Northwest Teaching for Social Justice (www.nwtsj.org)

- Rethinking Schools (www.rethinkingschools.org)
- Teachers 4 Social Justice–San Francisco (www.t4sj.org)
- Teachers for Social Justice–Chicago (www.teachersforjustice.org)

You don't need to travel far to build community. New 6th grade teachers Ryan Oto, Ngan Nguyen, Megan Custer, Peder Ericson, and Nick Liebelt (2021) have written about a support group they created at their school in Minneapolis. They started their "small collective . . . of support and solidarity" to counter the "toxicity of copy room conversations" and the troubling inequities in their district. "As individuals," they noted, "we may not have been able to wrestle with the daily struggles against white supremacy in our school environment without the sounding board and support we intentionally nurtured among our small group" (p. 2). They described their daily routine of carving out time to reflect on questions such as *What makes you feel human?* and *What brings you joy?* They shared,

> These small moments set a tone of compassion and presence . . . not felt before. It wasn't a space to pass through as a part of the labor of the day; it quickly became a critical moment to slow down and be with one another. These moments allowed us to clear our thinking and focus on what mattered to our work: how we showed up and what we stood for. As our intimacy with one another grew through these conversations, the business of school was replaced with a labor of community and love. (Oto et al., 2021, p. 6)

Despite their fears that they weren't doing their job well, fanned by more veteran colleagues entrenched and invested in the status quo, their collective enacted changes both big and small to create more equitable classrooms. They explained,

> This work of building an intentional collective of teachers striving to become critical educators was purposeful, strategic, and forced us to confront the oppressive political dynamics of adults in ways that no teaching program had prepared us for. It was through our commitment to one another that we were able to persevere amidst the onslaught of pushback we faced from our colleagues, that brought us confidence when we needed it, and reminded us that justice and

humanity are inextricably linked. It was these spaces that frustrated us, brought us joy, and challenged us to imagine a more just vision of education that we could enact together. (p. 11)

This 6th grade team is a great example of how we can take care of ourselves by being in loving community with one another.

If You Feel Alone

Even if you feel alone in your school or district, there are always other people who are looking for that connection. As hooks (2000) reminds us,

> Those of us who have already chosen to embrace a love ethic, allowing it to govern and inform how we think and act, know that when we let our light shine, we draw to us and are drawn to other bearers of light. We are not alone. (p. 101)

"Letting your light shine" means showing up and taking risks and doing the work, showing the world what we're committed to and care about. People will respond for better or worse. It may not always be who we wish it was or who we expect it to be, but our support network is out there.

And don't forget to look beyond the walls of the school or the borders of the district for this kind of community. As the editors of *Rethinking Schools* (2021b) remind us in their introduction to an issue focused on defying bans on teaching racial justice,

> We recognize how demoralizing, scary, and destructive these attacks can be, particularly for educators already vulnerable in any number of ways: teachers of color, LGBTQ educators, early-career educators, and those working in states without strong unions. Overt resistance may not always be possible. That is why educators cannot wage this campaign of resistance on our own. We need parents, students, community groups, civil rights organizations, labor unions, and elected officials to join us. (para. 13)

Every community, state, or region has organizations dedicated to transformative equity in schools. We encourage you to look first for groups founded and led by people who are minoritized and marginalized: people who are pushing against the kind of injustice they experience.

What communities are you part of that help to sustain your commitment to equity? To whom have you been meaning to reach out to build your network? To whom will you reach out *right now*? What can you do to create more time for your staff to engage in equity-based community?

Conclusion

We are obligated to work as hard as we can to build a strong and healthy community with equity at its center, to create spaces of love and joy where transformative equity can thrive, where inequity finds no sustenance. Also, if we have any real chance to cultivate and sustain equity, we must take care of ourselves and of one other. We do that by rising above claims of divisiveness to embrace both the joy and the messiness that sustains a healthy, equitable community.

Figure 8.1 highlights some of the key points presented in this chapter. It summarizes the care, joy, and sustainability principle by illustrating, from a leader's point of view, the difference between mitigative equity and transformative equity in terms of actions and attitudes.

FIGURE 8.1

The Care, Joy, and Sustainability Principle: Comparing Leaders' Mindsets Related to Mitigative Versus Transformative Equity

Mitigative Equity	Transformative Equity
I am building a community rooted in similarities and commonalities.	I am helping to build a community rooted in interconnectedness and justice.
I show my love for staff and students by shielding them from conflict or difficult conversations.	I embrace honesty about inequity and accountability as fundamental elements of authentic, loving relationships.
I focus on improving school climate by celebrating staff and students, regularly voicing how much I appreciate and value them.	I am wary of toxic positivity and show my appreciation through words and actions that address problems staff and students face in conjunction with genuine appreciation and celebration.
I frame equity efforts only in terms of us/them binaries.	I frame equity efforts as "diverse us" versus "inequity and injustice."
I keep staff focused on what is realistic and practical when devising solutions to inequity.	I encourage dreaming and outside-the-box thinking about what equitable schools can and should be.
Inequity never takes a minute off, so neither do I.	I find healthy outlets for processing stress, and I support staff in doing the same.
I often feel alone in my equity commitments and work, but I am willing to push ahead regardless.	I have sought out or built support networks where I can be sustained and help sustain others.
I am surprised or discouraged by resistance and offer condolences when staff experience pushback.	I anticipate resistance and see it as evidence of equity effectiveness, taking proactive steps to provide personal and structural protections for staff—especially those at greater risk for attacks.

9

A Few Final Thoughts

Thank you for reading our book and engaging with our ideas. Of course, although you have reached the end of the book, the work never ends.

In fact, we don't want your engagement with this book to end. Now that you're well-versed in transformative equity and the basic principles of equity literacy, we invite you to take stock of how all that we've discussed in this book hangs together. We encourage you to to generate a transformative equity action plan for your school or district.

We hope you'll begin by reflecting on the role each principle plays in your leadership efforts and how it might strengthen your equity leadership abilities. Some aspects of some of the principles may not relate to your position or leadership role. That's OK. The point is to carefully reflect on each principle and consider whether your actions are rooted more in mitigative or transformative equity. Are you lingering in responsive actions, or are you digging out the roots and redressing inequity?

However you choose to reflect on what you've learned from these pages, we hope it helps you to move your equity efforts forward. Remember, reading this book is not the equity work in the same way attending a professional development session is not the equity work. The question is, what will you do with what you learned? What are the actions?

We're certain that many of our readers are already powerful equity leaders. To you, we say, *Thank you for all you're doing.* To those of you who are new to this work, we thank you too and welcome you to the community of equity leaders. Wherever you are, in whatever capacity you lead, we hope we've provided you with some of the tools that will enable you to be the most formidable threat to inequity, the most powerful cultivator of equity, you are capable of being.

If there's any way we can support you, please don't hesitate to reach out.

References

Alemán, E., Jr. (2009). Through the prism of critical race theory: "Niceness" and Latina/o leadership in the politics of education. *Journal of Latinos and Education, 8*(4), 290–311. https://doi.org/10.1080/15348430902973351

Alzate González, J. (2015). Anti-racist activism and community self-care at the University of Michigan. *Souls, 17*(1–2), 11–19.

An, S. (2016). Asian Americans in American history: An AsianCrit perspective on Asian American inclusion in state U.S. history curriculum standards. *Theory & Research in Social Education, 44*(2), 244–276. https://doi.org/10.1080/00933104.2016.117 0646

Apperley, T. H., & Gray, K. L. (2021). Digital divides and structural inequalities: Exploring the technomasculine culture of gaming. In R. Kowert & T. Quandt (Eds.), *The video game debate 2: Revisiting the physical, social, and psychological effects of video games* (pp. 41–52). Routledge.

Au, W. (2010). *Unequal by design: High-stakes testing and the standardization of inequality.* Routledge.

Banks, J. A. (1993). Multicultural education: Development, dimensions, and challenges. *Phi Delta Kappan, 75*(1), 22–28.

Bazzano, A. N., Anderson, C. E., Hylton, C., & Gustat, J. (2018). Effect of mindfulness and yoga on quality of life for elementary school students and teachers: Results of a randomized controlled school-based study. *Psychology Research and Behavior Management, 11*, 81–89. https://doi.org/10.2147/PRBM.S157503

Behnken, M. (2021, November 8). *Farewell address.* Ames Community School District school board meeting, Ames, Iowa.

Berliner, D. C. (2013). Effects of inequality and poverty vs. teachers and schooling on America's youth. *Teachers College Record, 115*(12), 1–26. https://doi.org/10.1177/016146811311501203

Bonilla-Silva, E. (2006). *Racism without racists: Color-blind racism and the persistence of racial inequality in the United States* (2nd ed.). Rowman & Littlefield.

Brazelton, B. (2021). On the erasure of Black indigeneity. *Review of Education, Pedagogy, and Cultural Studies, 43*(5), 379–397. https://doi.org/10.1080/10714413.2021.1968235

Bright, A. (2016). Education for whom? Word problems as carriers of cultural values. *Taboo: The Journal of Culture and Education, 15*(1), 6–22. https://doi.org/10.31390/taboo.15.1.04

Bryan, N. (2017). White teachers' role in sustaining the school-to-prison pipeline: Recommendations for teacher education. *The Urban Review, 49*(2), 326–345. https://doi.org/10.1007/s11256-017-0403-3

Carter, P. L., Skiba, R., Arredondo, M. I., & Pollock, M. (2017). You can't fix what you don't look at: Acknowledging race in addressing racial discipline disparities. *Urban Education, 52*(2), 207–235. https://doi.org/10.1177/0042085916660350

Castagno, A. E. (Ed.). (2019). *The price of nice: How good intentions maintain educational inequity*. University of Minnesota Press.

Chen, J., Hamilton, H., Iyer, V., Jarue, A., Samaniego, C., Wang, C., & Woodsmall, J. (2021). "It shouldn't be that hard": Student activists' frustrations and demands. In K. Swalwell & D. Spikes (Eds.), *Anti-oppressive education in "elite" schools: Promising practices and cautionary tales from the field* (pp. 219–228). Teachers College Press.

Child Trends. (2013). *Parental involvement in schools*.

Cineas, F. (2020, June 10). Merriam-Webster has a new definition of "racism." *Vox*. https://www.vox.com/identities/2020/6/10/21286656/merriam-webster-racism-definition

Cote, A. C. (2020). *Gaming sexism: Gender and identity in the era of casual video games*. New York University Press.

Cox, M. [@DrMonicaCox] (2021, July 8). *Instead of showing me your diversity statement, show me your hiring data, your discrimination claim stats, your salary tables, your retention numbers, your diversity policies, and your leaders' public actions against racism. End performative allyship* [Tweet]. Twitter. https://twitter.com/drmonicacox/status/1413136017754783752

Crabtree, L. M., Richardson, S. C., & Lewis, C. W. (2019). The gifted gap, STEM education, and economic immobility. *Journal of Advanced Academics, 30*(2), 203–231. https://doi.org/10.1177/1932202X19829749

Darder, A. (2011). The establishment of liberatory alliances with people of color: What must be understood. *Counterpoints, 418*, 81–91.

Davis, L. P., & Museus, S. D. (2019). What is deficit thinking? An analysis of conceptualizations of deficit thinking and implications for scholarly research. *NCID Currents, 1*(1), 117–130. https://doi.org/10.3998/currents.17387731.0001.110

DuBose, M. [@Due_East_Equity]. (2022, February 9). *Reframe feedback as a gift. Anyone who takes the time to slow down in their day and share with you that a choice you made had a ripple effect is giving you a gift. Of information. Of relationship. Of connection and caring. They haven't written you off yet* [Tweet]. Twitter. https://twitter.com/Due_East_Equity/status/1491520857377759235

DuBose, M. S., & Orseth, T. M. (2021). *No stone unturned: A journal for antiracist equitable pedagogy*. Voyage East Media.

Emdin, C. (2021). *Ratchetdemic: Reimagining academic success*. Beacon.

English, D., Lambert, S. F., Tynes, B. M., Bowleg, L., Zea, M. C., & Howard, C. (2020). Daily multidimensional racial discrimination among Black U.S. American adolescents. *Journal of Applied Developmental Psychology, 66*.

Evans, K., & Vaandering, D. (2016). *The little book of restorative justice in education: Fostering responsibility, healing, and hope in school.* Simon & Schuster.

Evans, R. W. (2006). The social studies wars, now and then. *Social Education, 70*(5), 317–321.

Ewing, E. L. (2018). *Ghosts in the schoolyard: Racism and school closings on Chicago's South Side.* University of Chicago Press.

Fan, X., & Chen, M. (2001). Parental involvement and students' academic achievement: A meta-analysis. *Educational Psychology Review, 13*(1), 1–22. https://doi.org/10.1023/A:1009048817385

Fergus, E. (2021). The beliefs about race and culture operating in our discipline strategies: A commentary. *Preventing School Failure: Alternative Education for Children and Youth, 65*(3), 216–222. https://doi.org/10.1080/1045988X.2021.1888686

Fernandez, M., & Hauser, C. (2015, October 5). Texas mother teaches textbook company a lesson on accuracy. *New York Times.* https://www.nytimes.com/2015/10/06/us/publisher-promises-revisions-after-textbook-refers-to-african-slaves-as-workers.html

Girvan, E. J., Gion, C., McIntosh, K., & Smolkowski, K. (2017). The relative contribution of subjective office referrals to racial disproportionality in school discipline. *School Psychology Quarterly, 32*(3), 392–404. https://doi.org/10.1037/spq0000178

Girvan, E. J., McIntosh, K., & Smolkowski, K. (2019). Tail, tusk, and trunk: What different metrics reveal about racial disproportionality in school discipline. *Educational Psychologist, 54*(3), 1–20. https://doi.org/10.1080/00461520.2018.1537125

Global Family Research Project. (2018). *Joining together to create a bold vision for next generation family engagement: Engaging families to transform education.* Carnegie Corporation of New York.

González, J. C. (2007). The ordinary-ness of institutional racism: The effect of history and law in the segregation and integration of Latinas/os in schools. *American Educational History Journal, 34*(1/2), 331–345.

Gorski, P. C. (2016). Poverty and the ideological imperative: A call to unhook from deficit and grit ideology and to strive for structural ideology in teacher education. *Journal of Education for Teaching, 42*(4), 378–386. https://doi.org/10.1080/02607476.2016.1215546

Gorski, P. C. (2018). *Reaching and teaching students in poverty: Strategies for erasing the opportunity gap* (2nd ed.). Teachers College Press.

Gorski, P. (2019). Avoiding racial equity detours. *Educational Leadership, 76*(7), 56–61. https://www.ascd.org/el/articles/avoiding-racial-equity-detours

Gorski, P. (2021). How trauma-informed are we, really? *Educational Leadership, 78*(2), 14–19. https://www.ascd.org/el/articles/how-trauma-informed-are-we-really

Gorski, P. C., & Chen, C. (2015). "Frayed all over": The causes and consequences of activist burnout among social justice education activists. *Educational Studies, 51*(5), 385–405.

Gorski, P., DuBose, M., & Swalwell, K. (2022). Trading baby steps for big equity leaps. *Educational Leadership, 79*(5), 26–31. https://www.ascd.org/el/articles/trading-baby-steps-for-big-equity-leaps

Gorski, P. C., & Erakat, N. (2019). Racism, whiteness, and burnout in antiracism movements: How white racial justice activists elevate burnout in racial justice activists of color in the United States. *Ethnicities, 19*(5), 784–808. https://doi.org/10.1177/1468796819833871

Gupta, P., Goldman, T., Hernandez, E., & Rose, M. (2018, December 19). Paid family and medical leave is critical for low-wage workers and their families. Center for Law and Social Policy. https://www.clasp.org/publications/fact-sheet/paid-family-and-medical-leave-critical-low-wage-workers-and-their-families/

Gutiérrez y Muhs, G., Niemann, Y. F., González, C. G., & Harris, A. P. (Eds.). (2012). *Presumed incompetent: The intersections of race and class for women in academia.* University Press of Colorado.

Haden, J. (2021, December 3). Why emotionally intelligent leaders avoid the "feedback sandwich." *Inc.* https://www.inc.com/jeff-haden/why-emotionally-intelligent-leaders-avoid-feedback-sandwich-to-improve-employee-performance-backed-by-science.html

Harris, F., III, & Wood, J. L. (2021, February 12). Racelighting: A prevalent version of gaslighting facing People of Color. *Diverse Issues in Higher Education.* https://www.diverseeducation.com/opinion/article/15108651/racelighting-a-prevalent-version-of-gaslighting-facing-people-of-color

Hartlep, N. D. (2021). *The model minority stereotype: Demystifying Asian American success* (2nd ed.). Information Age.

hooks, b. (2000). *All about love: New visions.* Morrow.

Hornsby, G., & Blackwell, I. (2018). Barriers to parental involvement in education: An update. *Educational Review, 70*(1), 109–119.

Irby, D. J., Green, T., & Ishimaru, A. M. (2022). PK–12 district leadership for equity: An exploration of director role configurations and vulnerabilities. *American Journal of Education, 128*(3), 417–453.

Johnson, D. C., & Johnson, E. J. (2021). *The language gap: Normalizing deficit ideologies.* Routledge.

Johnson, L. L., Bryan, N., & Boutte, G. (2019). Show us the love: Revolutionary teaching in (un)critical times. *Urban Review, 51*(1), 46–64.

Johnson, S. B., Arevalo, J., Cates, C. B., Weisleder, A., Dreyer, B. P., & Mendelsohn, A. L. (2016). Perceptions about parental engagement among Hispanic immigrant mothers of first graders from low-income backgrounds. *Early Childhood Education Journal, 44*(5), 445–452.

Jones, S. P. (2019). Ending curriculum violence. *Learning for Justice, 64.* https://www.learningforjustice.org/magazine/spring-2020/ending-curriculum-violence

Joshi, K. Y. (2020). *White Christian privilege: The illusion of religious equality in America.* New York University Press.

Keenan, H. (2020). Keep yourself alive: Welcoming the next generation of queer and trans educators. *Bank Street College of Education Occasional Paper Series.* https://www.bankstreet.edu/research-publications-policy/occasional-paper-series/archive/ops-45/keep-yourself-alive/

King, L. J., & Simmons, C. (2018). Narratives of Black history in textbooks: Canada and the United States. In S. A. Metzger & L. M. Harris (Eds.), *The Wiley international handbook of history teaching and learning* (pp. 93–116). Wiley. https://doi.org/10.1002/9781119100812.ch4

King, L. J., & Woodson, A. N. (2017). Baskets of cotton and birthday cakes: Teaching slavery in social studies classrooms. *Social Studies Education Review, 6*(1), 1–18.

Kohli, R. (2018). Behind school doors: The impact of hostile racial climates on urban teachers of color. *Urban Education, 53*(3), 307–333. https://doi.org/10.1177/0042085916636653

Kohli, R. (2021). *Teachers of color: Resisting racism and reclaiming education.* Harvard University Press.

Kohli, R., & Pizarro, M. (2016). Fighting to educate our own: Teachers of color, relational accountability, and the struggle for racial justice. *Equity & Excellence in Education, 49*(1), 72–84.

Ladson-Billings, G. (1995). Toward a theory of culturally relevant pedagogy. *American Educational Research Journal, 32*(3), 465–491. https://doi.org/10.3102/00028312032003465

Ladson-Billings, G. (2009). *Dreamkeepers: Successful teachers of African American children*. Jossey-Bass.

Ladson-Billings, G. (2014). Culturally relevant pedagogy 2.0: A.K.A. the remix. *Harvard Educational Review, 84*(1), 74–84. https://doi.org/10.17763/haer.84.1.p2rj131485484751

Lang, C. (2021, April 26). Extracurricular activities can play a central role in K–12 education. *Kappan*. https://kappanonline.org/extracurricular-activities-can-play-a-central-role-in-k-12-education-lang/

Lechuga-Peña, S., & Brisson, D. (2018). Barriers to school-based parent involvement while living in public housing: A mother's perspective. *Qualitative Report, 23*(5), 1176–1187. https://doi.org/10.46743/2160-3715/2018.3062

Lewis, A. E., & Diamond, J. B. (2015). *Despite the best intentions: How racial inequality thrives in good schools*. Oxford University Press.

Loewen, J. W. (2008). *Lies my teacher told me: Everything your American history textbook got wrong*. New Press.

Lofton, R. (2021). Plessy's tracks: African American students confronting academic placement in a racially diverse school and African American community. *Race Ethnicity and Education* (online preprint). https://doi.org/10.1080/13613324.2021.1924141

Lorde, A. (2017). *A burst of light: And other essays*. Ixia.

Love, B. (2019). *We want to do more than survive: Abolitionist teaching and the pursuit of educational freedom*. Beacon.

Lovinsky-Desir, S., Acosta, L. M., Rundle, A. G., Miller, R. L., Goldstein, I. F., Jacobson, J. S., Chillrud, S. N., & Perzanowski, M. S. (2019). Air pollution, urgent asthma medical visits, and the modifying effect of neighborhood asthma prevalence. *Pediatric Research, 85*(1), 36–42. https://doi.org/10.1038/s41390-018-0189-3

Low, S. (2009). Maintaining whiteness: The fear of others and niceness. *Transforming Anthropology, 17*(2), 79–92. https://doi.org/10.1111/j.1548-7466.2009.01047.x

Lustick, H. (2021). Going restorative, staying tough: Urban principals' perceptions of restorative practices in collocated small schools. *Education and Urban Society, 53*(7), 739–760.

Magwood, A. (2021). Unspoken rules, White communication styles, and White blinders: Why elite independent schools can't retain Black and Brown faculty. In K. Swalwell & D. Spikes (Eds.), *Anti-oppressive education in "elite" schools: Promising practices and cautionary tales from the field* (pp. 73–84). Teachers College Press.

Marcelo, P. (2022, February 8). Wellesley school district settles suit by conservative group over student affinity groups. *WBUR Online*. https://www.wbur.org/news/2022/02/08/wellesley-parents-defending-education-lawsuit-settlement-boston

Martins, L. B., & Gaudiot, D. M. F. (2012). The deaf and the classroom design: A contribution of the built environmental ergonomics for the accessibility. *Work, 41*(1), 3663–3668.

Mayorga, E., & Picower, B. (2018). Active solidarity: Centering the demands and vision of the Black Lives Matter movement in teacher education. *Urban Education, 53*(2), 212–230. https://doi.org/10.1177/0042085917747117

McCarty, T. L., & Lee, T. S. (2014). Critical culturally sustaining/revitalizing pedagogy and Indigenous education sovereignty. *Harvard Educational Review, 84*(1), 101–124. https://doi.org/10.17763/haer.84.1.q83746nl5pj34216

McGuire, L., Mulvey, K. L., Goff, E., Irvin, M. J., Winterbottom, M., Fields, G. E., Hartstone-Rose, A., & Rutland, A. (2020). STEM gender stereotypes from early childhood through adolescence at informal science centers. *Journal of Applied Developmental Psychology, 67*, 101–109. https://doi.org/10.1016/j.appdev.2020.101109

McNeal, R. B., Jr. (2012). Checking in or checking out? Investigating the parent involvement reactive hypothesis. *Journal of Educational Research, 105*(2), 79–89. https://doi.org/10.1080/00220671.2010.519410

Milner, H. R., IV (2013). Why are students of color (still) punished more severely and frequently than white students? *Urban Education, 48*(4), 483–489. https://doi.org/10.1177/0042085913493040

Mishel, L., Gould, E., & Bivens, J. (2015). *Wage stagnation in nine charts*. Economic Policy Institute. https://www.epi.org/publication/charting-wage-stagnation/

Moll, L. C., Amanti, C., Neff, D., & Gonzalez, N. (1992). Funds of knowledge for teaching: Using a qualitative approach to connect homes and classrooms. *Theory into Practice, 31*(2), 132–141. https://doi.org/10.1080/00405849209543534

Muhammad, G. (2020). *Cultivating genius: An equity framework for culturally and historically responsive literacy*. Scholastic Teaching Resources.

Nieto, S., & Bode, P. (2017). *Affirming diversity: The sociopolitical context of multicultural education*. Pearson.

Orozco, R. (2019). The method of avoidance: Niceness as whiteness in segregated Chicanx schools. *Whiteness and Education, 4*(2), 128–145. https://doi.org/10.1080/23793406.2019.1642795

Oto, R., Nguyen, N., Custer, M., Ericson, P., & Liebelt, N. (2021, Spring). Becoming a critical social educator: The power of a collective to counteract copy room conversations. *The Critical Social Educator, 1*(1).

Paris, D., & Alim, H. S. (2014). What are we seeking to sustain through culturally sustaining pedagogy? A loving critique forward. *Harvard Educational Review, 84*(1), 85–100.

Paris, D., & Alim, H. S. (Eds.). (2017). *Culturally sustaining pedagogies: Teaching and learning for justice in a changing world*. Teachers College Press.

Pashler, H., McDaniel, M., Rohrer, D., & Bjork, R. (2008). Learning styles: Concepts and evidence. *Psychological Science in the Public Interest, 9*(3), 105–119. https://doi.org/10.1111/j.1539-6053.2009.01038.x

Patterson, L. M. (2012). *The right to access: Citizenship and disability, 1950–1973* [Doctoral dissertation, Ohio State University]. OhioLINK Electronic Theses and Dissertations Center. http://rave.ohiolink.edu/etdc/view?acc_num=osu1342310475

Rethinking Schools Editors. (2021a, Summer). Right-wing legislators are trying to stop us from teaching for racial justice. We refuse. *Rethinking Schools, 35*(4). https://rethinkingschools.org/articles/right-wing-legislators-are-trying-to-stop-us-from-teaching-for-racial-justice-we-refuse/

Rethinking Schools Editors. (2021b, Fall). Confronting the right-wing attacks on racial justice teaching. *Rethinking Schools, 36*(1). https://rethinkingschools.org/articles/racial-justice-our-classrooms-and-the-right-wing-attacks/

Riddle, T., & Sinclair, S. (2019). Racial disparities in school-based disciplinary actions are associated with county-level rates of racial bias. *Proceedings of the National Academy of Sciences, 116*(17), 8255–8260. https://doi.org/10.1073/pnas.1808307116

Robinson, D. V., & Volpé, L. (2015). Navigating the parent involvement terrain—The engagement of high poverty parents in a rural school district. *Journal of Family Diversity in Education, 1*(4), 66–85. https://doi.org/10.53956/jfde.2015.64

Rodriguez, G. (2020). Suburban schools as sites of inspection: Understanding Latin youth's sense of belonging in a suburban high school. *Equity & Excellence in Education, 53*(1–2), 14–29. https://doi.org/10.1080/10665684.2020.1758245

Rodriguez, G., & González Ybarra, M. (2020). "This is what I go through": Latinx youth facultades in suburban schools in the era of Trump. *Race Ethnicity and Education* [online preprint]. https://doi.org/10.1080/13613324.2020.1753676

Rodríguez, N. N., & Swalwell, K. M. (2022). *Social studies for a better world: An anti-oppressive approach for elementary educators.* W. W. Norton.

Romano, A., & Almengor, R. A. (2021). It's deeper than that! Restorative justice and the challenge of racial reflexivity in white-led schools. *Urban Education* (advance online copy).

Sabzalian, L. (2019). *Indigenous children's survivance in public schools.* Routledge.

Safir, S., & Dugan, J. (2021). *Street data: A next-generation model for equity, pedagogy, and school transformation.* Corwin.

Saleh, M. (2021). "We need a new story to guide us": Towards a curriculum of *Rashma. Curriculum Inquiry, 51*(2), 210–228. https://doi.org/10.1080/03626784.2020.1860642

Salinas, C., & Blevins, B. (2014). Critical historical inquiry: How might pre-service teachers confront master historical narratives? *Social Studies Research & Practice, 9*(3), 35–50. https://doi.org/10.1108/SSRP-03-2014-B0003

San Pedro, T. (2015). Silence as shields: Agency and resistances among Native American students in the urban Southwest. *Research in the Teaching of English, 50*(2), 132–153.

San Pedro, T. (2018). Abby as ally: An argument for culturally disruptive pedagogy. *American Educational Research Journal, 55*(6), 1193–1232. https://doi.org/10.3102/0002831218773488

Sánchez Loza, D. (2021). Dear "good" schools: White supremacy and political education in predominantly white and affluent suburban schools. *Theory into Practice, 60*(4), 380–391. https://doi.org/10.1080/00405841.2021.1981075

Santiago-Rosario, M. R., Whitcomb, S. A., Pearlman, J., & McIntosh, K. (2021). Associations between teacher expectations and racial disproportionality in discipline referrals. *Journal of School Psychology, 85*, 80–93. https://doi.org/10.1016/j.jsp.2021.02.004

Schwartz, S. (2022, July 26). Conservative parent group sues school district over curriculum that discusses race and gender. *Education Week.* https://www.edweek.org/policy-politics/conservative-parent-group-sues-school-district-over-curriculum-that-discusses-race-and-gender/2022/07

Sensoy, Ö., & DiAngelo, R. (2012). *Is everyone really equal? An introduction to key concepts in social justice education.* Teachers College Press.

Shalaby, C. (2017). *Troublemakers: Lessons in freedom from young children at school.* New Press.

Simmons, D. (2019). Why we can't afford whitewashed social-emotional learning. *Education Update, 61*(4). https://www.ascd.org/el/articles/why-we-cant-afford-whitewashed-social-emotional-learning

Simmons, D. (2021). Why SEL alone isn't enough. *Educational Leadership, 78*(6), 30–34. https://www.ascd.org/el/articles/why-sel-alone-isnt-enough

Sisk, V. F., Burgoyne, A. P., Sun, J., Butler, J. L., & Macnamara, B. N. (2018). To what extent and under which circumstances are growth mind-sets important to academic achievement? Two meta-analyses. *Psychological Science, 29*(4), 549–571. https://doi.org/10.1177/0956797617739704

Solorzano, D. G., & Ornelas, A. (2004). A critical race analysis of Latina/o and African American advanced placement enrollment in public high schools. *The High School Journal, 87*(3), 15–26. https://doi.org/10.1353/hsj.2004.0003

Stevenson, H. C. (2014). *Promoting racial literacy in schools: Differences that make a difference*. Teachers College Press.

Stewart, D.-L. (2017, March 30). Language of appeasement. *Inside Higher Ed.* https://www.insidehighered.com/views/2017/03/30/colleges-need-language-shift-not-one-you-think-essay?v2

Stewart, D-L., & Nicolazzo, Z. (2018). High impact of [whiteness] on trans* students in postsecondary education. *Equity & Excellence in Education, 51*(2), 132–145.

Stovall, D. (2018). Are we ready for "school" abolition? Thoughts and practices of radical imaginary in education. *Taboo: The Journal of Culture and Education, 17*(1), 51–61. https://doi.org/10.31390/taboo.17.1.06

Swalwell, K. (2015). Mind the civic empowerment gap: Economically elite students and critical civic education. *Curriculum Inquiry, 45*(5), 491–512. https://doi.org/10.1080/03626784.2015.1095624

Tatum, B. D. (2017). *Why are all the Black kids sitting together in the cafeteria? And other conversations about race*. Basic Books.

Theoharis, G. (2007). Social justice educational leaders and resistance: Toward a theory of social justice leadership. *Educational Administration Quarterly, 43*(2), 221–258. https://doi.org/10.1177/0013161X06293717

Thomas Fordham Institute. (2021, April 9). Family engagement is critical to student success—especially now. https://fordhaminstitute.org/national/commentary/family-engagement-critical-student-success-especially-now

Thorsen, K., & Dempsey, D. (Writers and Producers). (1989). *James Baldwin: The price of a ticket* [Film]. Maysles Films.

Tuck, E., & Gaztambide-Fernández, R. A. (2013). Curriculum, replacement, and settler futurity. *Journal of Curriculum Theorizing, 29*(1), 72–89.

Venet, A. S. (2021). *Equity-centered trauma-informed education*. W. W. Norton.

Vickery, A. E., & Rodríguez, N. N. (2021). "A woman question and a race problem": Attending to intersectionality in children's literature. *The Social Studies, 112*(2), 57–62. https://doi.org/10.1080/00377996.2020.1809979

Walters, A. S., & Hayes, D. M. (1998). Homophobia within schools: Challenging the culturally sanctioned dismissal of gay students and colleagues. *Journal of Homosexuality, 35*(2), 1–23. https://doi.org/10.1300/J082v35n02_01

Wegmann, K. M., & Smith, B. (2019). Examining racial/ethnic disparities in school discipline in the context of student-reported behavior infractions. *Children and Youth Services Review, 103*, 18–27. https://doi.org/10.1016/j.childyouth.2019.05.027

Wheeler-Bell, Q., & Swalwell, K. (2021). "How could we solve that problem?" Cultivating a healthy democracy through democratic classrooms. In R. Evans (Ed.), *Handbook on teaching social issues*. IAP.

Winn, M. T., & Winn, L. T. (Eds.). (2021). *Restorative justice in education: Transforming teaching and learning through the disciplines.* Harvard Education Press.

Wozolek, B. (2018). Gaslighting queerness: Schooling as a place of violent assemblages. *Journal of LGBT Youth, 15*(4), 319–338. https://doi.org/10.1080/19361653.2018.14 84839

Yosso, T. J. (2005). Whose culture has capital? A critical race theory discussion of community cultural wealth. *Race Ethnicity and Education, 8*(1), 69–91. https://doi. org/10.1080/1361332052000341006

Zipin, L. (2009). Dark funds of knowledge, deep funds of pedagogy: Exploring boundaries between lifeworlds and schools. *Discourse: Studies in the Cultural Politics of Education, 30*(3), 317–331. https://doi.org/10.1080/01596300903037044

Index

The letter *f* following a page locator denotes a figure.

equity literacy, abilities of (*continued*)
    redressing inequity, 54–58, 74, 78–79
    responding to inequity, 50–54, 74, 77
    sustaining equity, 58–59
equity literacy, building blocks for leaders
    desire, 14–15, 37–38
    knowledge, 38–39
    skills, 39–41
    will, 41–44
equity literacy framework, 8
equity programs
    inadequate, 6
    magic vs. reality of, 11–14
equity statements, 18
evidence-based equity principle
    data collection instruments, limita-
        tions of, 182–185
    equity feedback, responding to,
        195–198
    equity feedback, soliciting, 185–187
    function of, 179
    introduction, 10
    leader mindsets, mitigative vs.
        transformative equity, 199*f*
    mining data to answer equity ques-
        tions, 180–182
    negative feedback, embracing,
        189–195
    no evidence of inequity does not
        equal equity, 187–189
    prioritization principle and, 185
    vignette, extracurricular participa-
        tion, 177–179
extracurricular participation, 177–178

family involvement gap, 95–96, 98–100,
    104–106
fear, rejecting, 211–213
feedback
    of benevolent honesty, 210
    critical, sharing and receiving
        skills, 40
    embracing negative, 189–195
    responding to, 195–198
    soliciting, 185–187
feedback sandwich, 210
fix injustice, not kids principle. *See also*
    injustice, responses to
    from deficit to structural ideology,
        119–120

fix injustice, not kids principle (*continued*)
    discipline inequity, 101–103,
        116–119
    homework example, 112–113, 115
    introduction, 9
    leader mindsets, mitigative vs.
        transformative equity, 122*f*
    leadership and, 101
    no excuses rhetoric, 115
    requirements, 13–14

gaslighting, 85–87
grit ideology, 99*f*

heterosexism, 109–112, 170–171
hiring for equity, 40, 145–147, 172
history classes, equitable, 163–164
holiday calendar, 130–131
homophobia, 109–112

ideological blockages, recognizing, 40
ideology
    deficit, 9, 97–103, 99*f*, 105–109,
        119–121, 179
    functions of, 97
    grit, 99*f*
    hiring process and, 146
    possibility of equity and, 97–103
    structural, 99*f*, 100–101, 103–107,
        109, 119–120
inequity. *See also* access and opportunity
    choosing, 107
    confronting without consensus,
        75–79
    data mining to answer questions of,
        187–189
    defining, 22
    in discipline, 5–6, 101–103, 116–119
    disparities, predictable, 24–25
    educational outcomes and, 21
    eliminating, 74
    naming, 84–85
    no evidence does not equal equity,
        187–189
    recognizing, 47–50, 72–73
    redressing, 54–56, 74, 78–79,
        137–147
    responding to, 50–54, 74, 77,
        135–137
    roots of, 93

About the Authors

 **Paul Gorski, PhD,** is the founder of the Equity Literacy Institute and EdChange. He has 25 years of experience helping educators, nonprofit workers, and others strengthen their equity efforts. He has worked with educators in 48 states and a dozen countries. He also is the research director of the Equity Literacy Institute, conducting and collaborating on research and other scholarship related to maximizing the transformative potential of equity efforts. Paul has published more than 70 articles and has written, cowritten, or coedited 12 books on various aspects of educational equity, including *Reaching and Teaching Students in Poverty: Strategies for Erasing the Opportunity Gap* and *Case Studies on Diversity and Social Justice Education* (with Seema Pothini). Paul spent nine years on the board of directors of the National Association for Multicultural Education and five years on the board of the International Association for Intercultural Education. He earned a PhD in educational evaluation at the University of Virginia. He was a teacher educator at several universities for 15 years. He is also a father, a published poet, a black belt in Tae Kwon Do, and the biggest fan of Buster, his cat.

 **Katy Swalwell, PhD,** is lead equity specialist for the Equity Literacy Institute and founder of Past Present Future Consulting & Media. Over the past 20 years, Katy has served as a classroom teacher in public and private schools at the elementary and secondary levels, teacher educator, researcher, and administrator. Her books include *Educating Activist Allies: Social Justice Pedagogy with the Suburban and Urban Elite*, *Social Studies for a Better World: An Anti-Oppressive Approach for Elementary Educators* (with Noreen Naseem Rodríguez), and *Anti-Oppressive Education in "Elite" Schools: Promising Practices and Cautionary Tales from the Field* (coedited with Daniel Spikes). As a faculty member at multiple universities, she spent several years in leadership roles with the Critical Educators for Social Justice of the American Educational Research Association and cofounded the open access journal *The Critical Social Educator*. Her PhD in curriculum theory, research, and design is from the University of Wisconsin–Madison. Katy is a proud wife and mother who enjoys podcasts, writing children's books, learning local history, and trying to crush the competition in word games.